SWALLOWS AND SETTLERS

關學東

SWALLOWS AND SETTLERS

The Great Migration from North China to Manchuria

Thomas R. Gottschang and Diana Lary

CENTER FOR CHINESE STUDIES
THE UNIVERSITY OF MICHIGAN
ANN ARBOR

MICHIGAN MONOGRAPHS IN CHINESE STUDIES
ISSN 1081-9053
SERIES ESTABLISHED 1968
VOLUME 87

Published by
Center for Chinese Studies
The University of Michigan
Ann Arbor, Michigan 48104-1608

⊗ The paper used in this publication meets the requirements
of the American National Standard for Information Sciences —
Permanence of Paper for Publications and Documents
in Libraries and Archives ANSI/NISO/Z39.48 — 1992.

Library of Congress Cataloging-in-Publication Data

Gottschang, Thomas R.

Swallows and settlers : the great migration from north China to
Manchuria / Thomas R. Gottschang and Diana Lary.

p. cm. —
(Michigan Monographs in Chinese Studies, ISSN 1081-9053)
Includes bibliographical references and index.
ISBN 0-89264-134-7
1. Migrant labor — China — Manchuria. 2. Migration, Internal — China —
Manchuria. 3. China — Economic conditions — 1912–1949. I. Title: Great
migration from north China to Manchuria. II. Lary, Diana. III. Title. IV.
Series.
HD5856.C5 G67   2000
331.5'44"09518 — dc21   99-086273
CIP

This book is dedicated to Ho Lian (Franklin Ho) and
Owen Lattimore, pioneers in our field.

CONTENTS

TABLES, FIGURES, AND MAPS

Tables

Figures

Maps

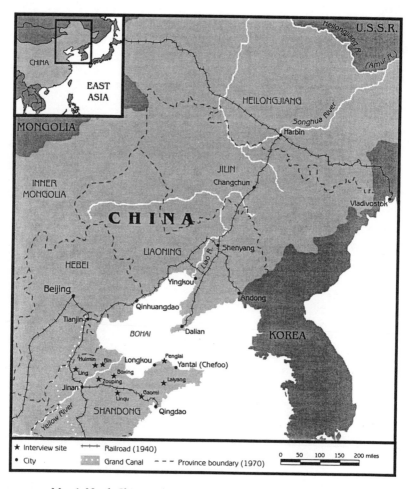

Map 1 North China and Manchuria: major railways and cities.

NOTE ON ROMANIZATION AND PLACE NAMES

We generally follow China's official romanization system, Hanyu pinyin. Exceptions occur for people from Taiwan, Hong Kong, Singapore, and other places that use the Wade-Giles system. We have spelled people's names the way they spell them in their own publications, including Chiang Kai-shek, who is Jiang Jieshi in pinyin. Quotations from works published in Western languages retain the romanizations used in the originals, which in some cases differ from both pinyin and Wade-Giles. A few places, like Manchuria, are familiar to readers in the English language by names that are not related to the current Chinese names; in these cases we have retained the more familiar names.

Most of the important places mentioned in this study are widely known by more than one name. We have, therefore, listed below the different names for prominent places that we encountered in the course of our research.

Manchuria is known in Chinese as either the Three Eastern Provinces (Dongsansheng) or the Northeast (Dongbei), the standard term used in China today. Manchuria is the most common term in international English language usage (e.g., "the Manchurian Incident") and no longer carries the imperialist flavor that it acquired when Japanese forces created the puppet state of Manchukuo (Manzhouguo, Manchoukuo) in 1932. Manchuria also has a looser meaning, which obviates the need to change the terminology for the period of the Japanese occupation or for boundary changes that have occurred since 1949.

Liaoning, Jilin, and Heilongjiang, the three provinces of Manchuria, have taken several different forms and names over the years. During the Republican period Liaoning was usually called Fengtien, but it was also known as Shengjing (Sheng-ching, Sheng-king) and Liaodong (Liao-tung). It encompassed much of present-day Jilin (Kirin) Province, while Jilin incorporated much of the territory of today's Heilongjiang Province.

Yingkou, the first treaty port in Liaoning, was widely known in Western languages as Newchwang (Niuzhuang), which was in fact a town inland of the port where the Customs station was officially located.

Dalian (Ta-lien), Manchuria's most important port, was pronounced "Dairen" in Japanese and appeared as Dairen in Western-language publications of the Japanese government. In Russian it was called Dalny.

Shenyang, the capital of Liaoning Province, was called Mukden by the Manchus and was also known as Fengtien.

North China traditionally includes the region containing today's provinces of Hebei (Ho-pei), Shandong (Shan-tung), Shanxi (Shan-hsi), Shaanxi (Shen-hsi), Henan (Ho-nan), and often the northern parts of Jiangsu and Anhui.

Hebei Province was part of Zhili (Chihli) Province during the Qing dynasty (1644–1911). In the Republican period (1911–1937) the northern third of Zhili was divided between Rehe (Jehol) Province and Chahar Province. In 1928 Zhili's name was changed to Hebei. After 1949 Hebei lost a narrow southern section but added much of Rehe to its northern border.

Qingdao, Shandong's main port, was known to Westerners before 1949 as Ch'ing-tao or Tsingtao, but Customs reports for Qingdao were filed under the name of the town of Jiaozhou (Kiaochow) where the Chinese Customs station was officially located.

Yantai (Yen-t'ai), the largest port on the north coast of the Shandong Peninsula, was known as Zhifu (Chih-fu) before 1949 and is commonly rendered Chefoo in Customs reports and other English language sources.

Beijing (Peking, Pei-ching—"northern capital") was changed to Beiping (Peping, Pei-p'ing—"northern peace") after Chiang Kai-shek established the capital of the Republic of China at Nanjing (Nanking) in 1927. The city became Beijing again in 1949.

Tianjin, the major port of Hebei Province, appeared as T'ientsin on most maps before 1949; the Wade-Giles spelling is T'ien-chin.

FOREWORD

This study examines the great movement of people from North China to Manchuria in the early twentieth century. It combines the results of our long-term research and draws on our different disciplinary approaches. On the one hand, we work from a statistical record of the migration, employing quantitative analysis to study relationships between fluctuations in the migration and economic influences. This element of the study builds on Gottschang's doctoral thesis in economics. He was drawn to the migration both because it was a major event in modern Chinese history and also because it provides an unusually clear example of the forces that stimulate population movements in the course of economic development. On the other hand, we highlight the effects of migration on individual families. This discussion is based on Lary's extensive examination of historical materials, many at the county level. The most valuable and unique component of the historical study is a series of interviews Lary conducted with former migrants in Shandong Province. She describes that research as follows:

> In 1984 I spent a wonderful spring moving around rural Shandong. I was received with the warm hospitality for which Shandong is famous. I interviewed former migrants to Manchuria, who were at first astounded and then pleased that someone wanted to hear about what had been, for most of them, the most important experience of their lives.
>
> The Chinese government had just begun to approve fieldwork projects by foreigners, and I went on the official Canada-China scholarly exchange. My trip came fortuitously at the time when many counties had started preparing new gazetteers, the first since the 1940s. There was already an interest in digging up materials about the local past and an awareness that much of this would have to be done through oral history. My field research was interrupted after 1984.
>
> I had hoped to return to Shandong the next year to continue; but instead I went to Beijing to serve as resident sinologist in the Canadian Embassy for two years. During that time I kept my investigation going

informally. The great spasm of migration in the 1920s and 1930s had dispersed Shandong people widely, and I seldom attended an official banquet at which there were not people from Shandong or Manchuria. Their migration experiences turned out to be an ideal dinner topic.

I returned to Shandong for a second field trip in May 1989. I was in Jinan on June 3 when the news came through that troops were firing on students and workers in Beijing. It was inconceivable to go out and carry on academic research when students were being killed and the whole academic endeavor was under harsh attack. In any case, the Canadian Embassy ordered all nationals to leave China, and within three days I was back in Toronto. Since then I have made one short visit to Shandong.

When we discovered in the 1980s that we were both working on the migration, we decided to work together. We felt that the vast scale of the topic warranted a collaborative effort, and it was clear to us that our approaches had much to offer in combination. The interviews and historical study supply personal stories and offer insights into the motivations and experiences of individual migrants. The statistical analysis provides numerical evidence and conclusions for the migration as a whole and its relationship to the larger forces at work in the Chinese economy. The purpose of this book is to use the personal stories to put a human face on the aggregate data, while the statistical evidence places the individual experiences in a broader context.

The resulting work combines two perspectives: Lary is a British-trained social historian, and Gottschang, an American-trained economist. We believe these different perspectives produce a richer and more nuanced picture of the migration than would emerge from a single disciplinary framework. Although every chapter is a product of long and intensive cooperative effort, some sections primarily reflect the work of one author. For example, Lary developed sections in chapter 1 that describe the migrants she interviewed and their home areas. She also took the lead in the chapters on family, local places, and return migration. Gottschang initiated most sections on statistics and the economy, particularly in chapters 1, 2, and 4.

Over the years we have worked on this project, many people and institutions have contributed valuable assistance. In China the Institute of Economics in the Chinese Academy of Social Sciences provided access to library resources and acted as our liaison to research institutions in Shandong and Manchuria. We would particularly like to thank former directors Dong Fureng and Zhao Renwei, and former assistant director

Huang Fanzhang for opening important doors. Professors Wu Cheng-ming and Mi Rucheng generously shared their extensive knowledge of Chinese economic history. Shang Lie provided tireless assistance and support. Other members of the Chinese Academy of Social Sciences to whom we owe special gratitude include Ding Weizhi, Duan Ruoshi, and Zhang Youyun. We would like to thank Ma Xiuqing of the Shandong Provincial Government for his help in arranging research visits and for assistance with interviews, as well as Lu Ren and Lu Yu of the Shandong Academy of Social Sciences and Nie Liming of Weifang, Shandong. At the College of the Holy Cross, Joel Villa provided technical expertise with maps and photographs. Anne Gibson, of Clark University's cartography service, prepared the final version of the maps. Several anonymous readers provided valuable guidance for reorganization and revisions. The calligraphy for the frontispiece was graciously supplied by Tse Shui Yim, librarian emeritus of the University of British Columbia.

This project would never have come to pass without the good services of our mutual friend and mentor, Thomas G. Rawski.

We owe special thanks to Karen Turner for reading and commenting on the entire manuscript, for serving as academic and stylistic arbiter, and for her unstinting intellectual and emotional support.

Thomas Gottschang
Diana Lary
February 2000

INTRODUCTION

On a chilly April morning in 1938, sixteen-year-old Zhang Zhenbao gazed at the docks of Dalian over the rail of the steamer he had boarded the day before at Yantai on the north coast of the Shandong Peninsula. Dalian was the gateway to Manchuria, China's rich Northeast, where he was to work as a coal miner. Zhenbao had known since he was a small boy that some day it would be his turn to go to Manchuria. That day had finally arrived, although Manchuria was now under Japanese rule. Zhenbao hailed from Dongguan Village, near the county seat of Laiyang, set among the hills of the Shandong Peninsula. For many years men from his village had journeyed to Manchuria in search of work. Over the past decade and a half more than a hundred young men had left the village of just over a thousand people, some for short periods, others permanently. They went in groups, usually in the late spring, often led by older local men who recruited workers for the Japanese mines. When they were able, they returned in the winter, in time for the lunar new year. These men were called swallows because of the seasonal cycles of their travels.

Zhenbao's family was very poor. His father, a farm laborer, could barely support his four children, and his mother and sister had to beg from time to time. By leaving home, Zhenbao spared his parents the expense of supporting him; if he managed to send money home, he would help the family even more. His departure, moreover, brought an immediate windfall for the family: A local labor contractor (*batou*), who was gathering men for a Japanese mining company, paid him a recruitment bonus (*anjiafei*, "money to settle the family") of 40 *yuan*—as much as many local men could expect to earn in a year. He gave 30 *yuan* to his parents and kept 10 for traveling expenses. Then he set off for the port of Yantai with the other young men from his village. This was the first time he had been further from home than the county seat. After four days they reached the port, where they were formally handed over to the Japanese mine authorities for the short trip to Dalian.

1

OVERVIEW OF THE MIGRATION

Zhang Zhenbao was typical of millions of workers who traveled to the Northeast from the 1890s to the beginning of the Second World War. During these years roughly 25 million people made the trip from the densely populated North China provinces of Shandong and Hebei. Two-thirds of them eventually returned to their home villages, while approximately 8 million remained in Manchuria.[1] This was one of the greatest population movements in modern history: Settlement of the western United States involved the migration of some 8 million people between 1880 and 1950; about 4 million people migrated from western Russia to Siberia from 1880 to 1914; and the exodus from Ireland between 1841 and 1911 was over 4 million. Only the great emigration of 52 million people from Europe between the 1840s and the 1930s was significantly larger than the migration to Manchuria.[2]

This migration was a crucial event in modern Chinese history. North Chinese workers settled the plains and forests of Manchuria and provided the labor that has made Manchuria a leading center of Chinese industry since the 1930s. Their presence also ensured that Manchuria would remain part of China, despite intense military and political maneuvering by Russia and Japan from the late nineteenth century until the end of the Second World War.

The migration to Manchuria seems at first glance to have a tidy symmetry. North China was seen as overcrowded (*renduo dixiao*), wretched, and poor, while Manchuria was considered empty (*diduo renxiao*) and ripe for exploitation. Migrants moved from the crowded place to the empty one, as naturally as water flows downhill. There is certainly truth to this description. North China, Shandong in particular, was terribly poor and brutally buffeted by nature. Out of the 268 years of the Qing dynasty (1644–1911), droughts occurred in 233, floods in 245, the Yellow River or Grand Canal overflowed in 127, and tidal inundations occurred in 45. Only two years passed without disaster striking some part of Shandong.[3] Nonetheless, the population of North China was huge and growing. Available statistics, though incomplete, suggest that between the time of the Xinhai Revolution (1911) and the early 1930s the population of Shandong grew from about 37 million people to about 40 million, while that of Hebei rose from around 32 million to about 34 million.[4] Shandong, always poor, seemed to get poorer still as its population boomed.

Manchuria, on the other hand, only 160 kilometers away from Shandong by the short sea crossing from Yantai to Dalian, was sparsely populated and potentially rich, with empty land, minerals, forests, and great rivers. In 1914 only 36 percent of the arable land in Manchuria was farmed, and though that percentage rose rapidly, by 1926 only 52 percent was under cultivation. Slightly under a quarter of Manchuria's 243 million acres was considered arable.[5] Finally, migrants from North China faced no major adjustments in Manchuria, save learning to deal with the fierce winters and the mosquitoes. They did not need to learn a new language or culture or even a new skill, since the development needs of Manchuria called for large additions of both skilled and unskilled labor.

The problem with this neat dichotomy is that it does not automatically produce migration; the equation is more complicated. Otherwise, a tidal wave of people from North China would have engulfed Manchuria as soon as the Qing dynasty removed restrictions on settlement in the late nineteenth century. Instead, the migratory flow generally remained a trickle to the end of the century, aside from brief bursts, as when hundreds of thousands of people fled the North China famine of 1876–1879. At the turn of the century, however, migration grew to a powerful stream that swelled in the late 1920s and 1930s to a true flood. The growth of the migration was clearly a response to new work opportunities in Manchuria—building railways, working in mines and factories, clearing the wilderness, and growing soybeans. It was equally spurred by the development of transportation, for while many people went to Manchuria by traditional means—by fishing boat or on foot—most twentieth-century migrants traveled by train or steamer.

The most spectacular aspect of the migration was its size. Yet the data should be looked at with some caution: They should be understood in light of China's huge population. Even so, the number of people making this move was enormous. The migration made it possible to open up a vast area, as did the late nineteenth- and early twentieth-century settlement of the western plains in the United States and Canada. While the settlement of the western plains in North America comes closest to the Manchurian migration, the political and social contexts were so different that the comparison can only be superficial, touching on matters such as terrain, climate, and natural resources.

The migration to Manchuria had one particular aspect that makes it difficult to categorize in terms of its overall form and thus to compare with other great migrations that may be classed as either urbanization or rural settlement. It was neither a movement from the land to the cities—urbanization—nor a migration from one rural setting to another, but a hybrid of the two. Some of the migrants did settle on the land while others moved from rural to urban areas, but these outcomes were incidental rather than preordained. Since most migrants were engaged as contract laborers or moved through personal channels, the outcome of their migration was determined by their employers rather than by their own decisions.

This migration is part of a continuum of population movement that has marked twentieth-century China. Some of the largest movements were refugee migrations. They included the flight into western China beginning in 1937 as Japanese armies invaded northern and eastern China, followed by the return migration after 1945, and then the exodus from China as the Communists took over in 1949. These movements were quite different from the economically driven migration to Manchuria. The huge internal migrations in the centrally planned era between 1949 and 1978 were often economic in intention—aimed at opening up borderlands and redistributing population from densely populated areas to less crowded ones—but they were orchestrated by the state and driven by political imperatives. Fundamental problems were often neglected, much to the migrants' detriment.[6] Most recently the migrations of the reform era, which have involved over 120 million people, have been overwhelmingly short-term movements from rural areas to the cities and industrial zones in eastern China. This current migration has many of the elements that characterized the Manchurian migration, including reliance on contract labor and personal networks. Likewise, Chinese emigration to Southeast Asia and to North America, which coincided with the Manchurian migration, also relied heavily on contract labor and personal ties. The major difference with these international migrations was the racism and immigration barriers the emigrants encountered wherever they went and the fact that they remained aliens in the places to which they moved.[7]

THE TEXTURE OF THE MIGRATION

Migration from Shandong and Hebei (Zhili) during the Republican period was summed up by the bleak expression *chuang guandong* (to escape hardship by going beyond the pass). "The pass" was Shanhaiguan (Mountain-sea Pass), the eastern terminus of the Great Wall, which marked the effective boundary between North China and Manchuria. The assumption was that people were forced to leave home by dire poverty. This assumption was grounded in harsh reality—the long catalog of suffering that was the life of many North China farmers. In the Shandong social and cultural context, which was strongly centered on family and home, to leave home for any reason but direst poverty was unthinkable. At some level people recognized the importance of economic opportunities elsewhere, but only to the extent that those driven out of their homes had to have somewhere to go, a temporary escape. There was no sense of the lure of a new land; migration was seen as something dismal but unavoidable.

A tabulated expression of this sense of expulsion from home emerges from an investigation conducted by the Nankai Economic Research Institute in April 1931. A team sent to various parts of Manchuria interviewed 1,149 migrant families, of whom more than 90 percent were from Shandong. Ninety percent had migrated after 1911, and two-thirds of that number between 1925 and 1930, from 69 of Shandong's 108 counties. They gave the following reasons for their migration:

Table I.1 Reasons for Migration

Reason	Number	Percentage
Economic (total)	793	69.0
difficult living conditions	569	49.5
too little land	109	9.5
no land	56	4.9
debts	8	0.7
desire to make money	8	0.7
homeless family	39	3.4
business problems	4	0.3
Disasters (total)	314	27.3
bandits	97	8.4
soldiers	28	2.4
drought	37	3.2
bandits and soldiers	25	2.2
bandits, soldiers, natural disasters	23	2.0
floods	22	1.9
hail	15	1.3
various natural disasters	65	5.7
Other (total)	42	3.7
family matters	6	0.5
summoned by family or friends	5	0.4
looking for brothers	5	0.4
an ill relative	2	0.2
looking for a friend	1	0.1
wanting to go abroad	2	0.2
other	24	2.1
Total	1,149	100.0

Source: Wang Yaoyu, "Shandong nongmin licun de yige jiantao," in *Zhong-guo jingji yanjiu,* ed. Fang Yanting (Changsha: Shang-wu, 1938), 180.

Although these statistics look only at families, not individuals, and allow only a single cause for migration, they still present an overwhelming internal unity: They give almost universally negative reasons for migrating. Only eight of the 1,149 interviewed said that they were moving to make money, and only two spoke of a positive desire to leave home.

Foreign missionaries in Shandong shared the view that migration was essentially negative; permanent emigration was seen as a sad but necessary solution to the province's overwhelming population problem. Writing in 1911, R. C. Forsyth had this to say:

> So scarce is the supply of food that many of the people are compelled to migrate to the Provinces of Shansi and Shensi, and thousands annually cross over into Manchuria. Under present conditions there seems to be little hope for the people unless the Government can organise emigration on a vast scale and so relieve the pressure of over-population.[8]

In the late Qing and early Republic, emigration did develop rapidly, though very little of it was government sponsored. In the early 1930s John Lossing Buck estimated an out-migration rate for the whole country of forty-four per thousand, with the much higher rate of 133 per thousand for males in North China.[9] In 1938 Wang Yaoyu, working at the Nankai Institute of Economic Research, estimated that migration from different parts of Shandong in the early 1930s ranged from a low of 10 percent of the population to a high of 60 percent.[10] The statistics in both cases have flaws: It is often not possible to discover who is included and who is not; some figures include local movements, such as girls marrying out of their home villages, while others do not. It is also difficult to disentangle short-term and long-term migrants. But even allowing for these deficiencies, it is clear that a great number of people in Shandong and Hebei were on the move.

Japanese writers presented a very different picture of the migration. If the Chinese viewed the migration as a dismal but inevitable result of poverty, the Japanese, who were creating many of the economic opportunities in the north, perceived the migrants as fleeing the nightmare of China for the joys of Manchuria:

> Warfare, prevalence of banditry, excessive taxation, and famines have so harried the native population [of Shandong] that in desperation those who can find the means to travel at all hasten to seek the benefits of peace and order and the chance for better living conditions which Manchuria offers.[11]

Both the Chinese and Japanese views give generalized, undifferentiated causes for migration, but in the most general sense they are right. Shandong was poor. Manchuria did offer many jobs. But these two factors explain only the basic preconditions for the migration, not who went, or whether the correlation between poverty and migration was cast in concrete. Nor do they explain why some people affected by the misery of North China migrated to Manchuria, while others went into the army, or moved to a town, or simply stayed in their villages and endured.

Our research shows that migration to Manchuria was a complex process. When seeking the motives to migrate, however, moving beyond stereotypes can be difficult because any large migration acquires a lore that designates motive. Sometimes the receiving society dictates the motive. The Statue of Liberty stands as the ultimate symbol of American lore that says immigrants to the United States seek political, religious, or economic freedom. Sending societies portray emigration in ways specific to their own cultures and social systems. For the Highlands of Scotland, emigration in the eighteenth century was a tragedy visited on the migrants by the cruelty of absentee landlords. For Ireland, the great nineteenth-century emigration was flight from a famine that the pitiless British had done nothing to alleviate. In both of these cases the freight of migration was a sense of expulsion. Scandinavians have viewed emigration more phlegmatically, as a sensible course to take in countries where land was scarce. In China in the late Qing and early Republic the prevailing lore held that migration was unnatural. Migrants were either desperately poor or morally dubious and moved away from home because they were in trouble.

Myths of migration tend to confuse what actually happened. This study will show that the image of desperate migrants driven by extreme poverty was a cultural construction and that migration took place not haphazardly, but within well-defined channels. Those channels were created by early migrants, and became conduits for further migration. We will examine the family and village connections through which people entered the migration stream, as well as the way migrants were selected within their home settings.

What economic characteristics were common to those who migrated? According to Buck's study, six out of seven families that produced migrants fell below the national median in terms of landholding (3.3 acres), and tenant families were four times more numerous among migrants than in the general population.[12] However, a large survey on out-migration conducted in 1935 by the National Agricultural Research Bureau of the Ministry of Industry found that 49.5 percent of emigrant families had 5 *mu* (.8 of an acre) of land or less, while another 37.4

percent had between six and ten *mu* (1 and 1.7 acres). In other words, most migrants were not from the lowest economic stratum.[13]

Figures on landholding are tricky to analyze. Landholding figures for a family in which only one male migrated (a very common phenomenon) make sense only if we also know the total number of family members. A family with many sons might send several away, even though it had an adequate amount of land, while a very poor family with only one son might not be able to let him go. Only when a whole family left could the amount of land held be a crucial factor. A survey of 150 refugee (*nanmin*) households conducted in 1928 shows that even refugee migrants were less land-poor than might have been expected:

Table I.2 Landholding of Refugee Migrants

Land held	Percentage
Landless	11.4
5–10 *mu*	66.3
11–15 *mu*	22.3

Source: "Gesheng nongcun jingji yu nongmin yundong," in *Cunzhi* 2.6 (October 31, 1931):17.

In general, we can assume migrant families to have been poorer rather than richer, but poverty was not a necessary condition for migration. Truly destitute people usually could not afford to migrate, except when forced to by disaster. Many migrants *were* poor, but others were not. Migration to Manchuria did not primarily originate in Shandong's poorest counties; some of the highest rates occurred in relatively wealthy counties. Nor was landholding a completely reliable indicator. Farmers in very poor counties often worked their own scant holdings, while farmers in richer areas were more likely to be tenants — yet either might decide to migrate. Additional factors came into play as well: Laiyang, a rich county on the Peninsula, had a high rate of land concentration and tenancy, and indeed many of the migrants from there were landless. But the major stimulus for migration in that county was its excellent migration networks. Gaomi County also had highly concentrated landholding, with much property controlled by absentee landlords. But in this case chronic banditry and military activity proved to be the major stimuli for migration. In Linqu, a desperately poor county but one in which many people owned their own land, it was natural disasters that forced large numbers to leave. Clearly, no single economic cause can provide a satisfactory explanation for this complex movement.

FAMILY TIES: THE ENGINE OF MIGRATION

If Manchuria had more natural resources per worker than Shandong, why didn't more Shandong people move every year? Why were there few migrants in some years and many in others? On the other hand, if Shandong society prized family and local ties above all else, why did anyone leave home? What did it take to overcome the desire to remain at home? The answers lie in two realms: economics and family relationships. Family interests decided who went to Manchuria; economic conditions determined the opportunities available at home and abroad.

The experience of sixteen-year-old Zhang Zhenbao in 1938 illustrates this study's central theme: The driving force behind the migration to Manchuria was neither the poverty of North China, nor the growth of the Manchurian economy, but rather the deep and unquestioned commitment of millions of North Chinese workers to aid their families by any possible means. A defining characteristic of Chinese society is the immensely powerful web of connections and obligations within the nuclear and extended family and a great reluctance on the part of individuals to be separated from family and home. Yet Chinese history is studded with massive voluntary migrations, including the first great movement into the Yangtze River valley in the fourth and fifth centuries A.D., the settlement of South China between the eighth and twelfth centuries, the repopulation of Sichuan in the seventeenth and eighteenth centuries, and the dispersion of millions of Chinese people—the Chinese Diaspora—around the world in the nineteenth and twentieth centuries.[14] The migration to Manchuria provides an opportunity to reconcile these apparently contradictory realities of Chinese society. Unlike other major Chinese migrations, historical or modern, the movement to Manchuria is sufficiently well documented to allow for analysis of economic influences and recent enough to permit interviews with former migrants. The Manchurian migration can thus provide a multidimensional perspective on the motivations and behavior of Chinese migrants generally.

The data and the accounts of the migrants interviewed for this study show that in the great majority of cases the decision to migrate was not an individual one, but part of a family economic strategy—a characteristic aspect of migration in many countries.[15] The primacy of family interests countered the individual's reluctance to migrate. In fact, the strength of family ties promoted migration for economic reasons. The wider the gap between income-earning possibilities at home and elsewhere, the greater the potential benefit to the family of sending off one of its members. The importance of the family relationship provides a standard against which we may measure the pressures for and against migration. Was the possibility of higher income an adequate incentive to leave the family? It apparently was. Was the presence of Japanese occupation forces in Manchuria sufficient to discourage leaving the family? Clearly not. Did the effects of disaster at home warrant departure? In many cases they did.

Personal motivation was not the issue. The migrants expected to fulfill a duty to their families—to leave home for part of their lives in order to bolster the family income. They were not seeking better lives for themselves as individuals, but were contributing to the survival, at modest levels, of the family at home. They were doing something that in qualitative terms was similar to taking a contract as a long-term farm laborer or servant.

A corollary of migration as a service to the family is that the individual expression of free will—the bold courage of the pioneer so celebrated in the history and lore of migration to North America—is absent here. There are no tales of triumph over nature or epic feats of endurance. Instead the famous feats of courage that these migrants celebrated had occurred in Shandong itself, in the Song dynasty (A.D. 960–1279) stories of the "heroes of the marsh" from the traditional novel *Water Margin* (*Shuihu zhuan*). The migrants saw themselves, and were seen by others, as stolid, patient, and undemanding. They took pride in their ability to endure hardship (*chiku nailao*), and they had very limited personal expectations.

Other reasons help to explain why this migration had so little drama associated with it. The distances many of the migrants moved were short. Trips to the southern parts of Manchuria took little time, and the journey itself was not the deterrent to return that stormy Atlantic crossings often were for emigrants to North America. Moreover, the migrants to Manchuria were moving within China. They had no sense of leaving their country or culture for another, and hence the psychological leap was smaller than it would have been in an international migration.

Finally, Shandong migrants—though they probably never made the comparison themselves—did not have to contend with the pervasive racism experienced by Chinese moving abroad during the same period. The majority of Shandong migrants moved into the bottom levels of Manchurian society, as laborers, factory workers, and farmers. Their dealings were with other Chinese, with labor contractors, and low-level officials. They had little contact with either the substantial Chinese merchant body in Manchuria or the Japanese managerial and military elite who held leadership positions in the ports, railways, and major manufacturing and extractive industries. They lived in an overwhelmingly Chinese world, where their social and economic status, not their race, determined their treatment or maltreatment.

THE MIGRATION AND OTHER HISTORICAL STUDIES

The broad outlines and many details of the economic and social history of North China have become increasingly clear through path-breaking research since the early 1970s. Several key publications include studies based on analysis of previously underutilized sources, such as the extensive materials produced in the 1920s and 1930s by the South Manchuria Railway Company (SMR), the national archives in Beijing, and local records. This study of the migration to Manchuria builds upon and complements many of these historical works, some of which describe the economic conditions from which the migrants emerged, while others examine protest movements engendered by similar circumstances, such as the Boxer Uprising and secret society activities.

Two of the most important studies of North China's rural economy were written by Ramon Myers and Philip Huang.[16] Both Myers and Huang find that farm family behavior was driven by market forces, one of which was the imbalance between the labor markets of North China and Manchuria. Labor shortages in Manchuria provided opportunities for workers from Hebei and Shandong; they could increase family income by taking advantage of the better wages and job opportunities that existed to the north. Huang notes that in Hou Jiaying, a village in northern Hebei near the border with Manchuria, cash tenancies increased in the Republican period as more and more people moved to Manchuria. Labor contracts shrank to only one year because so many young men anticipated that they might move to Manchuria and refused to be tied into long-term contracts. Huang also describes social changes in the same village caused by the migration. People moved to Manchuria to make money and when they succeeded, they brought their earnings home and invested in land. New families had risen to the top of the social pile by this process: Of the nine leading households in the village, five had acquired their status through money earned in Manchuria.[17]

Myers, too, comments that the migration affected local labor markets in Hebei and Shandong, reducing the labor supply, which led to an upward drift in wages.[18] However, he also describes the migration largely as flight from chronic violence:

> . . . the emigration of millions of peasants from north China to Man-
> churia during the 1920s was principally due to the breakdown of peace
> and order in the countryside and the great loss of property at the hands
> of warlord armies. Peasants could cope with poor harvests and floods
> by fleeing with their belongings to other areas, waiting until the
> disaster had passed, and then returning. But the ravages of these troops

was something else. It usually meant both loss of property and life, and so one of the largest migrations of this century took place in the 1920s.[19]

More recent works, including books by Prasanjit Duara and Kenneth Pomeranz, provide additional evidence on the economic causes of the migration, but focus particularly on the relationship between economic change, the national state, and local political structures.[20] Duara, in a vein similar to Myers and Huang, finds that migration made some contribution to prosperity in North China.[21] Pomeranz analyses the economic decline of the region along the route of the old Grand Canal in western Shandong, caused first by the depredations of the Taiping Rebellion in the mid-nineteenth century and then by the shift of long-distance commerce to coastal steam shipping in the late nineteenth century and to railways in the twentieth century. Pomeranz shows that the decline in the region's importance was accompanied by political neglect and the consequent weakening of the central government's flood-control efforts, which exacerbated the effects of both floods and droughts in the early twentieth century.[22] In the face of long-term regional recession and endemic poverty, migration became an important element in the economy of western Shandong. In fact, "... before 1931, remittances from Manchuria made up for the trade deficits of most Shandong counties that ran them."[23]

Analysis of rural protest movements has become another prominent theme in the field of modern Chinese history. Most rural movements grew out of conditions that were similar to those that fueled the migration to Manchuria and were based on long local traditions. Elizabeth Perry's work, for example, shows that in many parts of rural North China there were long histories of relatively small-scale, but persistent strains of spontaneous rural protest organizations, like secret societies.[24] Joseph Esherick has produced a detailed analysis of the origins in Shandong of the most famous rural protest, the explosive and tragic Boxer Uprising of 1899–1900.[25] Esherick demonstrates that the movement was based in popular culture, but that it was also related to poverty, uncertainty, and natural disaster, problems that drove thousands of other Shandong residents to migrate to Manchuria.

1

MEMORIES AND NUMBERS:
SOURCES OF MIGRANT INFORMATION

One overwhelming aspect of the migration to Manchuria in the early twentieth century was its scale. At its height, the only metaphors that made sense were watery ones—torrents, floods, tidal waves, inundations of migrants. Photographs of tens of thousands of migrants arriving in Dalian, all young men in farmers' clothing, portray a nameless mass of workers headed to the north (see p. 14). For Lary, following one of the major migrant routes—traveling by ship from Yantai to Dalian in 1984—the sight of the huge crowd waiting in the dark after the night crossing, standing silently on the same great circular flight of stairs at the old South Manchuria Railway wharf in Dalian, conjured up the vastness and anonymity of the earlier movements.

In a sense, the migrants *were* anonymous. All accounts of the opening up of Manchuria mention the critical importance of Chinese labor in neutral, inanimate terms. Workers are discussed in terms of wages, recruitment, and efficiency; occasionally they appear as troublemakers or labor organizers. Farmers are discussed in terms of the amount of land settled and agricultural production. Chinese also figure in the formal records as bandits, soldiers, Christian converts, or plague victims. Only rare observers, notably Owen Lattimore, describe them in fuller human terms.

Former migrants who were interviewed for this study bring distinct concerns, motivations, and aspirations to the story of the migration. The statistical record traces the ebbs and flows of the mass movement within which their stories took shape. This chapter first describes the circumstances under which the interviews took place and profiles the home counties of the informants. It then discusses the sources from which the aggregate statistical record was compiled.

13

Immigrants arriving from Shandong.

The South Manchuria Railway Wharf at Dalian, 1927.

WHO WERE THE MIGRANTS?

Little in the written record of the early twentieth century addresses individual migrants and their stories. The migrants did little to draw attention to themselves: They were not politically involved; the vast majority of them were illiterate—they wrote few letters and kept no diaries. They seldom appear in fiction. While the farmers of Jiangnan were portrayed in the writings of Lu Xun and Mao Dun, Manchuria was featured in the work of only one widely read author, Xiao Jun, and his output was tragically small. His most famous novel, *Village in August*, published in 1935, dealt with Manchuria in the context of Chinese resistance to the Japanese. After that, his voice was silenced by the Communist literary bureaucracy, which found his views too salty and forthright and so managed to destroy one of China's great literary talents. Chinese intellectuals of the 1930s, the group most likely to be vocally sympathetic to the oppressed, tended to see migrants as ciphers, not people. They saw the vast movement as a sign of rural China's bankruptcy: The migrants were forced to leave home because of poverty, oppression, and corruption. They were part of a movement that has been translated most evocatively as the "exodus from the villages" (*licun*).

The migrants got no more attention under the Communists, for they were not considered heroes of either resistance or class struggle. Their labor had fueled the Japanese drive for domination, and Communist expansion in Shandong took place largely without their participation. The migrants had left a province where major Communist base areas were clawed out during the late 1930s and 1940s, creating legions of real heroes whose memories were of interest to the new authorities.

Much of the social-science literature on migration is written in impersonal terms, as indeed is a good part of the literature on rural China. It tends to rely heavily on statistics and to avoid anecdotal and personal data. Statistics are comfortable and they seem less prone to distortion than personal stories, but they can be inaccurate. Of equal importance, statistics reveal only part of the story of migration, the numbers involved. Only personal sources, whether contemporary surveys or later interviews, can reveal other aspects—the bases of the decision to migrate, the channels of migration, and the success or failure of the migration.

No migration is made up of faceless ciphers. While common themes can be expressed statistically, there are also a myriad of individual, personal stories that give texture to a mass movement of people. It is these stories that can clarify details and explain variations within the migration. Since there are few contemporary written records about the individual migrants, we must rely on interviews with survivors and their descendants to tell us why and how they left home, what their intentions were, and how well they succeeded. Migrants to Manchuria came from all over North China, but the greatest numbers came from Shandong, where the interviews for this study were conducted.

Former migrant Wang Kongde. Ling County, Chengguan, April 12, 1984.

Former migrants Hou Shangjian, Hou Shangrui, Hou Shangyu, Hou Xiaolun. Ling County, Fenghuang Township, April 13, 1984.

Shandong People and Traditions

The people of Shandong have always believed that they were born into the most historic province of China. Shandong is the "sacred province," the home of Confucius and Mencius, and the "country of the rites" (*liyi zhi bang*), where Confucian rituals have been practiced longest and are most richly developed.[1] This tradition is reflected in a strong emphasis on family history, recorded in family records (*shipu*). Besides the celebrated Kong (Confucius) and Meng (Mencius) families, the Chunyu family of Huang County traces its line back to the Spring and Autumn Period (770–476 B.C.).[2] Family tradition has a deeper sense of antiquity in Shandong than anywhere else in China.

Shandong was also the birthplace of Zhuge Liang, one of China's few military heroes, the great strategist of the Three Kingdoms period (A.D. 220–280), who was later turned into a folk hero in *The Romance of the Three Kingdoms*. Normally Chinese tradition is unkind to military figures. Indeed, "military tradition" is a contradiction in terms, since tradition implies respect, something the military rarely enjoyed in China. But Zhuge Liang was an exception. He was famous for cleverness and stratagems, not brute force, so Shandong could be proud of him and enhance its cultural preeminence with martial fame.

The third distinct tradition that colors the Shandong character is that of Liangshanbo, the marshy area in the west of the province inhabited by the tough, swaggering heroes of the *Water Margin*. These heroes, though fictional, were vivid and exciting, whether they were killing tigers, getting drunk, or taking on corrupt officials. They were brave (sometimes stupidly so), strong, down-to-earth, and decent.

Each of the three traditions is grounded in a different part of the province, but Shandong as a whole counts all three its own. These traditions have given the people pride and a sense of self-worth that compensates for widespread material poverty. Shandong people think of themselves as brave, sociable, decent, and morally courageous.[3] They are good at enduring hardship, reliable, physically tough, strong, and handsome. Lenin, Stalin and Trotsky all had Shandong bodyguards, recruited in Vladivostok. The Hong Kong police force also recruited Shandong men.[4] Some of China's most notorious anti-heroes also came from Shandong, including three of the Gang of Four and Kang Sheng, head of the secret police, whose death in 1975 was greeted with as much rejoicing as the Cultural Revolution allowed.[5]

The first foreigners in Shandong also saw the local people in a positive light. Baptist missionaries who established the first Christian mission in Shandong in the 1870s saw the people as "the most stalwart and vigorous of all the Chinese."[6] The German colonists of the late nineteenth century had a high respect for them, especially the young men, who embodied Germanic ideals of manliness and courage. Baron Ferdinand von Richthofen, the intrepid explorer who "found" Shandong for Germany, described the Shandong people as "intelligent and upright, and fit to develop into an advanced generation."[7] His account was published two years before the Boxer Uprising, which might have changed his mind, but he would not have departed from the admiration expressed by a fellow German:

> The Shantung people distinguish themselves, in favorable comparison to the people of the southern provinces, by generally powerful physiques, tall, well-built, manly forms, fresh, healthy complexions (dark yellow-grey to brown-grey) and other external manifestations of superiority. The facial expression is intelligent.[8]

The characteristics that the Shandong people saw in themselves, and that others saw in them, made them ideal candidates for opening up the Manchurian wilderness. Just as "stout peasants in sheepskin coats" from Eastern Europe were enlisted to settle the Canadian prairies, the inhabitants of Shandong were deemed an appropriate labor force for the development of Manchuria, not just because they were geographically close to Manchuria, but because they were the right kind of people, physically and psychologically. The sturdiness, ingenuity, and positive outlook that enabled Shandong people to endure the rigors of life in Manchuria were abundantly apparent in the former migrants Lary interviewed in 1984.

Interviews and Informants

Eighty people, two of whom were women, gave interviews on their migration experiences. Generally the informants were elderly men who had spent varying lengths of time in Manchuria. They came from nine counties—Ling, Huimin, Binzhou, Boxing, Zouping, Linqu, Gaomi, Laiyang, and Penglai. The interviews were arranged by the Shandong Academy of Social Sciences (SASS), and Lary was accompanied first by an official from the provincial government, and then by a population studies scholar from SASS,[9] in addition to representatives of the district and county governments. Most informants were interviewed in their villages, or occasionally in the county *jiaodaisuo* (guesthouse). The villages were known to have been places of heavy migration or were close to the county town. Only two villages were clearly out of the ordinary— Zhangxilou Production Brigade in Ling County is a village with an average household income over three times the province average, and Fengjiacun in Zouping is the home of Feng Yuexi, a member of the National People's Consultative Congress.[10]

The interviews all took place in groups, for no woman, especially a foreign one, could meet privately with a man. The interviews were conducted without interpreters; when the local dialect was unclear, one of the entourage would translate into standard Mandarin. The group setting usually created a comfortable atmosphere; by the time tea, nuts, fruit, candy, and cigarettes had made the rounds, all were quite relaxed. There was a fair amount of joking and teasing, and when one person was speaking others often intervened to make corrections, or to amplify stories. The group setting seemed to encourage more accuracy and less hyperbole. Elaborate tales transparently bored other informants. One woman's rambling, emotional tale of being taken off into something close to slavery put two of the informants to sleep.

From the start it was clear that no one wanted to fill in a questionnaire. The informants regarded the collection of formal statistics with suspicion. Such a project would also have been unproductive, since their experiences were so different. As a consequence, each informant first was asked for basic details about leaving home and the size and condition of his or her family at the time. They were then asked to tell their own stories. Most were eager to do so. They launched into vivid descriptions of their experiences, often prefaced with a reproach that it took the visit of a foreigner for them to have a chance to tell their stories. The stories were not standardized, and few were bland or dull. The informants injected humor whenever they could, but reliving what had often been a hard and cruel past was not easy for many of them. The admissions of men unable to send home remittances, or the stories of exploitation, particularly at the hands of family members, were very moving.

The interviews revealed a great deal about how rural people coped with one major handicap, illiteracy, which shaped their consciousness in intriguing ways. They could not use maps to show where they had gone. Geography for them was not spatial; they measured distance by how long a journey took by a certain mode of transport: "I walked five days to get from my village to Yantai," or "I went by train to Sankeshu in three days." Their maps were their families and their connections at home and away, a network that linked known people, not places. This personal world was engraved on their minds. All informants could give detailed information about every family member, living or dead, without pausing or faltering. The family was clearly the critical framework of life.

The migrants showed great ingenuity in coping with illiteracy. First were the external ways: They relied on literate relatives or neighbors to help write letters or fill in forms or they paid for the services of letter writers. But illiterate people also develop different kinds of memory than those who can write down what they need to remember. Being illiterate made it essential for them to train their minds to store information accurately, since that is where all their personal and economic records resided. The informants had precise memories for money, the most important information they had to retain. They remembered exact figures and almost always stated, without prompting, the particular currency in which the money had been held. They had migrated during a period when multiple currencies were in circulation, and precise knowledge about the currencies and their relative values was crucial to avoid being cheated. Some coped with currency confusion by expressing money in terms of the amount of a commodity that a certain sum would buy. Zhao Qingfu's family sold their Gaomi County farm in 1939, before they left for Manchuria, for the cash equivalent of 1,250 *jin* (625 kilograms) of beans; this amount paid their fares and presumably gave them a chance at a new start in Manchuria.[11] In 1941 Hou Shangjian of Ling County brought back enough money after a year working in Manchuria to buy 90 *jin* (45 kilograms) of beans. This was not to say that he actually bought the beans, but that this was the easiest way for him to express how much he had earned.[12] Sometimes the migrant or family actually did use the money in the way its value was expressed. In 1945 Hu Huiliang's older brother sent home the proceeds of two years' work as a rickshaw puller in Dalian, enough money for his father in Zouping to buy an ox.[13]

The migrants were less accurate about chronological time. They remembered things that had happened to them in terms of their age at the time, and they often had to struggle to put a year to the age. They often got dates wrong, but never by more than a year. This problem seemed to arise when they switched from calculating age in terms of *sui*, where the child is one year old at birth, to chronological time counted in *nian* (calendar years). Many counted time in the traditional dynastic form: They remembered dates as they had been cited in different periods. Up to 1949, years were designated Minguo (after the Republic), and for post-1949 they used Western calendar years. One man, Zhang Guangwen, even announced the year of his birth as the Qing reign year, Xuantong 3 (1910).[14]

Most informants referred to places by the names they had when the migrants first went there—present-day Dandong was Andong, Changchun was Xinjing, the "new capital" of Manchukuo. Political correctness seemed not to be an issue. Few informants seemed to have much sense of the momentous events that had occurred during their lifetimes, including the Manchurian Crisis and Japanese expansionism. They had experienced

Japanese brutality as employees of Japanese companies, but there was no connection in their minds between their maltreatment and a Chinese nationalist response. They made *pro forma* expressions of gratitude to the Communist Party, especially for land reform, but real enthusiasm was reserved for the reforms that started in 1978. The great events of the past had receded or had never impinged on them. If this was true of events within China, it was even more so of international events. In Linqu there was a lingering memory of people who had gone away to Canada, but no knowledge that this was the migration of workers going to France via Canada during the First World War.[15] The events that were crystal clear in their memories were local ones—the activities of bandits, the marauding of warlord troops, and above all the brutality of the natural world. Their indifference or lack of awareness regarding larger events probably resulted from the conditions in rural society: They lived in a world not yet unified by mass communication; news and information were limited and difficult to come by even for the elite.

The political world also presented dangers. The modern history of Shandong has done nothing to dissuade people from avoiding political participation. In Republican China, Shandong politics meant the military. In living memory of the informants and their parents, Shandong had endured major military upheavals: the Boxer Uprising and its aftermath; Germany's aggressive development of the Peninsula; the Japanese incursion of 1914 to oust the Germans; Japan's departure in 1922 and return in 1928. These events took place against a background of incessant warlord conflicts and uninterrupted banditry. Shandong was a province beset by warfare. Civilians stayed as far away as possible from the military and thus from politics. Even though Shandong was a major target for the Japanese, it was not a major site for anti-Japanese agitation, at either the top or bottom of society. In late 1937 the Shandong governor, Han Fuju, withdrew his large armies in the face of the Japanese invasion from the north. He apparently considered this action prudent and was amazed to be treated as a traitor when he met with Chiang Kai-shek and other senior generals. He was executed soon afterwards. The Xuzhou campaign, fought in the first half of 1938 in northern Jiangsu and southern Shandong, was fought mainly by troops from southern and western China, under the command of the Guangxi general Li Zongren. Many Shandong troops, including Han Fuju's, had already joined with the Japanese.

The Chinese Communist Party had great difficulty developing political consciousness in Shandong. Only after long years of frustration, towards the end of the War of Resistance Against Japan, were they able to develop significant liberated areas in the central mountains, the eastern mountains, and the western marsh area. The Civil War was hard fought in

Shandong and swung back and forth several times before the Guomindang fled to Taiwan, taking large numbers of Shandong soldiers with them. The experience of politics after 1949 was different, but not much more encouraging. Shandong went through all the political upheavals visited on China as a whole, plus two specific to the province. One was the widespread building of dams during the Great Leap Forward; the second was the organized migration of large numbers of people to Manchuria in the late 1950s and early 1960s. Both events caused huge disruptions in local life.[16]

The informants had lived hard lives, and time had not been kind to many of them. Most looked older than they were; few had any teeth left; none had the sleek veneer of success. But they had a moving dignity and a quiet tranquillity (some of them may have been frozen with nerves), interlaced with humor. They could laugh about what had happened before because their children were leading better lives. That was enough reward for the hardships they had suffered.

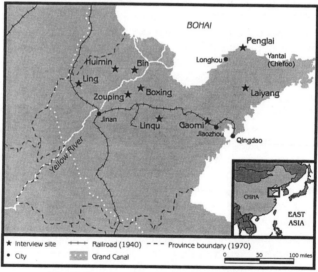

Map 2 Shandong Province with interview sites.

HOME AREAS OF THE INFORMANTS

Shandong looks like a well-defined natural entity on a map. The bold peninsula extends northeastward into the sea, pointing straight at Korea. Together with the Liaodong Peninsula of Manchuria it forms an entrance to the Gulf of Bohai. The Shandong Peninsula's base is anchored to the North China Plain in the northwest and southwest; in the center it slopes up into the imposing mountain range of the Central Massif, which includes China's most sacred mountain, Taishan. The Grand Canal crosses Shandong from south to north near its western border, while the Yellow River flows from west to east just south of its northern land border. The strongly etched lines of the coast and the waterways suggest a self-contained region.

This geography creates an appearance of cohesion not always mirrored in political reality, for Shandong has been a province of marked internal divisions throughout its history. During the Warring States period (475–221 B.C.), the area was divided into two large and several small states. Shandong's classical name, Qi-Lu, still frequently used, combines the names of its two large states, Qi and Lu. Geographical divisions are still important: Shandong has six administrative districts (*diqu*), but in popular thinking it is divided into four traditional regions: Luxi ("west Lu"), Lunan ("south Lu"), Lubei ("north Lu") and Jiaodong ("east Jiao").

The Yellow River's geographic reality also has to be approached with some caution, because it has changed its course often enough to make it difficult to think of as fixed in place. From the beginnings of recorded history until the Northern Song (twelfth century), the Yellow River entered the sea north of the Shandong Peninsula. It then moved south of the Peninsula, where it stayed, emptying into the sea through various mouths until 1854, when it moved north again. In 1938 it shifted to the south once more, after dikes were blown upriver in a futile attempt to halt the invading Japanese army. In 1947 it was redirected back north. With each shift came devastating floods and massive loss of life; in the 1938 flood almost a million people in Henan and Jiangsu were killed, and another twelve million injured or displaced. Each crisis necessitated a major rearrangement of the Shandong economy.[17]

The regions of Shandong differ considerably in prosperity. The Peninsula and the counties to the west of it on the northern slope of the Central Massif have always been prosperous, and a few counties actually rich. They benefit from the moderating influence of the sea on the climate, and from alluvial soils that support a rich agriculture. The Central Massif, on the other hand, has always been an area of great poverty, beautiful but barren and arid. These two regions are part of the same geological formation as the Liaodong Peninsula of Manchuria. Lubei, Luxi, and Lunan are part of the North China Plain, with a harsh continental climate, an agriculture perilously dependent on erratic rainfall, and, depending on the course of the Yellow River, threatened by floods. Lubei is plagued by soil leaching, evident in its famous "white fields," where the soil is frosted with alkalies. Lunan has a mountainous northern section, the southern foothills of which are fairly fertile; this is where Qufu, the home of Confucius, lies. In the 1920s Lunan's desperately poor southern area on the North China Plain was part of the Badlands, a zone of lawlessness and banditry that spread across parts of Anhui, Henan, and northern Jiangsu, as well as southern Shandong. Luxi was as poor as Lunan, but had a different topography; its land was low-lying, usually sandy, and often waterlogged. Here lay the marshes of Liangshanbo — today largely drained — home of the heroes of the *Water Margin*.

These conventional divisions between the regions of Shandong are not drawn on the map as the administrative divisions are, but they are the ones local people use. For discussing the migration, they make better points of reference than the administrative divisions.[18]

In the late Qing and early Republic, communications were poor through much of the province. The great north-south route of traditional China, the Grand Canal, had fallen into disrepair and was barely passable. The Xiaoqing River, just south of the Yellow River, was used for local traffic, but the Yellow River itself was not navigable. There were very few roads; in the late Qing there were really only two, one running north-south through the western part of the province, the other running east-west just south of the Yellow River and along the Bohai coast.[19] The road from Qingdao to Yantai did not deserve the name. The first automobile journey taken along it, a promotional gambit by the Qingdao Chrysler distributor, came only in 1926. It took two and a half days to travel about 150 kilometers. The distributor had these encouraging words to say about the car: "The motor took deep sand, dust, ruts, holes, plowed fields, river beds, rocks and water with wonderful ease."[20]

Shandong's first modern improvement in transportation came with the construction of two railways. The Jin-Pu Railway, which began operation in 1910, ran from the port of Tianjin in Hebei, south to the Yangtze River town of Pukou. It traversed Shandong from north to south, passing through the provincial capital of Jinan. In Jinan the Jin-Pu line connected to the Ji-Jiao line, which had opened for operation in 1904 to connect Jinan with the German leasehold at Qingdao.[21] The logical extension of that line, from Qingdao across the Peninsula to Yantai, was not built until the 1950s.

The home counties of the informants demonstrate the wide diversity of geographic and economic conditions within Shandong. They all boast a long history and strong provincial identity, but each has a clear local personality. While the counties described below do not constitute a comprehensive sample of migrant home localities, they do provide a good cross section of the types of areas from which a large portion of migrants came.

Ling

Ling County lies on the North China Plain southeast of Dezhou, about twenty miles east of the Jin-Pu Railway. The plain is flat, but deeply scarred with gullies and dry river valleys; as people say of Saskatchewan, "the parts that aren't flat are lower." Village houses, built of bricks or adobe of the same dun color as the soil, almost blend into it. The soil is alkaline, and there are patches of white frosting on many fields where the salts have leached to the surface.

The history of Ling County goes back to the former Han (206 B.C.– A.D. 220). It has always been poor, always exposed to droughts, floods, and locusts. In the 1920s and 1930s it was tortured by bandits. The gazetteer compilers recorded mournfully:

> It is not worth listing bandit troubles individually in the gazetteer. Some people think it would be better to say nothing about them. But in a hundred or a thousand years time, how will any reader know about the anguish of the bandit turbulence that has so disturbed the people?[22]

In the 1920s Ling County was a backward place.[23] Economic development was slow in coming—in fact the county had been through a process of economic contraction in the late Qing as loss of Grand Canal trade hit Dezhou and the surrounding district.[24] According to land reform statistics, in 1945 the county had just over 350,000 people in 93,000 households. There were 4,124 landlords, who owned 32 percent of the land; 68 percent of the population had some land, and 42,000 were landless. Fifteen percent of the population migrated at some point during the Republican period.[25]

Huimin

Huimin is a middle-sized county with poor, alkaline soil, located northeast of Jinan on the north bank of the Yellow River. It has the same harrowed landscape as Ling County. Its long history has been one of grim poverty. Here is a description of Wutingfu, the prefecture in which Humin lies, from just before the 1911 Revolution:

> . . . the country lies so low that from time immemorial it has suffered from the inroads of the waters of the Yellow River, and flood and famine have been frequently experienced in all parts of the prefecture. As a consequence, life is hard, the standard of living is low, the population, which is said to number some two millions, is probably

stationary, and from this part of Shandong there has always been a steady stream of emigrants seeking a livelihood in more favoured regions.[26]

The poverty was not evenly distributed. In the 1920s and 1930s, the north of the county was poorer than its south, and it was from the north in particular that people were recruited as migrant workers, through recruiting chains stretching north to Tianjin. There are no contemporary statistics on Republican-era migration, and the figure assessed from oral interviews, 1,948 for the entire period, is much too low for a population at land reform (1946) of 395,000.[27]

Binzhou, Bin County

Binzhou also lies north of the Yellow River, next to Huimin. It is a recent creation, a major expansion of the old town of Beizhen. The southern part of Bin County was hived off in 1982 to make Binzhou, and this area is still rural, though technically part of the city. Binzhou is important because it is the site where a ferry, and more recently, a bridge cross the Yellow River; this is a key route for people going to Beijing from southern China.[28] The land attached to the town is fertile, but vulnerable. Its villages lie between two great dikes along the Yellow River, the first actually holding the river in, the second a back-up in case of flood. When the river flooded in 1932, it inundated these villages. This danger made the land undesirable, and most of the populace have remained squatters.[29] People here have little sense of permanency, only an uneasy feeling that they are living where they really should not.

Boxing

Boxing is a small county south of Bin County, across the Yellow River. It is connected to Jinan by the Xiaoqing River, and is about thirty miles north of the Jinan-Qingdao Railway. A county administration has been here since the Warring States period (475–221 B.C.),[30] and historical remains go back even further, to the Shang Dynasty (sixteenth to the eleventh century B.C.).[31]

Boxing is not naturally blessed. The soil is poor and productivity is low; in the 1920s land had so little value that it was not concentrated in landlord hands; in 1922 there was a tenancy rate of less than 10 percent.[32] Parts of the district are waterlogged and produce only osiers, rushes, and willows, the raw materials for Boxing's major handicraft industry, woven baskets and furniture.

The Franciscan Order of Quebec maintained a small mission in Boxing. When Father Bonaventure Peloquin arrived there in 1915 he saw:

. . . an immense, denuded plain, reminiscent of those of the Canadian West, with, here and there, like so many baskets of greenery scattered over the surface of a tranquil sea, innumerable little villages and towns.[33]

Zouping

Zouping, located directly east of Jinan, is one of the most famous counties in China. Here in the 1930s the governor, Han Fuju, sponsored a well-known agricultural experiment that was run by Liang Shuming, the ranking expert on local development. The county's agricultural conditions were intensively studied at the time.[34] Since 1986 it has been a research site for the Committee on Scholarly Communications with China.

Zouping is a small county, with low hills in the south, and a flat plain stretching north almost to the Yellow River. In 1931 it had a population of just under 160,000 people, 95 percent of them farmers.[35] Its communication lines run west along the Xiaoqing River to Jinan and south to the Jinan-Qingdao Railway at Zhoucun. The building of the railway in 1904 turned the county town from a thriving center into something close to a backwater, with all the Jinan-Qingdao traffic passing along the railway rather than through the town.

Linqu

Linqu, situated to the southeast of Jinan, is a stunningly beautiful mountain county, with rich red soil, soaring peaks, and sheer cliffs. It is also terribly poor, because the mountains are arid and bare. The county sits in a cul-de-sac at the end of the road from Yidu; to its south lies the heart of the Central Massif, useless for agriculture, but a paradise for bandits.

Linqu is not only poor, but also has a long history of natural and manmade disasters. The following is a list of major disasters from the early part of the century:

Table 1.1 Disasters in Linqu, 1915–1932

Year	Disasters
1915	hail, locusts
1916	ice storm, locusts, drought
1917	harvest failure, drought
1918	earthquake, torrential rain and hail, bandits
1919	late snow, locusts, torrential rain, bandits
1920	hail, heavy rain
1921	continuous rain, bandits
1922	late frost, summer drought
1923	late frost, bandits
1924	drought, bandits, soldiers
1925	drought, bandits, soldiers
1926	heavy snow, bandits
1927	hail, bandits
1928	torrential rain, locusts, soldiers
1930	heavy rain, hail, bandits
1931	heavy rain, bandits
1932	extensive banditry

Source: Linqu xianzhi, 1935, 38–40.

In twenty-seven years only two passed without a natural disaster, and only six without some military or bandit trouble. The greatest disaster, a four-year drought, occurred in the early 1940s. The county got occasional help from the Red Swastika Society in Jinan before the Japanese invasion, but for the most part residents had to cope on their own. They either starved at home or left the area for a short time. At least half of the population—recorded at 380,000 during land reform (1945 and 1946)—migrated at some stage, most in the early 1940s.[36]

The silk industry that developed in the first years of the Republic gave new hope to the people of Linqu. By 1920 there were over a thousand looms in operation, providing plenty of employment and making Linqu appear to be a copybook example of diversification as a means to cope with agricultural uncertainty.[37] But the new industry was vulnerable to changes in distant markets: The success of artificial silk in 1920s Europe and Japan practically killed Linqu's silk industry. Prices that had boomed through the early 1920s collapsed, and by 1931 over a hundred silk merchants had gone bankrupt.[38] The Japanese invasion also had a devastating effect on trade with other counties and destroyed many sideline activities that had bolstered family incomes.[39]

The rugged terrain of Linqu.

The people of Linqu see themselves as straightforward and having a sense of humor; they are imaginative in dealing with the rough hand nature has dealt them. Indeed, the local cuisine includes a specialty derived from poverty—deep-fried scorpions. It is a specialty because courage, patience, and skill are needed first to catch the scorpions, then to remove the poison.

Gaomi

Gaomi lies on the plain that crosses the waist of the Peninsula. It is bleak terrain, flat land deeply scored with gullies; only in the west do low hills rise to break the flatness. Its recent history has been dominated by the Jinan-Qingdao Railway, which brought prosperity and allowed the people to leave easily, but also made them vulnerable to foreign pressure, first from the Germans and then from the Japanese. It also opened them up to press-ganging by Chinese armies. Military activity, especially of small irregular units (*zapai*), was almost indistinguishable from banditry. From the early 1920s on, the high level of insecurity drove the wealthier rural inhabitants into the county town or to Qingdao for protection.[40]

In the spring of 1928, for example, much of the countryside of Gaomi was infested with bandits. At first they demanded contributions only from the rich, and only every ten days or so, but soon they started to make daily demands from all households, rich and poor. The county authorities did nothing to help, except to provide weapons to villagers who asked for them. One village that did resist, Cuijia jicun, was destroyed and all the villagers murdered.[41] The local people's terror of bandits was so absolute that it drove many to flee to Manchuria.

Gaomi had a population in the mid-1930s of about 500,000, almost all of them farmers. Land ownership was heavily concentrated; only one-third of the land was owned by independent farm proprietors, while much of the rest was owned by absentee landlords living in Qingdao. In one township, Kangzhuangzhen, landlords and rich farmers owned 75 percent of the arable land. Tenant indebtedness was a serious problem and the cause of many sudden departures. The recorded migration figure for the Republican period was about 38,000, though this did not include seasonal migrants, another very large figure. Gaomi was politically more divided than many counties. There was strong support for the Guomindang in the county town, while the rural areas favored the Communists. The county was liberated twice, once in 1946 and again in 1949, and each time large numbers of people fled.[42]

Gaomi has a strong tradition of popular culture and a rich agricultural history. The movie *Red Sorghum*, based on a story by Mo Yan, a local writer, was made there. Set in the late 1930s just before the Japanese occupation, the film gives a sense of the tough, resourceful, cheerful farmers of the county, able to endure almost anything and still live their lives with gusto.

Laiyang

Laiyang is another beautiful area, with gentle hills covering 70 percent of the county. The remainder is a fertile plain, part of it boasting the golden "oil sand" (*yousha*) on which grow groves of ancient pear trees whose fruit has made Laiyang famous throughout China. The county lies on the Peninsula to the northeast of Qingdao and stretches to the coast at its southern end. Until recently its communications were poor; the long-planned Qingdao-Yantai Railway that now passes through the county was not completed until 1954.

Laiyang's agriculture has always prospered, given the richness of the land, but this richness also led to a concentration of landholding and an extensive tenancy system. Seventy percent of the land was controlled by landlords or rich farmers.[43] The county's huge population put pressure on the land and by the late Qing people were forced to go elsewhere for work. Young men were used to migrating by the time that the great movement to Manchuria got underway; they left Laiyang to work either as artisans or traders, but some also to set up substantial businesses in Manchuria.[44] The actual population during the Republican era is difficult to calculate, since the boundaries were changed several times. County authorities estimated that about 23,000 people, possibly 5 percent of the population, migrated. Ninety percent of these were poor farmers.

A pear orchard in Laiyang.

Laiyang has a strong cultural tradition and was known in eastern Shandong as a center of learning. In the late Qing the Wang family of Laiyang achieved the almost incredible feat of having three living *jinshi* among its members.[45] At that time the county center was described as "a well-built city, having substantial walls, and having numerous ornamental arches in its streets."[46] To this day the county town appears prosperous and attractive, its streets clean and tree-shaded, its buildings neatly painted.

Penglai

Penglai is a coastal county, at the juncture of the Gulf of Bohai and the Yellow Sea. It was formerly the seat of the prefecture of Dengzhou and a great historic center. Just outside the town is the sheer cliff said to have been the jumping-off point for the Eight Immortals; the islands of the immortals were said to lie somewhere off its coast and be visible to the fortunate. The cliff has always attracted tourists, including Qinshi Huangdi, first emperor of China, and Han Wudi, the most active emperor of the Former Han. Many visitors recorded their appreciation of the site in calligraphy. These inscriptions were later carved in stone and a great collection of them resides in the temple buildings on the cliff and in the gardens below. This collection is all that survived the destruction of this "center of feudal superstition" carried out by the Red Guards.

Dengzhou was also a major naval station during the Ming (1368–1644), but its harbor, Shuicheng (Water City), silted up and is only now being dug out again. During the Republican period there was no port because the water was too shallow for steamers. People going to Manchuria went either by sailboat from the beach or caught a steamer at Yantai, a treaty port where the harbor was maintained.

The agricultural areas surrounding Penglai must be among the most beautiful in the world. Hills slope up gently from white beaches, the soil is a soft red, and villages with solid stone houses nestle into the folds of the hills. The climate is gentle, nature is abundant, and it is hard to understand why the Immortals were looking for paradise elsewhere.

Penglai developed a mercantile tradition as early as the Ming dynasty. Large numbers of people were involved in trade as small shopkeepers and itinerant traders on the Liaodong Peninsula, less than a hundred miles across the mouth of the gulf. By the end of the Qing the tradition of leaving home permanently was well established and many villages had parallel settlements (*haiwaicun*) across the water in Liaodong.

The first foreigners in the area, American missionaries, liked the local people:

> The people of the *hsien* are. . . simple, kindly, well-disposed to foreigners, industrious and fairly reliable, with a good deal of character, yet slow to receive the gospel.[47]

STATISTICAL RECORD OF THE MIGRATION

Problems with the statistical record turn on two issues. The first is the technical question of how the statistics were collected and their reliability. It is always dangerous to put too much faith in statistics, but nowhere is this more true than in the records of Republican China. In the Republican era, statistical accuracy was still a novel concept, and the means of generating reliable data scarcely existed. No one understood this problem better than Franklin Ho (He Lian), who at the age of 30 returned from the United States with a Ph.D. in economics from Yale to establish the Nankai Institute of Economic Research in Tianjin:

> When I initiated my research in 1926, my chief objective was to acquire an empirical knowledge of the Chinese economy, which necessarily rests on quantitative measurement of economic facts. Through the years of experience in research at Nankai, however, I became convinced that quantification of the Chinese economy is hazardous and must be treated with extreme caution. Reliable statistics are the function of a

high degree of statistical consciousness by the public, on the one hand, and universally competent statistical staff on the other. In China, to say the least, we were extremely deficient in both. In collecting quantitative data oneself in China, one had to face the possibility of a misunderstanding of a numerical question by the subject. If one relied on statistics compiled by others, the possibility of error was compounded; one had not only to deal with the error inherent in the lack of a statistically conscious public, but also with the possibility of error stemming from the incompetency of the compiling statistical staff. Statistical time series in China are the most defective. In most cases they are not comparable from period to period. Coverage differs in each case, and I would hesitate to waste too much time on them. Even for a specific point of time, statistics are sometimes misleading. Before I attempted to employ such statistics, I should want to know how the statistics were compiled, who compiled them, and for what purpose they were compiled. Of the statistics compiled in China, statistics compiled for case studies, I found, were more reliable than others.[48]

The second question concerns where the figures were collected, and by which nationality, at the sending (Chinese) end or the receiving (Japanese) end. Chinese statistics looked at who had left. Data collected in Ding County, Hebei, in the 1930s, for example, focused on those who had left home but were still tightly connected to the family economy. The statistics did not include brides, and in fact registered only twenty-two females; but they did include men who had moved only short distances to another part of the county. They also included a large number of "unclear" responses, without specifying whether it was the family who did not know where the relative was, or the data collectors. The statistics for the nearly 700 men break down into four almost equal categories:

Table 1.2 Locations of Ding County Migrants, 1930s

Location	Number
Ding County	170
North China	164
Manchuria	153
Unclear	195

Source: Li Jinghan, "Nongcun jiating renkou fenxi," in Shehui kexue, 2.1 (Mar. 1931): 113.

These are some of the best statistics available, since they were collected at the Ding County experiment site of the Mass Education Movement and were published through the most reputable of the new social science journals. Still, they have to be treated with caution.

The Japanese statistics counted the number of people who arrived in Manchuria. They give a greater sense of security, since they are neat and were collected efficiently by a large staff and processed through a highly organized system. But they have their own inherent weaknesses. They were collected by the agents of a dominant foreign power that became an occupying force in 1931. There was no obvious trust between subjects and collectors. The data were collected in part to control people, to exclude them if they were sick, and to send them in specific directions. The interests of the subjects were often diametrically opposed to those of the collectors; if false information had to be given, it would be given. Finally, many people simply avoided being counted, usually by traveling overland or arriving in a vessel that did not go into the docks.

Is it then possible to find reliable data on migrant numbers? A good starting point is Franklin Ho's own work. In 1931 he published a description of the migration entitled *Population Movement to the North Eastern Frontier in China.*[49] Drawing his data from a series of studies produced by the Research Department of the Japanese-owned South Manchuria Railway Company, Ho noted: "Though the movement of population from other parts of China to Manchuria on the Northeastern frontier had grown steadily since the beginning of the Tsing [Qing] Dynasty, no systematic statistics, whether official or nonofficial, relating to the extent of such movement, had been compiled until 1923. In this year the Research Department of the South Manchuria Railway Company began the publication of annual statistics on the total volume of Chinese immigration into Manchuria."[50]

SMR Studies

The South Manchuria Railway Company (SMR), often referred to as Mantetsu, an abbreviation of Minimi Manshu Tetsudo Kabushiki Kaisha, was founded in 1906. Half of its original capital was provided by the Japanese government and half by private investors. The SMR leadership considered the company to be an arm of Japanese colonial management and employed the Research Department to gather intelligence for that purpose. Fortunately, the Research Department employed highly trained social scientists, who conducted some of the most insightful economic and social surveys carried out in North China in the 1920s and 1930s.[51] In his major study of the North Chinese rural economy published in 1985, Philip Huang concludes that while the SMR researchers neglected the "attitudes, values, and thoughts" of Chinese villagers, they nonetheless produced "the most precise and detailed body of information available to us on pre-Revolution Hebei-Shandong villages."[52]

The SMR's first effort to analyze the migration intensively took place in 1927 and produced a study called *Minkoku juroku nen no manshu dekasegi sha* (Migrant workers in Manchuria in 1927).[53] The researchers collected information from the Chinese Maritime Customs service, local offices of the SMR, and local government agencies at each of the four main points of entry to Manchuria: the ports of Dalian, Yingkou, and Andong, and the land route through Shanhaiguan. The study estimated total migration for the years from 1923 through 1927 by examining the data available for each of the entry points and making adjustments where the data appeared deficient.

For the port of Dalian, the SMR researchers used passenger data recorded by the port Water Police. They considered this series to be generally reliable even though it did not include infants and was inconsistent in its coverage of women. The only passenger data for the other two ports were the figures reported by the Maritime Customs, which the SMR researchers modified to allow for biases that were reported by local sources. Passenger data reported by Customs for the port of Yingkou were assumed to underreport the actual numbers by the same rate as the difference found each year between the Customs data and the Water Police reports at Dalian. They were adjusted accordingly. At Andong the passenger records and reports by local Chinese police revealed that about 10 percent of recorded arrivals and departures each year were on their way to or from Dalian rather than North China, while a further 20 percent were not migrants. The level of migration for each year was therefore estimated as 70 percent of the figure reported by the Maritime Customs.[54]

Movement in and out of Manchuria by the land route presented the greatest measurement difficulties. The largest number of land migrants traveled from Hebei on the Bei-Ning Railway to either Shenyang or Huanggutun. Most then continued their journeys to destinations north of Shenyang by rail or on foot. The Bei-Ning Railway did not keep complete passenger records, so estimates of this flow were based on surveys that counted passengers traveling north from Shenyang on the SMR during the annual peak period of in-migration, from February through June. There were also many migrants who simply walked from Hebei to Manchuria. No record was made of their passage, and the SMR researchers could estimate their numbers only roughly by referring to the volume of railway passenger traffic. For the first six months of 1927 it was estimated that 163,701 migrants arrived on the Bei-Ning line and that 36,372 entered on foot.[55]

The SMR Research Department published additional studies of the migration in 1928, 1929, and 1930.[56] Comparable data on migrant numbers were gathered and published in the SMR periodicals, *Manchu sangyo tokei* (Manchurian industrial statistics), and *Romu jiho* (Labor review), in 1931, 1932, and 1933.[57]

After the state of Manchukuo was established under Japanese control in 1932, an elaborate labor certificate system for immigrants was developed and put into effect in the late 1930s and early 1940s. The Manchukuo government first issued "Regulations Governing the Entrance of Foreigners" in 1933 for the purpose of excluding individuals considered undesirable.[58] Beginning in 1935 the regulations were enforced by an agency called the Dadong Gongsi (Ta-tung Kung-ssu, the Great East Company), which established offices at Tianjin, Dalian, Qingdao, Weihaiwei, Yantai, Longkou, Tanggu, and Shanhaiguan, with branch offices in several other towns and cities. It was responsible for examining all Chinese workers who wished to migrate to Manchuria and issuing certificates to "those who were deemed safe to enter Manchoukuo." In 1935 this system was strengthened by a new set of labor regulations which fined ship captains who carried migrants without certificates and required them to return such migrants to their ports of departure.[59] The new Labor Control Commission also specified the total number of migrants to be admitted in each year and the number in each of four occupational areas: farming, construction, mining, and unskilled labor.

Article V of the 1935 Regulations specified the content of the laborers' certificates as follows: "Every agent handling foreign laborers shall issue to each foreign laborer before the latter's entry into this country a certificate of identification containing the following facts: 1) Permanent place of domicile; name and age; 2) Kind of labor; 3) Place of entry; 4) Destination."[60] Migrant data gathered by the certificate system from 1937 through 1942 were published by the SMR in its economic reports.[61]

Customs Records

The SMR and Manchukuo agencies provided reliable data for the period from 1923 to 1942, but for the years before 1923 the only systematic data on the movement of people between North China and Manchuria were the numbers of sea passengers noted by the Chinese Maritime Customs Service in its annual reports on each of the treaty ports. The Maritime Customs Service of the late Qing dynasty was a curious institution, staffed at its upper levels by foreign nationals primarily from Britain, Europe, and Japan, who maintained a strict ethic of efficiency and loyalty to the Chinese government. Following China's defeat in the Opium War, the foreign powers imposed customs practices and terms on China, with the result that the Customs Service was insulated from much of the chaos that plagued the Chinese government during the late Qing and the Republican era.[62]

Before the 1890s the passenger data in Customs reports appears to have included only a small fraction of the migrants. In 1876, for instance, when drought and famine in North China caused hundreds of thousands of refugees to flee to Manchuria, Customs recorded only 618 passengers leaving Yantai for Manchuria and only 8,562 people embarking at Tianjin for all destinations.[63] At this time most migrants still made the crossing to Manchuria on sailing junks that were not subject to supervision by Customs. By the end of the nineteenth century, however, a major share of the passenger traffic was carried by steamships, which were bigger, faster, and more reliable than junks, and were more consistently monitored by Customs. In the 1890s the Maritime Customs reported passenger figures that were much closer to the levels of seaborne migration reported by other sources. In 1893 over 44,000 Chinese passengers were recorded leaving North China ports for Manchuria, and in 1900 over 120,000 passengers were reported.[64]

Some of the Customs commissioners believed that the annual reports seriously understated passenger figures. This suspicion was confirmed at Yingkou in 1899 and 1901. Outbreaks of plague at the port in these years resulted in medical examinations and enumeration of all departing passengers. These independent passenger counts found significantly larger actual numbers of passengers on each ship than the total reported.[65] In 1927 the South Manchuria Railway researchers found that ships routinely carried more than their authorized capacity of passengers, even though they always reported numbers within their rated limits.[66] The Railway researchers were able to estimate the size of the shortfall for the years from 1923 to 1928 by comparing Customs passenger data for Dalian with records maintained by the harbor Water Police. They found that the number recorded by the police exceeded the Customs total by an average of 18 percent in the six years from 1923 through 1928.[67]

Despite the persistent tendency to undercount, the Customs passenger series is consistent with the major historical events that influenced the migration. The number of passengers recorded entering Manchuria by sea rose steadily in the early 1890s, declined sharply during the Sino-Japanese War in 1894 and 1895, then surged at the turn of the century as construction of the South Manchuria Railway caused the demand for labor to explode. By 1902 the annual total was over 200,000. The only significant drop below that level occurred during the Russo-Japanese War of 1904–1905 and during the pneumonic plague epidemic in Manchuria in 1911.[68] After 1928 passenger data were no longer published in the annual Customs reports.

Of course, the passenger data include some travelers who were not migrants and do not include migrants who traveled by routes that did not go through the treaty ports. Fortunately the SMR studies from the 1920s explain how the passenger data related to the total numbers of migrants. By following the Railway's adjustments, it is possible to reconstruct migrant data for 1891 to 1922 that are consistent with the series for 1923 to 1942, resulting in a continuous statistical description of the migration for the fifty-two years from 1891 to 1942. The numbers are illustrated in Figure 1.3 and appear in Appendix Table 1.[69]

Observations on the Data

Figure 1.1 shows that annual migration numbers rose substantially at the turn of the century, when the first railways in Manchuria were constructed. From 1895 until the early 1940s there was a steady increase in migrant numbers, from an average of less than 40,000 a year between 1891 and 1895, to over a million each year in the late 1920s and again in

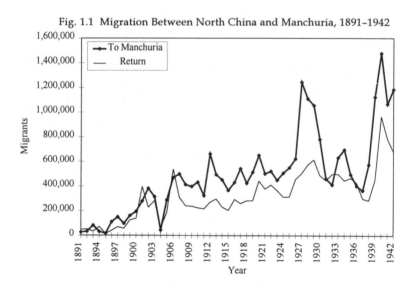

Fig. 1.1 Migration Between North China and Manchuria, 1891–1942

the late 1930s. The rising flow was interrupted only by the Russo-Japanese War in 1904 and restrictive immigration policies of the Manchukuo government in the early 1930s. The figure also shows that return migration closely followed out-migration in most years, but that the difference between the two could vary considerably, from net losses for Manchuria in a few years, to gains of over half a million in 1928 and the late 1930s. (For details on return migration, see chapter 4.)

Because the data were gathered at the relatively few routes into Manchuria, the annual flow can be divided into migrants coming from two broad home areas. Most migrants who lived on the Shandong Peninsula to the east and north of the railway between Jinan and Qingdao departed from the ports of Longkou and Yantai (Chefoo) on the north coast of the Peninsula. This was the case with Zhang Zhenbao and his companions. Migrants from western Shandong and Hebei—many from areas on the North China Plain—could either make the entire trip by land, or they could take ships from Qingdao or Tianjin. The separate streams of migration from the Shandong Peninsula and Hebei-West Shandong appear below in Figure 1.2. The numbers are given in Appendix Table 2.

Figure 1.2 shows that the level of migration from the Shandong Peninsula was remarkably stable, reflecting the area's proximity to

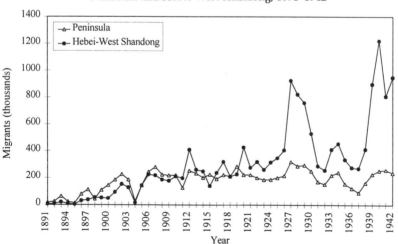

Fig. 1.2 Migration from the Shandong
Peninsula and Hebei-West Shandong, 1891–1942

Manchuria and its long tradition of sending off "swallows" each spring. After the turn of the century annual migration rarely fell below 200,000 and only once rose above 300,000. The average number of migrants per year for the entire 52-year period was 181,000, and the standard deviation was 79,000, less than half of the average. The flow from Hebei and western Shandong, on the other hand, was much larger, averaging over 300,000 migrants per year, but it was also much more variable. The numbers after 1902 ranged erratically between a minimum of 15,700 in 1904 and a maximum of over 1.2 million in 1940, with a standard deviation of 276,000, nearly as large as the average.

The importance of migration to an area depends not just on the numbers of migrants, but also on the size of the population. In 1933 the population of Hebei, including the Beijing Metropolitan District, was reported as 34.6 million, and the population of Shandong was reported as 40.6 million, of whom 14.3 million resided in Jiaodong District—the Peninsula. In other words, although less than 20 percent of the combined populations of Hebei and Shandong resided on the Peninsula, it supplied almost 40 percent of all migrants. Figure 1.3 shows the portion of the population of each of the two broad home areas that migrated each year, expressed as the rate of migration (migrants per thousand population).

Fig. 1.3 Rate of Migration from the Shandong Peninsula
and Hebei-West Shandong 1891–1942

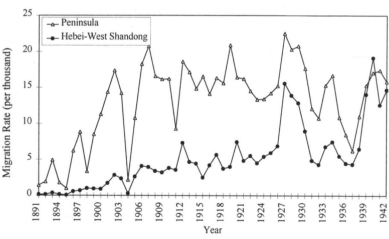

The data appear in Appendix Tables 3 and 4. On average, over 2.5 times as many people per thousand went to Manchuria from the Peninsula each year as from the other home areas, demonstrating again the more permanent role of migration in the Peninsula's economy.

The importance of circular migration[70] to the population of the Peninsula is emphasized in the Longkou *Trade Report* for 1916:

That emigration is the keystone in the whole life-structure of the entire population of this vast and populous district will be understood when it is realized that of three sons in a family invariably two leave home to seek their luck for a shorter or longer period in the North.[71]

In the 1860s, Ida Pruitt said of Penglai:

From almost every family a son went to Manchuria to seek his fortune, for trade was in their bones and the rocks of the homeland were bare. A good sailboat could get there, threading between the islands, in two or three days if the weather was fair.[72]

For much of the Peninsula, particularly the coastal regions, migration was not just a reaction to hard times, it was a basic element of the local economy.

2

PUSHES AND PULLS: FORCES
THAT SHAPED THE MIGRATION

The former migrants interviewed for this study traveled to Manchuria because they believed they could earn more money there than at home. As with most voluntary migrations in other times and places, the various forces that observers reported were important to the migration primarily because they affected income-earning possibilities.[1] And income prospects at both ends of the migration were most directly influenced by economic growth—or the lack of it. In the case of early twentieth-century China, the most dynamic improvements in the economy were stimulated by the arrival of modern production methods, modern transportation, and international trade. At the same time, the economy was often damaged by natural and manmade disasters that retarded growth over wide areas and pushed many migrants from their homes.

Other considerations pushed some migrants toward Manchuria and pulled others away. For many potential migrants the decision to venture far from home was eased by signing on with a recruiter. Recruiters removed the uncertainty and risk of going through a job search in Manchuria, although they also took part of the migrants' earnings— sometimes a very substantial part—as their fees. Some migrants were drawn to destinations other than Manchuria, including places as distant as South Africa and France. Job prospects in Manchuria were also affected by the arrival of immigrants from other countries, including Russia, Japan, and Korea.

MIGRATION AND THE ECONOMY

Economic change in China and abroad during the late Qing brought opportunity for some but removed it from others. After the Taiping Rebellion cut off trade between north and south China in the 1850s, many people in western Shandong lost their livelihood as the grain trade on the Grand Canal dwindled to nothing.[2] Linqing, on the Grand Canal at the Shandong-Zhili border, declined from a considerable trading center into a backwater after the Taipings captured it in 1855.[3] Traffic on the Grand Canal was not restored with peace, but was supplanted by faster and cheaper steam transportation, first by ship, then by rail. The vagaries of foreign trade and export-led production also produced instability in employment. Wei County, in central Shandong, was one of the first areas in China to grow substantial amounts of the "bright tobacco" used in manufactured cigarettes. The crop promised great profits, but also exposed growers to a range of risks from disease to price gouging to price fluctuations on international markets.[4] Yantai (Chefoo) was hit by a permanent foreign market disaster, when after the First World War women in Europe and North America started bobbing and shingling their hair, thus drastically reducing the demand for hairnets. At Yantai, the center of the hairnet industry, workshops that had once employed 17,000 people by 1926 employed only 2,000. Former workers in the industry and their families had to look for another source of income.[5] For many people, migration to Manchuria was the answer.

Incomes

Numerous studies have documented the job opportunities and higher income levels in Manchuria.[6] Franklin Ho, writing in 1931, remarked, "As a distinct pioneer belt and with the growth of industrialization, Manchuria is in need of more laborers than they themselves can supply for the development of industry, mining, and agriculture. Opportunities for employment are plentiful and wages are relatively high." He found that in Jilin and Heilongjiang Provinces a migrant from Shandong working as an assistant farm hand could earn "about $130 Harbin currency a year, or almost three to four times as much as he could earn in his native district."[7]

An SMR study on migrants published in 1940 compared real wage levels of Chinese workers in Manchuria and North China by calculating the portion of daily wages that was required for eating expenses in each area. Among the Chinese construction workers and coal miners surveyed in Manchuria, an average of 46 percent of each day's wage was spent on minimal food needs, while the comparable figure for single cargo

handlers and spinning mill workers in Qingdao was nearly 60 percent.[8]
Another SMR study published in 1941 divided total wages by living
expenses for six occupations in North China and Manchuria, then
compared the ratio of this "real wage" rate in Manchuria to that in North
China. In the occupations surveyed, net income rates in Manchuria were
between 47 and 118 percent higher than in North China.

Table 2.1 Ratio of "Real Wages"
Manchuria Over North China, 1941

Occupation	Wage ratio
Waiter	1.47
Laborer	1.66
Construction worker	1.96
Stone mason	1.67
Sawyer	1.52
Coal miner	2.18

Source: Toiku Shiro, "Hokushi ni okeru tai man
rodo ryoku kyokyu no kinkyo" (Recent condition
of the labor supply for Manchuria in North
China), in Mantetsu chosa geppo 21.1 (January
1941): 178, Table 1.

History, Geography, and Jobs

Why did Manchuria offer more jobs and higher wages? The
fundamental reason was that there were far fewer people relative to the
available natural resources in Manchuria than in Shandong and Hebei.
Population density was low in Manchuria for several historical and
geographic reasons, the most basic of which was that there were few
natural transportation routes, particularly in the north. Although
Manchuria had been linked to North China from the earliest eras of
Chinese civilization, it was also sufficiently isolated to prevent full
integration with China before the twentieth century. Archaeological
evidence indicates there were close ties between North China and
southern Manchuria as early as the prehistoric and Yin-Shang (roughly
1766–1122 B.C.) Chinese cultures, and when the Great Wall was first
pieced together by the Qin dynasty at the end of the third century B.C.,
the eastern end is said to have encompassed the southern tip of
Manchuria, including the Liaodong Peninsula.[9] Nonetheless, for most of
its history Manchuria was only tenuously connected to the periphery of
the extensive North China marketing networks.[10] Manchuria did not
develop dense regional marketing systems like those that had emerged
centuries earlier in the other major regions of China until railways were
introduced.

Manchuria was historically divided by its geography into two distinct economic and cultural zones. The southern half of the fertile Manchurian Plain is drained by the Liao River, which flows south to the Gulf of Bohai, providing transportation toward the markets of North China. This region was inhabited from ancient times primarily by Chinese farmers and was controlled in some periods by strong Chinese empires. The northern part of the plain, however, is drained by the Songhua (Sungari) River, which flows north to the Heilongjiang (Amur) River, away from China. This region and the mountainous areas to the east and west of the central plain were home to nomadic and semi-nomadic tribes that Chinese governments rarely controlled.[11] In three periods when the Chinese state was weak, coalitions of tribes from Manchuria invaded China and established dynasties. The last of these occurred in 1644, when the group of tribes that called itself the Manchus seized control of all China and ruled as the Qing dynasty until the Republican Revolution of 1911.[12]

The Qing controlled all of Manchuria, but intentionally hindered its economic development. The labor shortage that drew migrants into the region from North China in the twentieth century had its origins three-and-a-half centuries earlier, when the prolonged series of campaigns waged by the Manchu banner armies against the forces of the Ming dynasty decimated the population of Manchuria. By the time the conquest was completed, the population of Manchuria had dwindled to around three million people.[13] For a brief period the Qing government encouraged resettlement of southern Manchuria by willing migrants and thousands of convicts and political exiles. In the 1660s, however, Manchu leaders decided to prohibit Chinese migration in order to preserve the Manchu way of life and to retain control over valuable products of the region, notably ginseng root and furs, especially the sable. To enforce the ban on migration, two lines of willow trees, known as the "Willow Palisades," were planted along the periphery of the traditional area of Chinese settlement in southern Manchuria. Troops were stationed at checkpoints along the palisades.[14] The penalties for ships' captains who helped migrants move to Manchuria were harsh; the mid-Qing legal code stipulated 90 strokes of the bamboo, two-and-a-half years' exile, plus confiscation of the boat as punishment.[15]

Nonetheless, the official prohibition did not completely stop migration into Manchuria, a fact the Qing court was well aware of. An edict from the Kangxi Emperor in 1707 noted that in Manchuria, "We saw people from Shandong everywhere, some hundred thousand living as merchants or working on the land."[16]

Few of these people were officially sanctioned settlers; most hoped to quietly make a reasonable living as squatters on the rich land and avoid detection by the authorities in their remote locations.[17] A Japanese journalist later gave a lyrical description of the historical process that had brought the settlers there:

> When the Chinese entered Manchuria they walked with the furtive steps of a thief. Indeed, they were law-breakers—criminals in the eyes of the Manchu law. They bowed in the dust before the Manchu landlord: got the job of a petty farm labourer. Their one passion seemed to be patient, eternal toil. Nothing stopped them in their work. And in that manner they laid the foundation of economic and financial power. But they never made speeches over it. When their Manchu landlords wished to lease the land they spoke, for they were ready to put up the money. When the land changed hands, it was from the hand of the original Manchu owner to that of a Chinese tenant farmer. Settled on their own piece of land, they called across the Yellow Sea to their kinfolk whom they had left in their home villages in Shantung. The kinfolk came and joined them. The history of the Agricultural Development of Manchuria is the story of the Shantung Coolie, nothing more.[18]

Many banner troops and local officials regarded settlers as an asset. Banner garrisons were expected to support themselves by farming, and bannermen on active duty were sometimes rewarded with pieces of land rather than money. Thus many bannermen in Manchuria held tracts of land which they were eager to rent or sell to Chinese farmers. In addition, Chinese farmers, artisans, and merchants supplied the bannermen highly desired goods and services, and they were a valuable source of taxation revenue for local governments.[19]

The prohibition on immigration was officially relaxed in times of famine in North China.[20] A massive wave of refugees entered Manchuria during the great drought and famine of 1876 to 1879, one of the worst natural disasters in Chinese history. It devastated much of Shaanxi, Shanxi, Henan, Hebei, and western Shandong, with a death toll believed to number over ten million people.[21] In 1876 Chinese officials told the Customs commissioner at Yingkou (Newchwang) that nearly 900,000 migrants arrived in South Manchuria that year: some 80,000 arrived by boat at Yingkou, around 600,000 landed on the Liaodong Peninsula, and about 200,000 entered by the land route through Shanhaiguan.[22]

The settlers, legal or otherwise, concentrated most densely in the Liaodong Peninsula; further north government efforts to keep the Manchu heartland free from Chinese settlement, plus the inhospitable climate and the lack of efficient transportation routes, kept the population far below what the land could support. At the end of the Qing, most of the land in the north was still virgin and was beginning to attract unwelcome attention from Russia and Japan. When the Qing authorities finally decided to open Manchuria to settlement—the northern parts in 1860, and the whole area in 1887—it was to counter the growing threat of Russian expansionism.[23]

Once Manchuria was opened, it inspired great excitement, not only among Russians and Japanese, but among other foreigners who saw it as one of the last frontiers in the world. The scarcity of labor was seen as one of the few obstacles to rapid development. By the end of the Qing the population of Fengtian, the southern part of Manchuria, was reported to be around 18 million.[24] But the central and northern zones remained so seriously short of labor that in 1901 Alexander Hosie, the British consul at Yingkou, estimated that only one-fifth of the arable land in Manchuria was under cultivation.[25]

Railways and Migration

The most important barrier to economic growth in Manchuria was removed at the turn of the twentieth century when the Chinese Eastern and South Manchuria railway lines brought steam-powered transportation to the Manchurian Plain. In 1896 the Qing court granted Russia the right to build the Chinese Eastern Railway across northern Manchuria to the port of Vladivostok. In 1898 Russia also received the rights to lease Dalian and Port Arthur (Lushun) and to build the South Manchuria Railway to connect the Liaodong Peninsula to the Chinese Eastern Railway.[26]

Ironically, while Russia intended the two railways to extend its control over Manchuria, they actually provided the means and the stimulus for the massive influx of Chinese settlers that ensured Manchuria would remain Chinese.[27] When construction began in 1898, migration from Hebei and Shandong soared as tens of thousands of laborers sought work on the railways. In that year the Newchwang Customs commissioner at Yingkou remarked in his annual report, "The increase apparent in the number of those who arrived is owing to the engagement of numbers of coolies required to build the Russian railway. Each steamer that arrived from Chefoo [Yantai] and Tientsin was literally packed with coolies, some of the steamers which came in from Tientsin to this port being specially chartered to convey coolies." Between 1897 and 1900 the number of migrants recorded entering Manchuria from North China ports grew from about 42,000 to over 122,000, and in 1902 the total exceeded 213,000.[28]

When the railways were opened to traffic in 1902, migrants were able for the first time to travel quickly and relatively inexpensively from the docks at Yingkou and Dalian all the way north to Heilongjiang. The influence of the railways on the settlement of Manchuria was profound. At the end of the nineteenth century Jilin and Heilongjiang were still relatively lightly populated, with an extensive, frontier-style economy as opposed to the intensive agriculture characteristic of the North China Plain.[29] The completion of the Chinese Eastern and South Manchuria lines linked Jilin and Heilongjiang to the ports of Vladivostok, Dalian, and Yingkou. Steamship traffic quickly drew Manchurian products into regional and world markets, fostering lively trade with Japan, western Europe, and North America. With growing markets for agricultural exports—dominated by a booming trade in Manchurian soybeans—and easier, cheaper transportation, large numbers of farmers from North China streamed onto the plains of northern Manchuria during the next three decades.[30]

Russia's dominance over railway development in Manchuria was brief. The Treaty of Portsmouth, which ended the Russo-Japanese War in 1905, awarded Russia's rights over the Liaodong Peninsula and the South Manchuria Railway line between Changchun and Dalian to Japan.[31] From 1906 until 1931 Manchuria was a complex patchwork of Chinese, Japanese, and Russian spheres of authority. Northern Manchuria was dominated by the Chinese Eastern Railway, which remained under Russian control until the Russian Revolution of 1917. In the 1920s the railway was managed jointly by a Chinese-Soviet board, but it became a subject of dispute and finally the cause of an undeclared border war between China and the Soviet Union in 1929. Meanwhile, Japan held the Liaodong Peninsula, the South Manchuria Railway, the strip of land through which the SMR ran, and a host of smaller rail lines, mines, and other industrial and commercial projects.

The Russian and Japanese enterprises received the most attention, but there was also a growing number of railways under Chinese control, including the important Bei-Ning (Beijing-Shenyang or Peking-Mukden) Railway. In addition, commerce, agriculture, and light industry were mostly Chinese-owned, and the civil government and military forces in all but the leasehold areas were also Chinese. This Chinese government was not, however, the national government, but the warlord regime of Marshal Zhang Zuolin. When he was assassinated in 1928 by elements of the Japanese Army in Manchuria,[32] he was succeeded by his son Zhang Xueliang, the "Young Marshal," who was driven out of Manchuria by the Japanese Army in the so-called Manchurian Incident of 1931.

The importance of the railways to economic growth is illustrated by the following data on the "average cost of transportation of agricultural products to markets outside the *hsien* [*xian*, county] in silver dollars per ton-mile" in the early 1930s:

Table 2.2 Transportation Cost per Ton-Mile

Transport mode	Cost/ton-mile (in silver dollars)
Junk	0.14
Human portage	0.71
Wheelbarrow	0.30
Camel	0.37
Cart	0.36
Donkey	0.56
Mule	0.48
Horse	0.53
Railway	0.09
Steamboat	0.08

Source: L. Buck, *Land Utilization in China: Statistics,* Chapter 9, Table 5. *Note:* Similar figures from a variety of sources are given in Ralph William Huenemann, *The Dragon and the Iron Horse: The Economics of Railroads in China, 1876–1937* (Cambridge, Mass.: Harvard University Press, 1984), 222–25.

The lower cost of railway and steamship transportation opened new markets for many traditional Chinese products, such as peanuts, eggs, and sesame seeds.[33] The most dramatic impact was on the soybean trade. By 1929 Manchuria produced 61 percent of the world's total soybean output.[34] Many of the jobs migrants obtained—in farming, transportation, or oil pressing—were directly related to the soybean trade, while thousands of others worked in service trades supplying everything from shoes to meals for the bean workers.

Even traditional forms of transportation that had declined so precipitously along the old Grand Canal were stimulated in most areas by the rise of railway and steamship traffic. While trains and steamships took over much of the long-distance hauling, nearly all local transportation still relied on sampans, junks, carts, porters, and pack animals. The rapidly growing volume of regionally and internationally traded farm products still had to be moved from the farms and towns where they were produced to the sparse network of rail lines and steamship ports.[35] In 1900 the Customs report for Yingkou commented that "the growth of commerce induced by cheap and speedy conveyance in steamers must surely demand many more junks to feed the Treaty Ports from non-treaty places on the coast."[36] In 1908 British consul Alexander Hosie reported a tripling of the boat traffic on the Liao River, which carried produce from the South Manchuria Plain to the port of Yingkou and returned with salt, iron, and general cargo.[37] The Customs decennial report for 1922 to 1931 remarked that traditional shipping continued to function with surprising success in the face of steam competition, due mainly to the overall increase in commerce, and also to a reduction in piracy achieved by the steamships and the presence of modern gunboats.[38] In fact, Customs data on junk entries in the annual reports indicate that junk traffic in the Gulf of Bohai more than doubled between 1910 and 1928.

Table 2.3 Average Number of Junks Entering Port Annually

Years	Tianjin	Yantai	Dalian	Yingkou
1910–1914	524	7,794	4,937	4,051
1915–1919	535	7,590	9,863	3,625
1920–1924	877	14,831	17,977	7,826
1925–1928	1,096	16,206	21,449	9,759

Source: CMC, Returns of Trade and Trade Reports for Tianjin, Yantai, Dairen, Yingkou, 1910–1928.

Railways and steam shipping also contributed significantly to increased employment in China's small modern sector. The railways themselves were important employers of labor, particularly during the construction phase. In 1899 the Customs commissioner at Yingkou reported that over 200,000 Chinese laborers were at work constructing the Chinese Eastern Railway (CER).[39] In 1935, when administration of the CER was transferred from Soviet authorities to the SMR, it employed 10,716 Chinese workers.[40]

Modern industry constituted only a small part of the Chinese economy in the early twentieth century, but it grew rapidly where it was served by rail or steamship transportation and had access to foreign trade. Coal mining, for instance, was directly linked to railway expansion. The first railway in North China was built in the late 1870s to service the Kaiping Mines at Tangshan in northeastern Hebei.[41] As early as 1899 the CER opened several coal mines along its route in Manchuria.[42] A major goal of the German colonial plan for Shandong was to exploit the mineral resources of the Peninsula; coal mines were developed within the zone of the Shandong Railway concurrently with construction of the track. German mining activity in Shandong also generated concerted competition from Chinese-owned mines at the urging of the provincial authorities.[43] The Fuxun coal mines near Shenyang, the largest mining operation in China, were first developed in modern form by the SMR,[44] and their rapid expansion directly affected migration through a recruiting system instituted to alleviate shortages of mine labor in 1918. Between 1918 and 1921 an average of 15,000 mine workers were recruited in Shandong and Hebei each year.[45]

Describing itself as "the carrier of the light of civilization into Manchuria,"[46] the South Manchuria Railway Company operated a wide range of modern enterprises including hotels, harbors, a shale-oil distillation plant, the Anshan iron works, and a host of public works such as schools, hospitals, and research facilities. Between 1907 and 1936 over 60 percent of SMR capital outlays were invested in holdings other than railways, and between 1933 and 1936 less than half of the company's receipts were railway revenues.[47]

Railways were also introduced in Hebei and western Shandong— but not the Peninsula—around the turn of the century. The Beijing-Hankou Railway, which ran south from Beijing through western Hebei, began carrying limited freight in 1901 and was completed in 1906 (see Appendix Table 5). The Beijing-Liaoning Line, originally begun in 1878 at the Kaiping Mines north of Tianjin, was extended in stages north to Shenyang and south to Tianjin and then Beijing. When it was completed in 1907, it became the main artery between North China and Manchuria. The Tianjin-Pukou Line ran south from Tianjin through Jinan and southern Shandong and thence to the Yangtze River valley. It began to carry traffic in 1910 and was completed in 1912. The Shandong Railway, also known as the Jiao-Ji (Kiao-tsi) Line, was the most significant economic result of Germany's endeavors in Shandong. Running from the port of Qingdao across the base of the Peninsula to Jinan, it began carrying traffic in 1901 and was completed in 1904. Taken together, these lines formed a very sparse network for the size of the area and the population they served, but as in Manchuria, they restructured the economic landscape, opening domestic and world markets to products that previously had been traded only locally or not at all.

Figure 2.1 shows that the volume of rail traffic in Hebei–West Shandong was very close to the volume in Manchuria until the 1920s, when warlord conflicts caused freight tonnage in North China to stagnate and decline, while growth in Manchuria went on unabated. The effect on employment and incomes, however, was much larger in Manchuria because each ton of freight served a considerably smaller

Fig. 2.1 Rail Freight Volume in Hebei–West
Shandong and Manchuria, 1891–1931

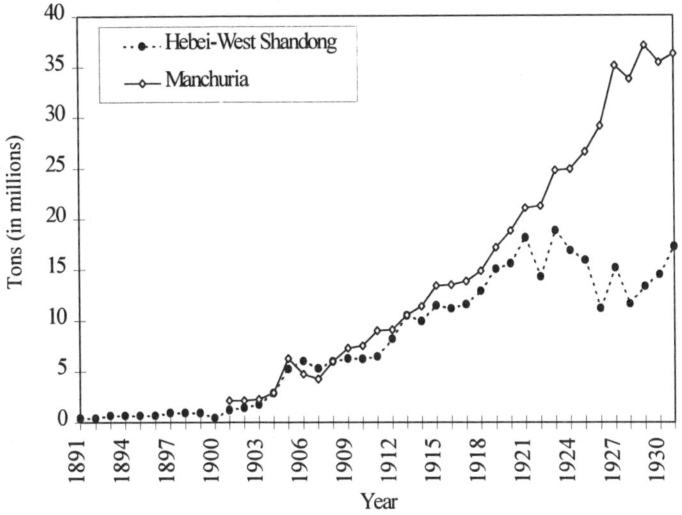

population. At the turn of the century the combined population of Hebei and Shandong was around 66 million, while the number of people in Manchuria was about 24 million. By the mid-1930s the population of Manchuria reached some 40 million, while Hebei and Shandong held about 76 million.[48] Figure 2.2 shows that as soon as the Chinese Eastern and South Manchuria lines went into operation, railway freight per capita in Manchuria was over four times as large as in Hebei and Shandong and was never less than twice as large.

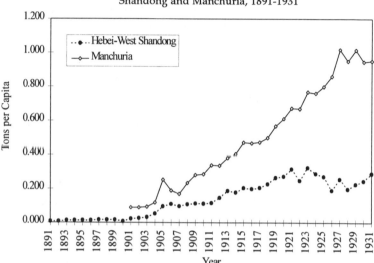

Fig. 2.2 Railway Freight Tons per Capita, Hebei-West
Shandong and Manchuria, 1891-1931

· *Foreign Trade and Migration*

The rise in foreign trade that accompanied the growth of modern
transportation also increased income-earning opportunities for many
workers. Figure 2.3 shows the growth of total net foreign trade (imports
plus exports minus re-exports) in Manchuria, the Shandong Peninsula and
Hebei-West Shandong.

As with the railways, the impact was greater in Manchuria than in
North China. As the source of modern production technology, foreign
trade was closely linked to the growth of modern economic activities.[49]
Many of the materials and machines required for the construction of
industrial facilities were imported from abroad. Of 1,244 engines
delivered to railways in China proper between 1897 and 1930, only 58
were constructed in China—all at the Tangshan workshop of the Beijing-
Liaoning Railway—while the others were imported from America,
England, Germany, France, and Belgium.[50] Between 1913 and 1936
imports supplied approximately 44 percent of the iron and steel and 70
percent of the machinery used in China.[51] Machinery, transportation
materials, iron, steel, and other metals accounted for a steadily rising
share of China's imports, from 7 percent in 1913 to 14 percent in 1920 to
25 percent in 1936.[52]

Fig. 2.3 Total Net Trade: Shandong Peninsula,
Hebei–West Shandong, and Manchuria, 1891–1931

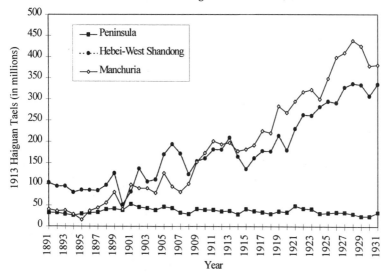

Fig. 2.4 Trade per Capita: Shandong Peninsula,
Hebei–West Shandong, and Manchuria, 1891–1931

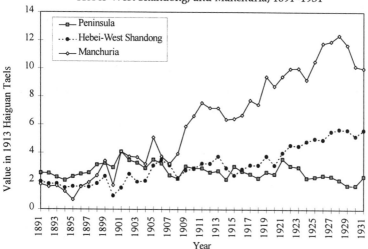

In foreign trade as in railway traffic the advantage enjoyed by Manchuria in most years after the turn of the century was even larger in per capita terms. Figure 2.4 demonstrates that beginning in 1901 the importance of foreign trade relative to population size was substantially greater in Manchuria than in either the Shandong Peninsula or in Hebei–West Shandong. In fact, over the forty-year period from 1891 to 1931 there was no growth at all in the foreign trade of the Shandong Peninsula. Trade at the northern Peninsula ports reached its peak in 1901 and the figures for the 1920s are nearly the same as those for the early 1890s. In other words, people living on the Peninsula received none of the benefits of the expanded foreign markets that generated thousands of new jobs in Manchuria.

Disasters and Migration

Disasters exerted perennial pressure to migrate. In a survey of over a thousand migrant families conducted by the Nankai Economic Research Institute in 1931, 27 percent of the respondents identified disasters of various types as their reason for leaving home.[53] Natural disasters ran the gamut from flood to drought to insects to disease. Manmade disasters were usually associated with warfare. There was constant lament about military turbulence and the related disruption of daily life, especially in areas frequented by *zapai*—small military units independent of any superior command. Sometimes the damage was done by actual fighting, for example, that which accompanied the Northern Expedition of 1927–1928,[54] or the earlier Russo-Japanese War of 1904–1905, in which some 20,000 civilians died in southern Manchuria.[55] More often, however, devastation was brought about by the demands the military made on the civilian population for food, labor, animals, money, and taxes.[56] In 1925 there were a quarter of a million soldiers in Shandong, eating up three-quarters of the provincial budget and making constant additional demands on the areas in which they were stationed.[57] In 1929 a map of Shandong showed six distinct military commands, including those of the central government and the Japanese; about a third of the province had no single command, but was "overrun with brigands and remnants of armies."[58]

Civilians especially feared military press-ganging—men being seized not to be soldiers but to serve as porters.[59] The danger of press-ganging was greatest near major roads or railway lines or close to a port; the military "recruiters" did not want to go further than they had to. Press-ganging took place with depressing regularity along the railway line from Jinan to Qingdao, and the fear of press-ganging forced many young men to flee.[60]

But no area was immune. In 1930 a student who returned for the summer to his home in Lu County (southwestern part of the Peninsula) found the place beset by soldiers involved in the war between Nanjing and the combined forces of Feng Yuxiang and Yan Xishan. The greatest fear for the local people, as it had been for the past decade, was press-ganging, which had led about 20 percent of the young men to leave the district over the previous decade.[61]

An immediate economic result of warlord-era fighting was the serious disruption of transportation as armies commandeered all available vehicles.[62] The detrimental impact of the civil wars on Hebei and western Shandong is plainly evident in Figure 2.1 in the reduced railway freight traffic of the 1920s. A less direct economic result was disruption of the nationwide financial market. In 1911, for instance, fighting related to the Republican Revolution did not touch Manchuria, but Chinese banks throughout China and Manchuria all suspended operations, and merchants were unable to obtain the credit they needed to purchase stocks of goods, causing a serious decline in trade.[63]

North China was notoriously vulnerable to natural disasters. Floods often wreaked tremendous physical destruction in the low-lying regions of Hebei and western Shandong, particularly along the Yellow River. Topsoil was washed away. Houses, crops, and animals were destroyed, reducing not only the size of the harvest and levels of trade in the year of the flood itself, but also jeopardizing the ability of the population to return to normal economic activities in subsequent years.[64] Canals and navigable rivers became blocked by silt, and roads and railways were washed out. Floods had the greatest impact when they were followed by one or more additional years of natural disaster. The terrible famine of 1920 resulted from a sequence of catastrophic events which began with a flood that inundated 15,000 square miles in Hebei in 1917, continued with poor harvests in 1919, and culminated in a lethal drought in 1920–1921.[65]

The most deadly disasters were droughts. The drought-famine of 1876–1879 killed between nine and 13 million people in the provinces of Shaanxi, Shanxi, Henan, Hebei, and Shandong. The drought-famine of 1920–1921 affected nearly 25 million peasants in roughly the same area. Mortality was greatly reduced due to railway food deliveries, but the number of deaths still reached approximately 500,000.[66] Desperate measures taken during drought-famines inflicted lasting damage on farm resources, since farm families were sometimes forced to eat their livestock, their seed grain, and even weeds and the leaves of the trees that helped to prevent erosion.[67]

Disasters were not limited to North China. In both North China and Manchuria dense population concentrations and primitive sanitary conditions allowed communicable diseases to spread with great speed. The most severe disease to affect the migration was pneumonic plague. Several times in the early twentieth century it swept down the railway lines and trade routes from Mongolia and northern Manchuria, where trappers were infected by fleas from plague-carrying marmots and rats. The rate of mortality was high. The worst epidemic of plague occurred in the winter of 1910–1911, causing an estimated 70,000 deaths in Manchuria.[68] Cholera and influenza also caused extensive fatalities.[69] In some cases afflicted areas were quarantined, as at Yantai, where, during the epidemic of 1910–1911, ships were prevented from calling at the port for four months.[70]

Banditry also afflicted both North China and Manchuria. Even a small number of bandit raids could virtually paralyze commerce over a wide area, as happened in response to the activities of the brigand called White Wolf in North Central China in 1913 and 1914. Reductions in commerce were reportedly caused by increased bandit predation in Hebei and Shandong in 1918.[71]

The severity of the bandit problem in North China rose during the warlord era of the 1920s, as the numbers of the destitute increased, swelling the ranks of potential desperadoes, and as modern arms became more readily available from the warlord armies.[72] In Manchuria the bands of mounted brigands known as *hong huzi* (red beards) terrorized settlers in the hills and forests and in some cases were strong enough to defeat regular troops.[73]

A representative picture of the incidence of different types of major disasters in the Shandong Peninsula, Hebei-West Shandong, and Manchuria between 1891 and 1931 can be drawn from the "conditions affecting trade" sections of the annual trade reports written by the Maritime Customs commissioners for the treaty ports and Customs stations in North China and Manchuria. The following table lists the years in which events occurred that caused one thousand or more deaths or affected at least 25 percent of the Shandong Peninsula, Hebei-West Shandong, and Manchuria:

Table 2.4 Major Disasters, 1891–1931

Disaster	Shandong Peninsula	Hebei-West Shandong	Manchuria
Warfare	1895, 1914	1900, 1920, 1922, 1926, 1928, 1930	1894, 1895, 1900, 1904, 1905, 1931
Military disruptions	1912	1912	
Insurrections	1916		
Banditry	1914, 1929	1922	
Drought	1914, 1929	1908, 1917, 1920, 1926, 1928	
Flood	1914	1908, 1912, 1917	
Famine		1920, 1928	
Plague	1911		1910, 1911

Sources: CMC, *Returns of Trade and Trade Reports* (annual), from the following treaty ports and Customs stations: Yantai (Chefoo); Longkou (from 1916); Qingdao (Kiaochow) (from 1899); Tianjin (Tientsin); Qinhuangdao (Chinwangtao) (from 1901); Yingkou (Newchwang); Harbin (from 1907); Jilin (Kirin) (from 1907); Shenyang (Moukden) (from 1907); Andong (Antung) (from 1907); Dalian (Dairen) (from 1907). Harbin district included the border crossings of the CER at Manzhouli on the west and Suifenhe on the east, as well as the Heilongjiang River port Aihe (Aigun), and the Songhua River port Sanxing. Shenyang (Moukden)and Jilin (Kirin) were not border points, but Customs officials were stationed there and made annual reports.

Several points emerge from Table 2.4. First, since large-scale disasters took place in only six years out of forty on the Shandong Peninsula and in nine years in Hebei and western Shandong, they cannot account for the high level of migration that characterized the entire period. Second, Manchuria actually experienced more years with major disasters (eight) in this period than the Peninsula, and only one fewer than Hebei and western Shandong, another indication that fear of disasters was probably not the most important motivation for most migrants.

RECRUITMENT

Much of the migration from Shandong and Hebei consisted of "self-starters" (*zifa*), people who left home on their own or went with groups of friends or relatives. But many other migrants were formally recruited by people who needed labor. Among the people who recruited large bodies of labor in Shandong and Hebei were foreigners. One of the earliest foreign enterprises to recruit labor in North China was the Kaiping Mining Company, in Tangshan, Hebei. The mines began operation in the late 1870s, and at first tried to recruit labor directly. However, the company encountered so many difficulties finding suitable workers and getting them to work hard that it moved to a system of contract labor, under which a labor contractor signed up to cut coal from a specific area of the mine and provided his own labor to do so. By the turn of the century the contract labor system was fully established, and two-thirds of the labor force neither worked for the company nor were supervised by them.[74]

The contract labor system was cheap and convenient for the employer. It seemed a new system, given that the foreign companies using it were new, but in fact it emerged from traditional systems of recruiting short-term agricultural labor. The recruiter, commonly known as a *batou*, was a local man whose specialty was making connections between those who needed labor and those who wanted work. Landlords and rich farmers made use of these labor suppliers to find workers for the busy periods of agriculture. The system had worked traditionally as a "rational, indispensable feature of the countryside."[75] As new demands for labor arose, often in a sporadic way, the contract labor system expanded to supply labor for industrial and mining ventures and even for work abroad.[76] An employer contracted with a supplier of labor for a certain number of men, left all the arrangements to the contractor, and paid the workers' wages directly to him. It suited everyone's interests, even in one sense the workers. Although they were left open to maltreatment and gouging by both contractors and employers, it was a reliable method of getting work in a system that had no impersonal means of recruiting labor, such as advertisements or labor exchanges.

When it came to labor recruitment for foreign countries, Shandong was a favored place because it had a reputation for producing strong, hard-working men with high levels of endurance. These advantages, coupled with the presence in Shandong of foreign missionaries and businessmen who could supervise recruiting for special purposes, such as laborers for the trenches in France during the First World War, made it an ideal place to find workers.

An early example of direct foreign recruitment occurred from 1889 to 1903, when laborers were recruited in Shandong and Hebei and shipped north to build the Chinese Eastern Railway.[77] Other recruiting efforts for a variety of purposes soon followed. At the end of the Qing, British agents started recruiting workers from the Jiaozhou area for the mines in the Transvaal,[78] while the Japanese recruited in Qingdao for the coal mines in Fengtian through the Fuxun Coal Mines Worker Recruitment Office set up there. As the range and scale of labor migration grew, the recruitment process became more complex. Additional layers developed, including labor companies, supercontractors, and subcontractors. Labor contractors still found the men in the villages, but now instead of supplying them direct to an employer, they supplied them to foreign agencies and firms based in China. By the late Qing there were several foreign firms based in Tianjin and Yantai (Chefoo) whose main business was supplying labor.

Through the 1920s foreign agencies continued to recruit Shandong men. One of the more improbable recruiters was the Agricultural Department from the tiny Spanish colony of Fernando Po. Male workers were offered five-year contracts, at U.S. $12 per month. It was not difficult to find people willing to go at that wage, and 1,700 volunteers showed up. However, the new Nanjing government, full of nationalist fervor, opposed such a blatant example of the coolie trade, and the men had to be paid off—they got $10 Mexican, essentially as a windfall.[79]

Recruitment for Manchuria's Mines and Factories

In the early stages of the migration, before personal networks were established, formal recruitment was an important means of marshalling labor for the mines and the factories of Manchuria, as it had been in other parts of China when modern mining and manufacturing started. Three systems were used. First, direct recruiting offices were established in cities in Shandong and Hebei. The Fuxun Mines maintained recruiting offices in four cities in Hebei and three in Shandong.[80]

Second, Chinese agencies provided an indirect recruitment system. The Japanese used Chinese recruiting companies, particularly in Tianjin, which acted as brokers for them. These companies subcontracted to professional labor contractors. Recruitment through labor contractors became standard practice for China's mines, accounting for up to 80 percent of the workers hired. The contractor was often hired by the mine as a foreman and paid directly by the company. He kept at least 10 percent of the workers' wages as his commission, but he made most of his money by supplying food and lodging at inflated prices, and by advancing workers money to send home, or to gamble.[81]

At its worst, when it lacked any moderating personal connection between the contractor and his workers, this form of recruitment led to serious abuses. Workers could be treated virtually as slaves. In 1935 local authorities discovered a group of 200 destitute men at Tianjin Station. They had been recruited from Hejian (southwest of Tianjin) for road work in Heilongjiang by a contractor who gave each of their families a 200 yuan recruitment bonus. When they met men returning from Heilongjiang who told them that they would not be paid up north, the new recruits refused to go on. But they did not have enough money to return home.[82] In Dalian a Japanese recruiting company headed by Aioi

Yoshitaro began developing a massive complex of worker dormitories in 1911. Eventually he built a string of eighty-nine dormitories, which could house 13,000 men. Although the management claimed that this was a model facility with heating and sanitation, in fact it "closely resembled a jail" in which the jailers were 300 *batou*, each controlling his own group of workers, most of whom came from Shandong.[83]

Third, a more personal version of the *batou* system, called the *oyakata* (head coolie) system, paid an existing employee to produce a group of workers, feed them, manage them, and have them ready for work each day. Under this system, Japanese companies gave the employee money to return to his native place at the end of one season to recruit workers to come back with him to Manchuria at the beginning of the next.[84]

In 1930 SMR officials carried out a demographic survey of a small group of migrants. Out of 2,571 groups (11,284 men) arriving at Dalian and Yingkou, 884 were groups of new workers being transferred by "people who had gone back to escort them to Manchuria."[85] This was the least exploitative form of recruitment, since the new laborers were recruited by people from their own native place (*laoxiang*). Long-standing personal connections made excessive exploitation difficult, especially if the *batou* wanted to recruit men the next year.

None of these systems helped to put together a strong labor force. They were cheap ways of recruiting labor, but inefficient over the long run because few men signed on for more than one year. Each season much of the new crop of workers had to be trained. Some Japanese companies, such as the Fuxun Mines, decided that these systems were too old-fashioned, "an obstacle to rational production"; by the 1930s they hired almost all their workers directly.[86]

But most employers found that they saved so much money in wages and so much trouble in management that they continued using them. One of their greatest attractions was that the indirect systems supplied labor without complications. It was unnecessary for managers to learn Chinese — workers could be dealt with entirely through intermediaries. The companies needed labor to staff their new enterprises, and they bought it just as they did any other input for the production process.

Management treated most labor impersonally even though the ties that produced the workers were often personal ones. At one remove, the Japanese relied on the tight Chinese system of personal connections to get them the workers they needed. The Japanese were not, however, doing anything novel. The contract system was the mainstay of Chinese recruitment for the construction of the North American railways, the Panama Canal, and the Trans-Siberian Railway as well.[87]

And Chinese contract labor is still supplied abroad today, though now by the state rather than through personal connections, to areas such as the Middle East that need cheap temporary labor. Today it is the state that makes the profits: Laborers work for Chinese wages, but the government collects at much higher levels.

Recruitment for the Land

People moving to settle on the land seldom went through the formal recruitment processes that workers and miners did. Some responded to official proclamations from Manchurian government agencies that were posted in Shandong and Hebei, as well as in Manchuria itself, describing officially sponsored colonization projects. The Lobei project, for example, almost on the Heilongjiang border with the USSR, was widely advertised in North China and offered over a million *mu* of land for settlement.[88] Much more commonly the new migrants went through established personal channels to join relatives or people from their native places who had migrated earlier. By the mid-1920s, the Lobei settlement was so well established that recruitment of new migrants was largely done through personal channels, and special inducements were hardly relevant.

OTHER MIGRANT DESTINATIONS

Manchuria was the major destination for Shandong and Hebei migrants, but migration streams to other places also developed. To the extent that other destinations became attractive, the pull to Manchuria was somewhat reduced. The eastern parts of Mongolia were considered almost a part of Manchuria and took the overflow of rural settlers into northern Manchuria.

There were also significant movements into Shaanxi from southern Shandong at the end of the Qing. Shaanxi had been devastated and depopulated by a succession of tragedies in the second half of the nineteenth century: the Taiping Rebellion, the Moslem Rebellion, and the great famine of 1887–1888. There was plenty of uncultivated land and empty houses and villages. The Qing government officially encouraged Shandong people to move there, and some did, though the overland journey took up to two months.[89] Other people went further afield.

Siberia

Beginning in the 1890s some thousands of workers traveled by steamer each year from the Shandong port of Yantai to Vladivostok, where they were employed on the Chinese Eastern Railway and in other Russian enterprises in far eastern Siberia. The recorded number of passengers averaged 7,900 per year in the 1890s and swelled to average over 22,000 per year from 1900 to 1916, with several thousand a year added from the port of Qingdao after 1908. This traffic peaked at nearly 70,000 in 1907, but fell off sharply after the Russian Revolution in 1917 and eventually dried up altogether due to the border dispute between Russia and China in 1928.[90]

Transvaal

Immediately after the Boer War, the demand for workers in the Witwatersrand gold mines increased rapidly, while the number of Africans willing to work in the mines declined. Business interests proposed a scheme to bring in large numbers of Chinese workers, who were thought to be cheap and docile. The new British administration concurred, for it was desperately concerned to see postwar South Africa become prosperous to give ex post facto justification to their claims for supplanting the Boers. Between 1904 and 1907, 63,695 Chinese laborers landed in South Africa, 93 percent of them from Shandong and Zhili, shipped out through Qinhuangdao in Hebei and Chefoo in Shandong. This was an easy time to recruit labor, since the Russo-Japanese War had just broken out in Manchuria, putting economic development, and therefore job growth, on hold.[91]

The scheme did not go well. The Chamber of Mines Labor Importation Agency, which handled the recruitment, expected Cantonese-speaking workers from South China and hired organizers and interpreters accordingly. When the northerners arrived, it was almost impossible to have any contact with them or to "manage" them well. Far more serious was the virulent opposition to the scheme from two quite different sources: one was the nativist anti-Asiatic movement, both in the Transvaal and in Britain; the other was the liberal antislavery group, who regarded the coolie trade as being very close to slavery.

The superintendent of foreign labor, an experienced hand with Chinese laborers in the Straits Settlement, to meet the difficulties of managing obstinate laborers, decided to permit 'slight corporal punishment' in 'cases of breaches of discipline and trivial offenses, for which it was not considered necessary to prosecute'. It was impossible to draw the line between slight and severe punishment, and, besides, any such punishment was contrary to law and contract. Cases of flogging were reported in England where the whole Chinese question had entered domestic politics. The defeat of the Unionist Party, and the taking over of the reins of government by the Liberals in January 1906 was largely caused by the Chinese labor question.[92]

The opposition to the scheme became so strong that in 1907 it was formally canceled, leaving a two-year period for those in the system to get home.[93]

France

During the First World War recruitment for labor in foreign countries reached its height in Shandong. The British, French, and Russians all recruited Shandong workers to replace their own young men who were at the front. The British recruited at first in Weihaiwei, taking about 50,000 men, and then moved their recruitment westwards. The British Consulate in Jinan was responsible for recruiting men in that district and sending them to Qingdao, where they departed for Europe. All along the railway from Jinan, offices run by missionaries were set up to recruit workers. Their job was to give health tests, cut the men's hair (queues), have them wash, outfit them with new clothes, inoculate them, and then have them put their marks on contracts. The men were then sent off in a paramilitary organization. Between April 1917 and February 1918 twenty-two vessels left Qingdao for Europe, taking 50,315 men. Later contingents brought the total to 150,000.

The contracts stated their name, place of residence, and the recipient of their recruitment bonus.[94] The terms of their service were detailed, listing all items the men were entitled to, from a bonus paid to the family of 10 *yuan* per month, to wages of 1 to 1.5 francs a day, to their gear on departure (an overcoat, a set of clothes, boots, hat, scarf, wash basin, tea bowl, kettle, palliasse, life belt, etc.), to their food while in France (10 ounces of meat, bread, and flour per day; 8 ounces of rice and vegetables; 2 ounces of pork; 1 ounce of sugar and butter; and 1/2 ounce of salt, tea, peanut oil). Tobacco and matches were issued twice a week, and dried fruit, tooth powder, soap, towel, toothbrush once a month. The men worked ten hours a day, with half a day off each week.

The French used a Chinese company, the Huimin Company, to recruit some 40,000 workers for them. The contracts were more generous than those arranged by the British, stipulating 5 francs a day, but with deductions for food, lodging, clothing, and life insurance, so that the men actually got 2 francs a day.

These terms may have seemed generous enough to encourage men to sign on, but not everything was supplied as agreed. The living conditions in France were bad, and many of the men died of the damp and cold in northern France. But at least their fate was known. Nearly all were returned to Shandong soon after the end of the war, unlike the thirty-three skilled workers recruited in 1917 to work in an airplane factory in Russia. Those men went off on a two-year contract and were never heard from again.[95]

The Transvaal situation was more exploitative and the trenches of France more dangerous than conditions encountered by migrants to Manchuria. Manchuria was also less foreign, with no language or cultural barriers. But it is unlikely that potential migrants made informed comparisons between Manchuria and other possible destinations before deciding where to go. Those who went beyond the Chinese world were almost always recruited. The recruitment schemes were localized, and people had one choice—whether to go or not. They could not choose where to go.

Recruitment of Shandong workers for exotic sites like the battle-fields of France and the mines of Africa received a great deal of publicity, but never constituted a major alternative for family survival strategies because they were always limited in size and duration. The largest single case was the one-time movement of 150,000 men to France, a number smaller than the average annual migration to Manchuria from the Shandong Peninsula alone.

MIGRATION TO MANCHURIA FROM OTHER COUNTRIES

Workers from North China were not the only people drawn to Manchuria. Economic opportunities and political rivalry between Russia, Japan, and China motivated substantial numbers of Russians, Japanese, and Koreans to move to Manchuria in the early twentieth century.

Beginning in the late 1890s Russian workers, engineers, technicians, administrators, and military personnel were brought into Manchuria to build and operate the Chinese Eastern Railway and to administer the railway zone and towns through which it passed. Russian officers and engineers also operated a large fleet of steamships on the Songhua and Heilongjiang Rivers. Harbin was established as a base for the railway and remained predominately a Russian town until the late 1920s. In 1930 there were 140,554 Russians in Manchuria.[96] By 1937 their numbers had declined to around 60,000.[97]

When Japan acquired the South Manchuria Railway and the Liaodong Peninsula, the Japanese counterpart of the Russian migration brought thousands of Japanese technicians, administrators, and other urban workers to southern Manchuria. By the end of 1937 there were nearly 400,000 Japanese living in the towns and cities of Manchuria.[98]

The goal of settling large numbers of Japanese farmers in Manchuria fared less well. At least five major official programs for "mass immigration" from Japan were planned, beginning in 1914 with a scheme for subsidized settlement of former Japanese soldiers in the SMR zone and culminating in 1936 with the adoption of a grandiose twenty-year plan to locate five million Japanese farmers in Manchuria.[99]

In each case detailed surveys were carried out in the prospective settlement areas, the farmers received subsidies of money, land, equipment, seed, and livestock, and supporting facilities such as training institutes and research centers were established.[100] Even after such painstaking preparations, however, few Japanese farmers could be enticed to leave their homes. Those Japanese farm families who did go to Manchuria found a harsh environment and an agrarian economy thoroughly dominated by Chinese farmers and merchants. By the end of 1937 there were only 21,000 Japanese living in the rural areas of Manchuria.

The largest number of non-Chinese immigrants were Koreans. In the early years of the twentieth century Korean farmers began to establish rice-growing communities in the lightly populated valleys along Manchuria and Korea's mountainous border. Unlike the politically fostered migrations from Russia and Japan, the migration from Korea was motivated simply by the desire for farmland. Of the three groups, only Koreans remained a significant element in the population of Manchuria after 1949. By the end of 1937 there were 988,000 Koreans living in Manchuria, of whom 76 percent were farmers.[101]

In 1910 Japan annexed Korea to the Japanese empire. From that time on Japanese officials took particular interest in the affairs of Korean immigrants in Manchuria; in at least one case Japanese troops were sent across the Yalu River to defend Korean settlements in Manchuria from Chinese bandits. In another instance a clash between Chinese and Korean settlers, known as the Wanbaoshan Affair, contributed to the rising tensions that resulted in the Manchurian Incident of 1931.[102] After the formation of Manchukuo in 1932, Japanese leaders devised plans for large-scale Korean immigration, similar to the "mass-immigration" schemes for Japanese farmers. But like the Japanese farmers, few Koreans were tempted to move into the Manchurian Plain. The great majority remained in the eastern regions of Liaoning and Jilin, where they are still the predominant population today.[103]

STATISTICAL INSIGHTS INTO MIGRANT MOTIVATIONS

When we view the migrant data presented in chapter 1 in light of the economic and disaster information outlined here, it is evident that the overall course of the migration closely followed the growth of economic opportunities in Manchuria. Statistical analysis finds strong correlation between migration numbers and levels of railway traffic and foreign trade in Manchuria.[104] The data also indicate that when economic conditions in North China improved, as reflected in railway traffic and foreign trade volume, migration tended to decline. The economic correlation is strongest for the migrant flow from Hebei and western Shandong, and weakest for the Shandong Peninsula, where the economy was largely stagnant, with neither railway development nor growth in trade. It appears that people from Hebei and western Shandong tended to go to Manchuria in larger numbers when conditions at home declined or those in Manchuria improved, and were more likely to stay home when circumstances improved. Migration from the Peninsula, however, tended to vary little except when Manchuria was afflicted by major disasters, indicating that migration was a deeply ingrained element of the local economy.

The data also shed light on the effects of disasters. Many migrants did indeed move to Manchuria to escape drought, flood, famine, warfare, and disease, but migration continued unabated in most years when disasters did not occur. However, disasters in Manchuria — particularly the wars and the epidemic of pneumonic plague in 1910-1911 — caused significant declines in migrant numbers. In other words, while disasters at home constituted a contributing push, they were not the major motivation to migrate.

The economic motivations that appear to be characteristic of the migration as a whole are brought into even sharper focus in the accounts of the migrants themselves. Conditions at home and the prospect of higher incomes to the north persuaded families throughout North China to send out their sons to supplement the family livelihood at home.

3

Family and Migration

The Role of the Family

The social and economic confusion that accompanied the decline of the Qing dynasty and the chaos of the early Republic put great strain on the Chinese family. As the bedrock of support and protection for Chinese rural society, the family had to survive intensified pressures as other social structures weakened with the crumbling of traditional society. Modern-minded intellectuals and revolutionaries might denounce the family and family-centered attitudes (*jiating guannian*) as part of the incubus of backwardness that oppressed the poor, but for most Chinese, the family was still their only frame of reference, and it determined their lives and livelihood.

The family was the major source of economic security and emotional comfort in an increasingly hostile world. In return it made great demands on its members. It was their duty to serve the family, to make whatever contributions they could to the family economy. In an uncertain world this meant they had to help diversify the family's income. Family members had to seek and grasp any opportunities to earn extra money; if such opportunities were limited at home, then they had to be sought elsewhere. This might mean working as a hired hand nearby, or it might mean going further, to the cities or into an army. From the late Qing on a new opportunity for enhancing family welfare emerged: migration to Southeast Asia from Guangdong and Fujian, or to Manchuria from Shandong and Hebei.

Migration could mean the departure of the whole family, but most often it meant sending single young men away so that most of the family could stay at home. Migration promised to benefit the family through remittances and the reduction of mouths to be fed at home. Family

69

interests decided who would go and who would stay in much the same way that they determined other key decisions for individuals, such as when and whom a person should marry. The life course of many young men in areas that produced migrants was largely set: they were born, grew up, went away for a while, returned, got married, and thereafter stayed put. Migration was simply a stage of life. In Ling County the local authorities estimated that during the Republican period one in three men migrated to Manchuria at some stage of their lives.[1]

The inarticulate Confucianism of the masses—the belief that the family had to be preserved in its native place at all costs, close to the graves of the ancestors—mitigated against permanent emigration. Ironically, at the same time, family togetherness and warmth was sacrificed in migration; the welfare of the family demanded that individual members suffer long periods of separation for the greater good of the family. It also demanded that individuals go away without being consulted about their own desires; the family had to send the most suitable person out. Collective family needs took precedence over the wishes of the individual. This was not a peculiarly Chinese feature of migration. Tamara Hareven's description of Quebec workers moving to Massachusetts in the late nineteenth century is strikingly similar:

> Both career choices and economic decisions were made within the family matrix. Families might be described as being composed of units that were switched around as the need arose. Each unit was relied upon and used when appropriate. Following such strategies, families timed the movement of members in response to both individual schedules and external conditions.[2]

In Shandong, as in Quebec, the individual's moral obligation to the family went without question:

> The sense of duty to the family was a manifestation of family culture— a set of values that entailed not only a commitment to the well-being and self reliance or survival of the family but one that took priority over individual needs and personal happiness.[3]

The demands that the family put on the individual in migration were paradoxical. The family obliged individuals to go away, for uncertain prospects of gain, while at the same time cutting them off from the immediate comfort of home. This might seem to weaken the family, but in fact the effects were to strengthen it. Migration was a sign of commitment; rather than lounge around at home the young man was doing something useful. The prolonged absence of husbands, fathers, or sons seemed often to strengthen the ties of affection rather than weaken them, because migration inevitably brought homesickness. And economically migration was a sure winner; the migrant was a net saving to his family while away, and, if he did not disappear altogether, might enrich the family on his return.

The Shape of the Family

Shandong farm families in the late Qing and early Republic were not large. In 1935 the average number of "mouths" per household in Zouping, a relatively affluent county, was 5.1.[4] Most were two-generation, nuclear families—a couple and their children. While this was the immediate economic and emotional unit, the one which made direct demands and for which direct responsibility was felt, it was not the full extent of the family. This was the "small family" (*xiao jiating*) or household (*hu*). Beyond it were close relatives—parents, brothers—living in the same village, and beyond these ties were kin connections. In a province where most villages were single-surname villages, the tie to the village was a close family tie. Other connections, which encompassed a larger sphere of more distant relatives and included neighbors, will be discussed in chapter 4.

The extended family connections, those beyond the household, had direct implications for migration: They provided a support system. Migrants could leave without disaster facing those who remained. Brothers could look after elderly parents or help sisters-in-law left alone. A new bride could live with her in-laws until her husband returned. The extended family also provided a haven in case of failure. If dire necessity dictated, the migrant had a home to return to. The support system made it easier to migrate when the opportunities arose.

Inheritance and Migration

The strong sense of family identity ensured the return of many migrants. The Confucian ideal of a large family of many generations living harmoniously together was buttressed by an inheritance system that gave equal shares to all sons. This created a powerful bond. So long as the family still possessed property, each male had some material expectation from it. In Western systems, second and subsequent sons were "spares," who would inherit only if the elder brother died without sons. Others had to leave home once they were adult, going into the army, the church, the cities, and as emigrants to foreign countries. No expectations kept them at home. But under the Chinese system, permanent departure from home was unthinkable, unless the family was completely destitute.

The sense of continuing connections and inheritance rights could survive over long periods of time. Reginald Johnston, as administrator of Weihaiwei, Shandong, in the late Qing, presided over a case in which the lapse of a century had not extinguished the rights to inheritance:

> Another litigant whose long residence abroad had had no apparent effect on his general outlook, came to me very recently with the complaint that on his return from Manchuria he had found his land in the possession of a neighbour. "I went to Manchuria as my family had not enough to eat," he said, "I came home this year and wished to redeem the land I had mortgaged before I went away. But I found it had already been redeemed by my neighbour, a cousin, and he refuses to let me redeem it from him." On being asked when he had mortgaged his land and emigrated, he replied, "In Chia-ch'ing 3" — that is in 1798. He was merely identifying himself with his own great-grandfather.[5]

The inheritance system, however equitable, had a built-in flaw: It was a system of partible inheritance. Although the ideal was that inheriting males would stay together and hold their property in common, there was no formal or legal mechanism to force them to do so. Instead it was possible at the time of inheritance to split the family and divide its possessions, a procedure known as *fenjia* (dividing the family).

Fenjia is regarded as something undesirable and is discussed with regret, because it means a departure from the ideal of a large family. Another problem with dividing the family and its possessions is that division can leave every member of the family with inadequate land holdings unless it is a wealthy family. The inheritance system of primogeniture widely used by landowners in Europe was designed to ensure that land holdings never got too small to support a family; it sacrificed the prospects of younger sons to make sure that land passed intact from oldest surviving son to oldest surviving son. A modern version of the system prevents the subdivision of farm land in English-speaking Canada. In China the Confucian system valued all sons, treated them with a degree of equality and gave each the right to a part of the family property. But too many sons could damage a family irretrievably. After one or two transfers of property the slices of the pie became too small to support individual families, unless they found extra income elsewhere. This situation was the stimulus for several informants' migration.

In a large family, division of assets might send one or more sons away. Wang Bingguang's father was one of six sons; at the *fenjia* on the death of his father, he got only one *mu* (.16 acre) of land, not enough to support a family. When he heard of a possibility of work in Manchuria, he left instantly. He had another, more pressing reason to leave; he was being harassed by his employer because of the accidental destruction of some farm equipment. His departure left his family destitute until they were able to join him in Manchuria some time later. A chain of disasters that had started with the prolific procreation of his parents finally came to an end.[6] Meng Jingen came from a family impoverished by a combination of too many sons and a *fenjia*. His grandfather's land had been divided among six sons; Meng's father had six children of his own and then died. At that point the family could no longer feed all its members, so fourteen-year-old Meng was sent away to work in Manchuria.[7] Jiang Lanqi's father was one of six brothers, each of whom got only 2 *damu* (a local version of the *mu*) at the *fenjia*. This was not enough land to support a family. Jiang had to go to Dalian to work and sent money home regularly.[8] Wang Yuxiang's grandfather had to migrate because after his family's *fenjia* between five brothers, his part was only 1.2 *damu* of land, not enough to support his own children.[9] Gao Xuchang's family could not live on the three *damu* of land his father inherited at the *fenjia*, so Gao and three of his brothers were sent to Manchuria, leaving only the youngest son at home.[10] In all these cases division of family property exacerbated an existing problem—the shortage of land. A supposedly equitable system of inheritance turned a holding that had once supported all family members into separate units that were not viable.

FAMILY MIGRATION STRATEGIES

Migration was seldom a casual affair. Families usually had an implicit strategy, tied to the family's future, which determined their decisions. They thought about migration long before it was undertaken. Relationships and connections came into play, and decisions were made, usually in terms of enhancing the family income. The process was seldom open and explicit, and few informants identified a specific person who made the actual decision about who was to go. The usual expression was "it was decided in the family." However vague the identity of the decision makers, families of the migrants had specific goals. The most important was supplementing the basic family income through remittances, but there were other compelling goals as well.
Raising Money for Specific Purposes
Families often sent members off as migrants in order to acquire land—not in the place to which they migrated, but back home in

Shandong. The opportunities for greater earnings outside the home province made this a logical way to accumulate capital. It was, however, logical only so long as it was limited to a few people. Too many people sending home money to buy land could push up prices, thus negating the whole exercise:

> One consequence of the foreign remittances from overseas labourers was a steady increase in the value of agricultural property in Weihai-wei, and the redemption of mortgaged land.[11]

Another common purpose for migration was to raise bride price for the marriage of a son. Marriage was an expensive business. As a son approached marriageable age, parents had to think carefully about accumulating sufficient money, especially in a family with many sons.[12] Despite the desirability of having many sons, such families could seldom afford to pay bride price for all their sons, or meet the standards of a girl's family, without extra income. According to Martin C. Yang's 1930s study of Taitou (near Qingdao), a family could be quite selective about a daughter's partner, since it was accepted that young men might marry girls from lower social backgrounds than their own:

> The prevailing opinion is that one should not select a daughter-in-law from a family that is much more prosperous than one's own, otherwise the bride may compare the new household unfavorably with the house she has left, complain about the deprivations, and feel superior to the other daughters-in-law.[13]

A girl's family had considerable range in looking at a boy's family — its wealth, the number of sons, the boy's character. The boy's family would have to be able to provide well for a girl before her parents agreed to a marriage. Temporary migration permitted the boy's family to raise funds for the wedding and for setting up the new couple within the groom's home or as a separate household. Either way new quarters had to be constructed.

Another reason young men had to make good offers for brides lay in the unequal ratio between men and women in Shandong. According to the population statistics compiled by the Minzhengting (Civil Administration Department) in 1930, the ratio between men and women was 116:100. This figure was not broken down by age group, but if it prevailed among individuals of marriageable age, it suggests that some men may have had difficulty finding brides.[14]

Typically young men went away for two to three years in their late teens, then returned and married immediately. This produced a relay migration within families, in which each son would go out at the appropriate stage of his life cycle. If the migrant failed to earn as much as expected, then the marriage was delayed. Some migrants married very late, though few as late as Guo Baofu. Guo migrated in 1927, just after he had gotten engaged at age eighteen. He worked as a rickshaw puller in Harbin, never earning more than a pittance. In 1935 he came home after his parents died, but just long enough to pawn the land he had inherited. He returned again when his grandmother died, and, to pay for a respectable funeral, he sold his house. He went back to Harbin again, this time as a back scrubber in a bath house. He continued at this job until 1955, by which time demand for back scrubbers had fallen off dramatically. At last he returned home for good and *finally* married his fiancee, who by this time was 54.[15]

Risk Splitting

In response to the insecurity of Republican China, many families in Shandong engaged in partial family migration. This was a longer-term strategy than the search for remittances to keep the family afloat or for money to cover specific expenditures. Those who left might be gone for a long time. With some members away and some at home, a single disaster could not destroy the family. The Zhao family were artisans in Laiyang; there were four sons. The father worked as a glazier in Benxi, Liaoning, for thirteen years, between 1913 and 1940. The oldest son, a bank clerk in Dalian, stayed there permanently. The second and fourth sons stayed at home, working as shoemakers, while the third son (the informant) spent four years in Benxi with his father. Having little confidence in long-term security at home, the family divided, although their ultimate aim was to maintain themselves in Laiyang. Splitting up seemed to give them a better chance of doing this than simply staying at home.[16]

Splitting the risk could develop into a local pattern. When enough families in one village followed this strategy, they often created a separate kin-village in the Northeast—a "village across the sea" (*haiwaicun*). Many villages in Manchuria were set up by one small family or a group of villagers with the same surname; their new villages bore names such as Tangjiacun (Tang family village) or Fanjiacun (Fan family village).[17] This strategy combined relay and partial family migration. Those who migrated permanently were the anchors for the relay migrants as well as risk insurance for the family if times were hard at home.

Migration by part of the family also provided advance protection, a kind of insurance, for a family that might need an escape from a future crisis at home. In some cases a private tragedy tipped the balance. In 1939, for example, Zhao Qingfu's mother died in Gaomi. His father could not manage the three children by himself and so sold his farm and took his family to join an older brother in Kaitong (Tongyu), Jilin.[18] The fact that he had a migrant brother helped him avoid difficulty at home. In other cases natural disaster created a crisis. Many of the Linqu drought victims in the early 1940s went to join relatives in Manchuria. Zhao Yongting's enterprising mother, a widow, took her four children to Liaoyang as the famine deepened at home. She sold her possessions for train fares and joined her late husband's cousin, who found them all jobs.[19] When the twin disasters of drought and locusts gripped Ling County in 1943, large numbers of people fled to family members in Manchuria. Five of the six members of Zhang Xincheng's family went off to join an uncle who was pioneering on the Heilongjiang-Inner Mongolia border. He had set up his own Zhangjiacun (Zhang family village) there and was glad to see his relatives. They were glad to be alive, but felt that life in the north was only marginally better than death. They went home as soon as they could, after seven long years.[20]

To escape famine or disaster was not easy — the totally destitute did not have the energy to move or the money to pay the expenses, however modest, of their journey. The head of the chamber of commerce in Harbin in the early 1930s, Zhang Fengting, reported that almost all refugees from southern Shandong had been able to pay their own travel expenses, sometimes by selling or mortgaging land or possessions, and had close relatives in Heilongjiang. Otherwise, they would have had to "stay home and die in misery"(*kunsi zai benxiang*).[21] The splitting of the family could make the difference between life and death.

Moreover, splitting the risk worked both ways. When hard times hit in Manchuria, as they did after the Japanese occupation in 1931 and the Japanese defeat in 1945, families could in turn flee to their relatives in Shandong. Inevitably, though, splitting the risk for the family also changed the nature of the family. The ideal of a large family living together could no longer be attained and gradually lost some of its appeal.[22]

The classic family strategy in migration elsewhere, chain migration, where one member of the family establishes a bridgehead and the others follow one by one until the whole family is reunited in the new land, was not particularly common. The first choice of Shandong families was to support the family at home, not to move it.

Chain migration was also impeded by the difficulty of getting brides for men who settled permanently in Manchuria. It was considered a rough, crude place, especially dangerous for women, who were thought to be susceptible to a malady colloquially referred to as "cold disease" (*hanbing*). Owen Lattimore reported on the scarcity of women in the frontier areas in the early 1930s and the very high bride prices there.[23] Gao Puchun's whole family fled from the famine in Linqu to Kaitong (Jilin) in 1942. Almost destitute, they were forced to beg to survive, even though they could have resolved their financial problems by marrying off Gao's two elder sisters. His mother, however, refused to let them marry in Manchuria. She insisted on waiting until they could return home to find husbands for her daughters.[24] One poor man from Laiyang, Wu Liantian, who had settled in Manchuria and was desperate to marry someone from home, succeeded only by marrying, almost in secret, a widow with five children. Theirs was such a disastrous match that the woman was willing to join him rather than remain on her own at home. The couple subsequently had four more children and never returned to Shandong. To judge from the comments of relatives, this was partly due to the shame of their marriage. But a more important reason was that Wu Liantian still had not repaid the money he had borrowed from his cousin fifty years earlier to pay for his fare.[25]

Some families of girls living in Manchuria were willing to lower their standards in their search for a match. Wang Xibiao went to Fuyu, Jilin, in 1934 when he was nineteen to marry the girl he had been engaged to since he was eleven. He came from a poverty-stricken family, his father was dead, and there were three other brothers to look after his mother. He was married off to save money for the family, since his marriage required no bride price. His telling of his story made clear that he had been the surplus son in the family and that he had been sacrificed for the good of his family, leaving a wound that time had not healed.[26]

MIGRATION AND FAMILY COMPOSITION

The family member most likely to migrate was the young male, old enough to work, young enough to be adaptable, and not critical to the family economy at home. Young men were also the people in demand for the hard, tough work in the mines and factories and on the railways and the virgin lands of Manchuria. In most parts of Shandong, migration was overwhelmingly male. The figures from Deping demonstrate this pattern:

Table 3.1 Migrants from Deping, 1919 and 1934

Year	Total number	Number of men	Male percentage of total
1919	26,386	22,301	84.5
1934	14,307	12,766	89.2

Source: Deping xian xuzhi (1935), 310–12.

Data gathered by the SMR at the other end of the migration show a similar breakdown; men accounted for 86 percent of all migrants receiving certificates to enter Manchuria from 1936 to 1941.[27]

Families had to have more than one son to send out a young man, for one son was still essential at home. A 1935 report of agricultural conditions in Zhaoyuan, an area of systemic migration, found that any family with two or more sons would send one away, usually one with some ability who would no longer "feel comfortable at home" after he heard about the world outside.[28] A report from Guangcong in southern Hebei divided the families in one village into two categories: those with one son who supplemented their farm income with handicrafts, and those with two or more sons who sent one out each year as a "swallow," a migrant who left in the spring and returned in the autumn.[29]

It might seem natural to choose the migrant by rank, with the oldest son staying at home to look after the parents, the younger, less important ones migrating. However, this pattern seems not to have been a strong one. In many parts of Shandong migration was a routine stage in the lives of all young men, a rite of passage that, like marriage, marked the beginning of adult life. Provided there was someone to leave at home, it made little difference which son went. In Penglai most young males expected to go to Manchuria after they had finished a few years of school. In 1935, 19 percent of the males between the ages of 15 and 24 were "somewhere else" (tawang), most of them in Manchuria.[30]

Often the choice of who went took into account a young man's ability to make something of himself. Suitability rather than rank appeared more often to be the basis of this decision; the son thought best able to adapt to the harsh conditions of Manchuria and most likely to make money was chosen. He might be physically stronger, or psychologically well adapted to endure hardship, or smarter. Gao Xuyuan, who left home when he was fifteen, was chosen for his intelligence as the family migrant by his own poor family, and relatives for whom he would work in Changchun. He worked in Changchun as a bookkeeper, then in Beijing as an accountant. He was away from 1930 to 1949, and for most of that period sent money home regularly—an ideal migrant.[31]

FAMILY HELP IN MIGRATION

The family played a key role in arranging migrations. Almost half of the informants interviewed for this study had migrated with family help:

Table 3.2 Migration Agents for Informants

Migration agent	Number
Family members	39
Fellow villagers	7
Formal recruiters	37
Total	83

Source: Lary interviews, spring 1984.

Early in the interviewing process it seemed likely that some family relationships would emerge as more important than others in terms of aiding migration, but in fact no consistent pattern appeared. While a clear distinction existed between close and distant family relationships (the latter falling into the fellow-villager or *laoxiang* category), even within the close family, many different relations came into play, maternal as well as paternal. Young men went off to join their fathers, older brothers, or paternal or maternal uncles. Sun Hongshan left home in 1934 to join his maternal uncle who was in Fusong, Liaoning, growing ginseng. It was a flourishing business, and the uncle spread the benefits among his relatives; his nephew made 230 yuan in three years, a huge income at the time. Wei Xianying, from the same village, made the journey to Manchuria at fifteen with a paternal cousin (*tangxiong*), to work at a job in Shenyang with one of his second cousins (*biaoshu*).[32] Yu Shulin went off to Shenyang in 1936 to join his cousin (*biaoge*) who had migrated the year before. Shulin had already been apprenticed to that cousin, a carpenter, and finished his apprenticeship in Shenyang. His cousin then got him a good job in a Japanese factory.[33]

Helping someone to move was the basis for further relay migration. The help one young man received, he repaid to other relatives younger than himself. In just a short time a person could move from being helped to helping others. Guo Baomeng migrated seasonally for five successive years. At first he needed help, but by the last two years it was he who was guiding his younger brothers.[34] At fourteen, Zhang Congchang left his village in Ye County and went with relatives to Yingkou, where he worked as a laborer. Then he moved on to Vladivostok, as a bodyguard in the Chinese Chamber of Commerce. Finally, still quite young, he started on his real career, first as a bandit, then as a soldier, and eventually as a warlord.[35] In the course of this career, he did many dreadful things, acquiring one of the worst reputations in the region. In 1925, for example, at the behest of Japanese industrialists, he used his troops to brutally crush a strike by Chinese workers in Japanese factories in Qingdao.[36] Nonetheless, he also made careers for thousands of other men from the Peninsula, first his own relatives, then people from his immediate neighborhood, then from Ye County, and ultimately from the Peninsula as a whole.

Departure Costs

Migration entailed certain costs, at a minimum travel expenses. The family members who stayed at home often had to assume these costs and take over the responsibilities of those who left; in effect, they made an investment in the migration. Reginald Johnston cites a case from Weihai-wei at the end of the Qing, where, after a *fenjia*, one brother took out a mortgage on a second brother's land to pay the fare for the second brother's migration to Manchuria. The brother who stayed at home eventually bought out the other, but when the migrant returned after many years, he still had the right to redeem his mortgaged land from his brother.[37] Mortgaging land was still a means to pay for fares forty years later. When Liu Zhengzhong left Binzhou in 1941, his family raised the fare by mortgaging two *mu* of land.[38] Many migrants left indebted to their families, a heavy moral burden that compelled them to make money before they dared show their faces at home again.

Arrival Arrangements

One of the most important ways in which family members who had already moved helped relatives was to provide services to new migrants, first sending information on jobs and wages before migration, and then finding jobs and shelter when the new migrant arrived. This greatly reduced the risks of migration, and migrants were more likely suited to work opportunities. Family members already settled in Manchuria probably had little interest in relatives from home arriving unless there was work available, for without work they might have to support them. If life was hard for the earlier migrants, which it usually was, their welcome for relatives might be less than enthusiastic. People who had migrated from Boxing did not encourage their relatives to join them, but if they showed up anyhow they helped them to find jobs.[39] If the migrant was doing well, the attitude might be quite different. Jing Wenguang's uncle did so well after his move to Shenyang in 1925 that twelve years later he sent fare money home for his younger brother and his family.

Two years later he did the same for another brother because he needed reliable labor for his vegetable business.[40]

Recruitment Bonuses — Anjiafei

The quickest way to provide financial help to one's family through migration was to be recruited by an agency, Chinese or foreign, which paid *anjiafei* to men as they left to work away from home. Some of the most generous bonuses came from foreign governments who recruited men to work as laborers during the First World War. The men were paid 10 yuan on departure; thereafter their families received 10 yuan a month, which was either sent to them by post or picked up by the relatives at a recruiting station — there were stations in Qingdao, Wei County, Zhoucun, and Jinan. Twenty thousand people were served regularly at Jinan, and 25,000 at Wei County. These stations also handled mail between the men in France and their families and provided information on how the war was going.[41]

The migrant could probably not keep the entire amount of his payment if he was recruited indirectly by a local labor contractor, for the recruiter would expect his cut. When Zhang Zhenbao went to Jilin in 1938, his total *anjiafei* was 60 yuan, of which the recruiter took 20, leaving 40 yuan for Zhang and his family.[42]

Anjiafei payments were especially attractive in hard times. In 1940 a large group of men were recruited in Huimin during a period of prolonged drought. The attraction was the 15 yuan *anjiafei*, which most of them turned over immediately to their families. Very few of these men came back from Manchuria at the end of the same year with any money in their pockets because they were cheated by their employers, but at least they had helped their families to get through the drought by giving them the money they received before they went away.[43]

The *anjiafei* was the only chance most farmers ever had to acquire a large sum of money. This fee was also paid for men going into the army and was the standard means to recruit soldiers in many areas. Normally the army or the labor contractor was careful to hand the money over only after the recruit was under custodial control, but there were instances when a bold man might get hold of the money and disappear. Usually though, this happened only when the local situation was chaotic. One enterprising fellow used his *anjiafei* from the army to finance his migration. In early 1945 Sun Zhiguo's father took money from the local puppet army, but then used it, presumably in some haste, to buy railway tickets to Manchuria for himself and his family.[44]

FULL FAMILY MIGRATION

Normally the strategy of preserving the family in its native place meant that the core family stayed at home, while certain members were sent elsewhere to work. But sometimes moving the whole family seemed the best course. This was the case with many migrants who settled on the land in Manchuria, for the promise of land was great enough to induce landless farmers to move. Exactly who these people were, in terms of their economic status, is hard to pinpoint. The settler families could not have been destitute, since the cost of migrating was so great that some capital was needed. Nor could they have been families with members too young or too old or debilitated by malnutrition, since the ferocity of the Manchurian climate would put their lives at risk during the pioneering stage. The most likely candidates were units of extended families that had been divided through a *fenjia*.

Family migration also occurred in times of disaster. In 1927 Shandong was ravaged by warfare as the old warlords resisted the northern movement of Guomindang troops. Many of the migrants in that year were refugees from manmade disasters (*renhuo*). A breakdown of the refugees arriving in Jilin indicates that the majority of them were traveling as families.

Table 3.3 Refugees Arriving in
Jilin from Shandong, 1927–1928

Category	Percentage
Male adults	31.2
Female adults	26.4
Children	42.4

Source: Chen Hansheng, "Nanmin de Dong-bei liuwang," 1934, 339.

Linqu, in the Central Massif, experienced two phases of family migration. One occurred in 1926–1927, when bandit violence forced many families to flee.[45] The second, much larger migration of families came during the dreadful drought that gripped the county in the early 1940s. At that time 49 percent of the population, or 168,000 people, were driven away by the complete lack of food. A few went to neighboring counties to wait out the drought, but the majority (128,000), probably aware that the drought would not end soon, left for Manchuria.[46] What happened in Daxingzhong village was typical. Of 163 families, ninety left, that is, 400 out of 730 people. One hundred of those who stayed behind died of starvation. When the drought was over, 190 people returned, but many stayed on in Manchuria. In 1984, when the village's population was 1,700, the village authorities were still in touch with 90 families living in Manchuria, about 400 people.[47]

Family Abuses

The role of the family in arranging migration was not necessarily altruistic or benign. In fact, as in other migrations, family exploitation of certain members was not uncommon. The warmth and affection one might associate with family ties were often absent; in their stead harsh, calculating arrangements were devised to exploit family ties for cheap, reliable labor. Frequently senior members of a family wanted to bring younger relatives over for their own convenience. Jiang Lanqi joined his father in Dalian when he was fourteen, in 1926, and worked at various jobs with him for five years. His father always took all his wages.[48] When Gong Wenxue joined his older sister in Dalian in 1936 at the age of twelve, her husband got him a job as an apprentice making Japanese snacks — and also kept all the money he earned over four years.[49] Gong felt doubly unfortunate: Not only did he never see the money he earned, he had also trained for a profession that became obsolete after 1945. Qu Rongyu worked as a carpenter for three years for his father's cousin (*shuboshu*) in the mid-1930s without ever receiving more than his board and lodging.[50] Wang Guiqian went with his father to Manchuria when he was seventeen, in 1939. His father took both his *anjiafei* and the wages he earned. He came home with no money.[51] Telling their stories more than forty years later, these men still felt a keen sense of injury that their relatives had exploited them. There was no question in their minds that they *had* been exploited.

Another form of family cruelty was to keep a married couple separated when they wanted to be together. Families often kept a young wife at home as hostage to guarantee her husband's return. The aunt of Ma Xiuqing, from the Yantai area, was married to a man who had gone to Manchuria. They were very attached to each other. When he came to fetch her to Manchuria, his mother refused to let her go because she feared she would never see her son again. Faced with another separation, the two committed suicide together.[52]

Escaping the Family

The ideals of Confucianism prescribed a united, orderly family, with harmonious relations based on respect, but not every family achieved this goal. Many families were full of anguish and animosity. Some people found family pressures unbearable, particularly in the case of unhappy marriages. The only way for a man to escape an unhappy marriage was to migrate, but there was no such escape for a woman. Reginald Johnston described a common practice in Weihaiwei:

> If his wife's family is numerous and wealthy, the unhappy man who is wedded to an untamable shrew is often driven to desperate expedients to break his chains. He may, indeed, emigrate to Peking or Manchuria — the usual resorts of persons who find life unbearable in Weihaiwei.[53]

Li Yunsheng abandoned his wife in 1934, when he got into financial trouble. She and their daughter had to return to her natal family. Their marriage had not been happy because of her fierce (*lihai*) temper. He took some time to get on his feet in Manchuria, but eventually married again and had three children. Only in old age did he return, in 1975, after his second wife had died. He tried to resume his first marriage. The two old people lived together for six months, but their relationship was as disastrous as ever, and they split up again.[54]

Migrations were also explained by unhappy relationships between incompatible relatives forced to live in the same household. Informants most often mentioned quarrels between brothers. Relations could get so bad that even dividing a household did not solve the problem. A single village could not contain the warring factions, and one or both parties would have to leave.[55] Departures were also blamed on bad relations between sisters-in-law. In Laiyang it was reported that two brothers and their wives had migrated because the relations between the wives and a third sister-in-law were so appalling.[56]

Effects of Migration on the Family

The process of migration changed the family and its roles. In the most obvious way it created distance between members. But the distance was most often physical, not economic or social, and the process of migration sometimes actually articulated and pointed up family ties. Family roles became very clear when they were no longer performed. Although migration was frequently designed to enrich and strengthen the family, it often took little account of present needs, either economic or emotional, and could have devastating effects.

Married migrants often left their wives and children behind because the purpose of migration was to allow the family to continue at home. But who cared for their wives while they were away? The ideal of the family support system was not always realized. Some wives depended on remittances, a precarious source of income. Others lived as part of their husband's extended family, but often in pitiful conditions, especially if the husband had migrated soon after the marriage. Dependents might be abandoned: In Taitou, a widowed father was forced to live by begging, to the great shame of the family, because one son had gone off to Manchuria and sent no money home because he was "idle," while the other was "unfilial" and had married a widow who refused to look after her father-in-law.[57] An equally tragic story told to Reginald Johnston underlines the separation anguish that migration could cause:

> My second son, Ts'ung Chia-lan, went to Manchuria a few months after his marriage. This was eight years ago. He went abroad because the family was poor and he wanted to make some money. His wife was very miserable when he went, and begged him not to go, but he promised to come back to her. He disappeared, and for years we heard nothing of him. His wife made no complaint, but she was unhappy. A few months ago a returned emigrant told us that he had seen my son in Manchuria. When I saw that this news made his wife glad, I sent my elder son, Chia-lin, to look for him and bring him home. My elder son was away for more than two months, and never found him. Then he returned by himself and told us there was no hope of our ever seeing Chia-lan again. His wife heard him say this. We tried to console her. She said nothing at all, but two hours after my elder son had come home, she took a dose of arsenic and died. She was a good woman, and no one ever had a complaint to make against her. She had no child.[58]

The wives of many of those interviewed had an equally harsh lot. Liu Huanwu left his wife of three months with his parents when he migrated in 1940. He did not return for ten years and sent money home only once, though he worked all the time in Xinjing (Changchun) and lived with people from the same village.[59] Some wives returned to their natal families, but among the informants only when the husband had had to flee. Feng Yuexiu's grandfather had to flee from creditors one night in 1927; he had his own brick kiln, but got into financial difficulties when a load of bricks was spoilt. He was away for twelve years, during which time his wife had to be supported by her own family. He returned one day without warning, and the family went back to the life it had lead before, as if the twelve-year hiatus had not occurred.[60]

The most pathetic wives were those who had to fend for themselves, without help from either relatives or their husbands. Some managed to get by with handicraft work, usually spinning and weaving. Li Chuan-zhen married at the age of twenty-three in 1935 and migrated to Man-churia immediately after his marriage. He did not see his wife again for seventeen years. He wandered around Manchuria all that time, never earning enough money to send home. His wife lived with his mother and eked out an existence by weaving.[61] Zhang Shuyun left his wife and two children to work in the Fuxun Mines. While he was away they had to beg to survive, since he could not send any money home.[62]

Separation was often a hard, lonely period for both husband and wife. Husbands, however, had much greater access to comfort and entertainment than did wives, since rural society was puritanical and regarded a woman on her own as an invitation to disaster. One of the main arguments in a contemporary attack on migration was that the separation of married couples would lead to rape, seduction, adultery, jealousy, and marital disharmony.[63]

In Nanyang (South China), men who were separated from their wives at home might take a second "local" wife if they were doing well enough to afford it. Among the Shandong informants there were only two such examples, both from Zouping. Li Yunsheng's case is described above. Zhang Xuefu, a tinker, left his wife and three children in 1939 for Manchuria. He never sent any money home, and it soon became clear through the grapevine that he had taken up with another woman. He eventually had four more children with the wife in Manchuria. Some of these children came to Shandong for visits, but Zhang never returned. His disapproving neighbors made it clear that "never returned" meant "never dared to show his face again."[64]

One side effect of separation was birth control. Yu Shulin went off in 1936 at age twenty-five, leaving his wife and a small child. He did not come back for eleven years and sent money only once. Once he returned two more children were born.[65] Liu Zhengzhong married when he was seventeen and migrated when he was twenty, in 1941. He did not come back until 1946, though he was good about sending money. Only after his return did his family start to grow — eventually he and his wife had four children. Liu Huanwu, from the same village, did even better; though his first child was not born until eleven years after his marriage, he eventually had six children.[66]

The demands of the traditional family on the migrants were particularly acute. Migration for many people was the start of a period of loneliness and deprivation, financial and emotional, endured in the expectation, not very often fulfilled, that the migration would make the family rich. Men lived in extreme discomfort and had to be prepared to put up with harsh treatment from their employers. Nonetheless most informants did not criticize a system which could be seen to have victimized its members. Although the pain of their experience was still vivid, they did not blame the family, except in cases where the family relationship had deteriorated into that of employer and unpaid servant. Nor did departure from home weaken control by the family over absent members. There were plenty of rebels against the family system in Republican China, but not many among the poor of Shandong.

Keeping In Touch

If migration was to strengthen a family, then the people who went away had to be able to keep in touch with those who stayed at home. This was made possible through the extraordinarily efficient Chinese post office, the only truly national institution to survive China's period of warlord turmoil and division. There was, however, one major problem with corresponding: almost all the migrants and their families were illiterate and could not write or read letters themselves. But letters did go back and forth. Some were prepared by professional letterwriters, others by friends and *laoxiang* with some education. Liu Huanwu, who had had three years of schooling, wrote letters to his own family and for other migrants from the same village. Some of these were sent by post; others were carried by relatives or friends going home.[67] The uncle of Cui Dengwen, however, was out of touch with his family for thirty-four years because he could not write.[68] His example was cited as extreme, but other informants told similar stories. Wu Benzhi was away from 1928 to 1969, with only one visit home in all those years. He did not send money, and his family assumed that he had died. But he virtually rose from the dead—out of the blue, 50 yuan arrived at his parents' house in 1956 and contact was resumed. By 1969 he was ready to retire. His brother, who had no son, wanted Wu's son to be his heir, so the family moved home to Laiyang.[69]

The local authorities today feel a responsibility to keep in touch with people who are away. In 1984, the Pangjiaxiang authorities knew about all the people and their descendants who were "outside"; they knew where each one was and had maintained direct contact by letter (*tongxin*) with one-third of the thousand or so households that traced their roots to Pangjiaxiang.[70] Many villages had detailed information about former inhabitants, which assumed considerable significance when long-term land leases were being distributed (see chapter 5).

Village and township authorities keep track of internal migrants, while county authorities generally run a bureau known as the Office of People Abroad (*qiaowuju*). In 1984 the Gaomi Qiaowuju had precise details of 500 local people living abroad, including one Sun Lansheng, who worked for Air Canada.[71] The office in Laiyang was aware of one man, surnamed Nie, still alive in France at age ninety-seven, who failed to return from digging trenches in the First World War.[72] Ostensibly these offices exist to maintain contacts with people from the community, as a reinforcement of local loyalties; but in the background is a hope that if local people do well elsewhere, they may be persuaded to make a generous donation to their hometown.

REMITTANCES

There was no clearer way of underlining the continuing connection to home than the sending of remittances (*huidui*). This was the primary purpose of many individual migrations; money was either sent home or brought home at the end of the work season. Migrants could send money home in many ways, none of them perfect. Several methods, however, were good enough to risk. Had the transfer of money been too risky, the migration would have very likely dried up.

Post Offices
The most obvious way to send money was through the Post Office. By the mid-1930s, Shandong had more extensive mail lines (48,677 kilo-meters) than any other province except Sichuan (55,507 kilometers). Third highest was Henan, with 35,631 kilometers. Shandong lines were divided as follows:

Table 3.4 Postal Lines in Shandong

Type of line	Kilometers
Main courier lines	11,271
Minor courier lines	32,814
Steamer	192
Railway	1,154
Automobile	3,246

Source: Chu Chia-hua, *China's Postal and Other Communications Services* (Shanghai: China United Press, 1937).

The Post Office had an unusual reputation in Republican China for honesty and efficiency. With a network of offices across the country, it was often the most convenient way to make financial transfers. Its couriers were considered reliable:

What Herodotus wrote twenty-three centuries ago of the Greek messengers of his time "neither snow, nor rain, nor heat nor the gloom of the night stays these couriers from the swift completion of their appointed rounds" is as fittingly applicable to the humble couriers of the Chinese Post Office today.[73]

Large amounts of money passed through the Shandong postal system. In 1926, at the beginning of a peak period of migration, Shandong post offices handled 18,543,400 silver yuan in various kinds of postal transfers, with a net inflow of 11,261,200 yuan.[74] Commercial transactions accounted for much of this money, but at least some was sent home by migrants. The county post offices of Ling County, not a commercial center, handled 158,961 yuan that year, with a net inflow of 131,833 yuan.[75] We can assume that a large part of this came from migrant remittances.

Some migrants used the Post Office regularly. Zhang Hongbao sent money home to Zouping two or three times a year by postal order; altogether each year he normally sent about 30 to 40 yuan (Manchurian) or about 10 percent of his income. His family cashed the postal orders at the district post office. Li Gongshui, from the same village, sent 50 to 60 yuan a year. Both men were dockers in Dalian, earning about the same amount of money.[76]

Migrants to Manchuria had to find other means of sending money home after 1932, when the Chinese Post Office network in Manchuria was closed down, with the loss of 50,278 kilometers of mail line.[77] Although an agreement to restore postal traffic was signed in 1934 between Nanjing and the Manchukuo government, the service did not reach earlier volumes, and in 1937 it was again interrupted by war.

Banks

By the mid-1920s the three main cities in Shandong—Jinan, Qingdao, and Yantai—all had branches of most of the major banks in China as well as a few foreign ones. But these banks were not interested in the small sums migrants sent. Migrants who did use banks—mainly people from Jiaodong (the Peninsula)—turned to traditional local banks or "money shops" (*qianzhuang, qianpu*).[78] In many of the Jiaodong counties local banks had branches in Manchuria. The Tianhexing *qianzhuang*, for example, had its main offices in Yantai, with branches in Jinan, Tianjin, Beijing, Dalian, and Qingdao. It was run by people from Ye County.[79] The Fuxunde *qianzhuang* had its headquarters in Penglai, with branches in Dalian and several Manchurian towns.[80] These banks were reliable and convenient, but they charged very high fees on each transaction, sometimes as much as 20 percent.[81] It was much cheaper to use other methods.

Transfers In Kind

Migrants sometimes sent or took their earnings home in kind, rather than in cash. In part this was because the rural population, used to dealing in silver dollars (*xianyang*) or copper cash (*xiantong*), distrusted paper currency. Another problem was the number of currencies in circulation. In the late Qing, Alexander Hosie, the British consul at Yingkou, reported, "Many of the labourers returning to Chefoo [Yantai] before the closing of the port in winter invest their savings in opium and smuggle it across to Chefoo."[82]

Sending money, or traveling with it, made one vulnerable to robbery. One complex scheme to send money home to an area where banditry was widespread involved sending money orders (*huipiao*) to a bank in Jinan, where they were cashed by a Binzhou merchant. He then used the money to buy inventory in Jinan and paid the families in Binzhou with cash he had in his Binzhou store.[83]

Goods were not necessarily safer than cash, nor were migrants necessarily good at doing business. When Zhao Yonghu's father came home in 1943, his stratagem of loading himself down with pens and shoes to sell along the way did not work—they were stolen from him.[84]

Friends and Connections

Some migrants relied on neither the Post Office nor the banks, but handled their transactions instead through people they could trust. Hou Shangjian, for example, sent his money from Harbin through the post to Jinan, where one of the local merchants picked it up and took it home for him.[85] Others sent money home with "swallows." This was a relatively reliable method, but it had the disadvantage that one had to reveal to one's friend—and therefore to the whole world—how much money one was sending. Even though they were talking about times long past, many informants were still reticent to talk about how much they had sent back.

Bringing Money Home Personally

Short-term migrants often brought money home with them in cash. This seemed the simplest thing to do, and for some it was. Guo Baomeng came home every year for the New Year, bringing money each time. He was a tinker and earned good money, but the Japanese authorities never allowed him to convert more than 50 yuan.[86] Sun Hongshan, who had sent money home to Laiyang through a bank in the early 1930s, brought money with him when he came back in 1938. He was searched in Dalian by Japanese border guards, who took all but 50 yuan from him. His only consolation was that he still had 20 yuan sewn into the sole of his shoe.[87]

Migrants bringing money home faced a major difficulty with currency exchange. The currency situation in Manchuria, as in the rest of China, was chaotic in the early twentieth century. Coins and notes were issued under the authority of the Chinese central government, the provincial governments, private banks, and foreign banks. At the end of 1929 the most widely circulated currencies in Manchuria included the following:

Table 3.5 Major Currencies Circulating in Manchuria, 1929

Currency	Exchange rate (per 100 silver yuan)	Circulation area
Silver *yuan (dayang qian)* – silver dollar coins issued by central government; generally stable	yuan 100	All Manchuria
Silver *yuan piao (dayang piao)* – dollar notes issued by various banks; based on silver yuan coins; generally stable	yuan 100	Liaoning Province and along railways
Feng piao – yuan notes issued by Manchurian government; very unstable	yuan 6,000	Liaoning Province
Harbin *dayang piao* – silver yuan notes issued by Harbin banks; fairly stable	yuan 140	Harbin and Chinese Eastern Railway Zone
Heilongjiang *dayang piao* – silver yuan notes issued by Heilongjiang Province government; generally stable	yuan 140	Heilongjiang Province
Jilin Yongcheng *dayang piao* – silver notes issued by official bank of Jilin Province; fairly stable	yuan 145	Jilin Province
Xiaoyang *qian (jiao)* – silver coins smaller than 1 yuan, issued by provincial mints; debased but relatively stable	yuan 114	All Manchuria
Yokohama Specie Bank silver yen notes – issued by Yokohama Specie Bank branches in Manchuria; stable	yen 100	Guandong Leased Territory (Liaodong Peninsula), SMR Railway Zone
Bank of Chosen (Korea) gold yen notes – issued by Bank of Chosen branches under Japanese supervision; stable	yen 100	Guandong Leased Territory, SMR Railway Zone

Sources: Sakatani, *Manchuria,* 20–31. See also "The Currency Situation," in *Chinese Economic Journal* 1 (May 1927): 5; Hitano Kenichiro, *The Japanese in Manchuria,* 265–338. *Note:* The "normal" exchange rate for the silver yuan was 0.50 U.S. dollars and 1.00 Japanese yen.

Inevitably migrants returned with earnings in a currency different than that used at home, which was itself subject to wide and frequent variation over time and between regions. In his study of western Shandong, Kenneth Pomeranz found persistent and erratic discrepancies in exchange rates between copper and silver Chinese currencies at different market centers in Shandong and other parts of North China between 1905 and 1935.[88]

Events as distant as the Bolshevik Revolution of 1917 had devastating effects on exchange rates in Manchuria and Shandong. A large proportion of the money that migrants brought to Shandong early in the century was in the form of Russian rubles because many had found work on the Russian railways in northern Manchuria. According to the Longkou Customs report for 1917, the fall in the value of the ruble—from 66 coppers in January to 10 coppers in December—"has brought the once wealthy emigrant to the verge of bankruptcy and has seriously affected the prosperity of every village in the district."[89]

Most intermediate-size markets in Zouping, serving populations of eight to nine thousand, had money changers.[90] But changing money was fraught with risks for the inexperienced. People who changed money at most once a year were easy prey for unscrupulous money changers. Migrants could lose as much as half of the money they brought back. Even the seasoned traveler could be caught out. The economist Franklin Ho recalled his experience in Manchuria in the late 1920s:

> . . . when I was carrying out field investigations in Manchuria on the problems of migration, I found that Manchurian currency differed from city to city and place to place. I started out with a $10 national bank note, and exchanged it for local currency at each of the places where I stopped. When I got back to Tientsin I exchanged it again for national currency. In the process of exchange the ten dollars in national currency was reduced to two dollars.[91]

After 1931 the Japanese ran strict controls on money leaving Manchuria. Hou Xiaolun lost 40 of the 100 yuan (Manchurian) he had earned in 1936 when he left Manchuria, through the artificial exchange rate. He lost again when he made his second return in 1944. The anguish he suffered at the time was still vivid in his memory forty years later.[92]

Scale of Remittances

By some accounts remittances from Manchuria made Shandong rich. According to the statistics of the Chinese Post Office, the total amount of postal transfers received, in silver yuan, rose from 346,500 in 1910 to 18,535,400 in 1926.[93] It is not possible to sort out what percentage were migrant remittances, and what were other forms of postal traffic. In any case it accounts for only a small part of the total sums remitted by migrants. The gazetteer for Deping County claims that in the late 1910s and early 1920s, migrant families received more than a million yuan every year.[94] The figure is so vague that it may well mean "a lot of money" rather than a precise amount. It is highly unlikely that county authorities knew exactly how much money was coming into their jurisdiction at a time when few were sure exactly how many inhabitants they had. Another factor working against precision was that few migrants would openly declare how much they were bringing back. They might reveal such information to their nearest and dearest, but they did not want to invite the attention of eager relatives or the tax collector.

An SMR study of Chinese workers in Manchuria in 1934 estimated the amount that workers in different occupations could save based on the differences between incomes and living expenses. The study concluded that, depending on the occupation, most Chinese workers could remit between 20 and 50 yuan a year and that the average annual remittance was probably around 40 yuan.[95] The remittances of most informants who succeeded in sending money home did indeed fall into this range.

How important was a sum of this size to families in Hebei or Shandong? A study of Chinese rural income distribution in the 1930s, based on a land survey carried out by the National Land Committee of China in 1935, concluded that average annual income for rural households was 88 yuan in Shandong and 124 yuan in Hebei.[96] An annual remittance of 40 yuan would have increased the income of a typical farm family in Hebei by nearly a third and that of an average Shandong household by almost half.

We can form a rough idea of the scale of total remittance payments if we take the SMR estimate of 40 yuan as the typical migrant's potential annual remittance. In an average year in the 1920s and 1930s, some 350,000 migrants returned home. If they carried 40 yuan, the total would have been 14 million yuan. If, in addition, around 20 percent of the labor force remaining in Manchuria (about 12 million in 1927) sent home remittances averaging 40 yuan each, a further 96 million yuan, the total remittance flow each year would have been around 110 million yuan. This was a large amount of money. Indeed, it was enough to cause considerable concern to the Japanese authorities, who feared that the wealth of Manchuria was being drained away and therefore implemented restrictions on the amount of cash people could take out of Manchukuo. However, the total sum was hardly enough to "enrich" Shandong and Hebei, since it amounted to only about 1.5 yuan per inhabitant of the two provinces. Nevertheless, for poor rural communities, the addition of even a few yuan could make a tremendous difference in family living standards.

There was variation in how assiduously migrants sent remittances, even among people with similar incomes. After more than forty years former migrants from Fucheng, Binzhou were still embarrassed about who had sent what. Some had sent money regularly, others scarcely at all. Liu Huanwu, who worked in a factory in Xinjing for ten years, sent money only once to his wife and parents, even though at his peak he was earning 70 yuan (Manchurian) a month. Li Dingjie's father, who worked in the same factory, sent money home every year. Other informants intimated that Liu might have been spending his money on less virtuous activities than caring for his family—probably gambling, the curse of single male migrants. He looked slightly shamefaced when his fecklessness was revealed.[97]

Many migrants failed to send any money home at all. For those who went as recruited workers (*huagong*) this was not surprising, because they were paid a recruitment bonus when they left, and their labor boss usually took a good part of their wages. People who moved as a family were unlikely to remit money. Others simply failed to make the amount of money they had hoped for. Not one of the informants became rich.

Table 3.6 Remittances from Informants

Category	Number
No money sent or brought home	41
Family migration	18
Money sent home	18
Money brought home	7
Not applicable	4

Source: Lary interviews, spring 1984.

It was clearly painful for the informants to admit publicly that they had brought no money home. Migrants who returned with nothing to show for their efforts had failed not only themselves, but also their entire family; and memories of the shame and disappointment that must have accompanied their return were revived. One informant told of a case that had gone beyond shame, to despair. Qu Rongyu's father had gone to Manchuria quite late in life, after losing his job in the Yantai Winery. He was deeply distressed at returning virtually empty-handed. He had been unable to continue working as a carpenter in Shenyang because his eyesight was failing, and he could not exchange the tiny amount of money he brought back with him because the currency was not convertible. Since he could not pay his taxes on returning home, he was put in prison for a few days. When he came out, he hung himself.[98]

4

LOCAL CONNECTIONS

HOME AND IDENTITY

A local identity is the birthright of every Chinese; in a formal sense, one has no identity at all without one. It is the second part of basic personal identification, after one's name: for example, Chen Zhirang, Sichuan Chengdu *ren* (Chen Zhirang, a person of Sichuan Province, Chengdu City). This identification spells out the province and locality to which a person belongs; it does not mean the place where he lives, but the place his family is from. Local identities descend through the male line and cannot be broken or changed; they endure long after people have left their native places. In the 1982 national census a majority of the people in Dalian declared their ancestral affiliation (*yuanji*) to be a county in Shandong, even those who were two and three generations removed from the forebear who had migrated.[1]

Among the regions of China is a recognized hierarchy of quality, within standardized categories. Some places are endowed with natural wealth, such as southern Jiangsu, the land of fish and rice, or the rich basin of Sichuan, or subtropical Guangdong. Other places offer their natives special access to connections and influence, none more so than the great metropolises of Shanghai and Beijing. Some places like Hangzhou and Suzhou are famous for their beauty. Others are steeped in history and culture. Shandong's ancient name, Qi-Lu, dates to before the unification of China. Lu, the native place of Confucius, is considered the birthplace of China's high culture. No place, however, is so poor, so barren, or so inconsequential that its inhabitants do not love it. Even places cheated by nature, such as the saline, lumpy plains around Ling County or the flood-threatened villages that sit between the two sets of Yellow River dikes at Binzhou, are loved profoundly by their

95

inhabitants—just as much as the ancient pear orchards of Laiyang or the fertile slopes overlooking the sea at Penglai are loved by theirs. Every place commands the respect and love of its children, whether it provides them with a decent living or not.

The migrants who left their families in Shandong to work in Manchuria were still tied to their home regions with strong bonds of emotion and tradition. While they were away they remained members of their home communities, which in turn provided wide networks of support through relatives, friends, and neighbors.

The Family—Jia

English has no adequate word to describe the object of this powerful sense of attachment. The English term "home" is quite broad. It may mean a house, a town, or a country. The Chinese term *jia* equates home with family; it can only refer to that precise place where one's family is. The German term *Heimat* is larger in scope, but it carries the same strong sense of emotional attachment to a place whose precise size is not defined, but which must be small enough for complete familiarity.

In places where there has been little migration, it is hard to separate the place where one lives from the people one is related to—they are the same thing. This overlap is often highlighted in village names. Many villages in Shandong, as elsewhere in China, carry single-family sur-names—Sunjiacun (Sun family village), Wangjiazhuang (Wang family village). Actually, only small or fairly remote villages are composed of families who all share the same surname; two or three surnames are more typical. Villages of families with many surnames are disparagingly referred to as *zaxingcun* or mixed-surname villages, with a definite sense that "mixed" means something improper. *Zaxingcun* were often situated in undesirable places: Chengnancun (South-of-the-Wall Village) in Laiyang, for example, had been an area of wasteland just outside the city wall. People who live in mixed villages were often displaced from their real homes by disaster or personal tragedy, misfortunes that are rather uncharitably interpreted as symptoms of personal laxity.

Laoxiang—"Fellow Locals"

If the family is the first level of local affiliation, the next level, which still commands a powerful loyalty, is the *xiang*. The term *xiang* has an administrative reality as a township, the level of administration between the county and the village. But in another sense *xiang* has a much more limited focus; it means local connections, an outer ring of personal ties, one step beyond close relatives. The area covered by this term is not precise: It could be a large village or a cluster of villages. The term is used in expressions like *tongxiang* or *laoxiang*, meaning the people who come from the same locale. While in German these terms are translated as *Landsmann*, and in Italian as *paesano*, English translates them clumsily as "fellow locals" or "people from the same hometown."

While the *laoxiang* connection is not as close as immediate family, it still often involves blood ties and is much closer than other recognized relationships, such as that between people from the same county or the same province. The informants clearly distinguished between people they were closely related to and those who were *laoxiang*. Close relatives were very carefully designated, as they have to be in Chinese kinship terminology. It is impossible to speak generally of "cousins"; one must distinguish between male and female, maternal or paternal, and between degrees of relationship (first, second, or third cousin). This means that in the case of small, single-surname villages, people's *laoxiang* are probably not from the same village, and anyone from their village is most likely a close relative. *Laoxiang* are either from the same (large) village or from the surrounding cluster of villages. They speak the same dialect, go to the same periodic market (*ji*), have regular, long-standing connections with each other, know all about each other, and have economic ties that require a certain amount of trust.

The *laoxiang* network is the means by which marriages are contracted, and it defines the radius within which girls can be married. Since people cannot marry someone of the same surname, girls are married out from their native villages to villages within the administrative *xiang* radius, close enough to maintain some connection with the family. In Taitou, Martin Yang reported that there had never been a marriage within the village, though there was more than one surname. This was because of the feeling that families related by marriage should not be too close to each other. Marriage to a neighboring village was the norm, often with several marriages in one family being contracted in the same neighboring village.[2]

Attachment to Home

Leaving home does not detach the person who leaves from family, village, or locality; nor does it cancel obligations to those left behind. Tradition held that the emigrant thought ceaselessly of the day when he could go home. The highest ideal was to "return home wearing brocade" (*yijin huanxiang*). Once a person made money, he *had* to go home; the whole point of going away was to find the means to return in glory. Returning to one's home was as natural as "the leaves of a tall tree falling close to its roots" (*shu gao qian zhang, ye luo gui gen*). Any other outcome was a misfortune or a sign of bad character.

The deep-seated attachment to home meant that migrants were reluctant to resettle permanently elsewhere. While some contemporary observers of the migration to Manchuria had supposed that emigration might solve problems of overpopulation in North China, this did not appear to be the case. As Walter Mallory noted in his important study of famine in China in the 1920s:

> There is an annual movement of labour from Shantung which reflects to a marked degree the love of home and unwillingness to leave it for new fields. Every year more than thirty thousand men [a major understatement] migrate from Shantung to Manchuria. They leave early in the spring and travel more than 500 miles to the rich lands of the north where they work during the summer; but in the autumn they all return to their homes in Shantung. In the days before the construction of the Peking-Mukden Railway, they made this trip on foot taking nearly a month on the road each way. It is almost unbelievable that such a practice continues year after year when good Manchurian farm lands are available and can be bought on easy terms and for a phenomenally low price from the railway authorities which are making an effort to settle this region. It cannot be said that the people do not realize the benefits, for they see them with their own eyes and share in them for a short time every summer; but they are unwilling to change their homes and their mode of life.[3]

Mallory's criticism of the Shandong farmers' refusal to migrate permanently contrasts with the widespread fear in the West at that time that Chinese were only too anxious to emigrate and would flood the world unless barred from admission abroad. He was writing in the same period when Canada and the United States passed legislation to bar Chinese immigration.

Mallory wrote about the migrants' intentions, but not about what actually happened. Many of those who migrated did not come back, and the growth in the Manchurian population reflected this. Some stayed because there was nothing for them to return to at home, others because political vicissitudes intervened, and still others because they found the life in Manchuria good enough to warrant staying—for a while. Others who did well enough to send regular remittances were urged by their families to stay, because they were a secure source of income. And then there were those who could not return because they did not make enough money to come home with their heads held high. On his travels through Manchuria in the early 1930s, Owen Lattimore found everywhere the phenomenon of "long-term temporary migration" and the widespread feeling that:

> . . . definite settlement in Manchuria was an expedient only for those destitute of other resources, a mark of exile, failure and defeat . . . the successful emigrant, and the one most respected was the one who went out, made his money and came back.[4]

Martin Yang reported the same phenomenon for his village, Taitou, across the bay from Qingdao:

> Several decades ago, a single man of a Yang family went to work in Manchuria. Because of his special ability in reclamation and farm management, he succeeded in acquiring a large farm of several hundred acres. He married there and had three or four children. Recently, however, the head of the family decided to move back to his ancestors' place. So, five or six years ago, a new family was added to the village of Taitou. But unfortunately, the local people, including his own kinsmen, and the land situation very much disappointed the once successful farmer. He could not buy the amount of land he wanted because land is more scarce and expensive than in Manchuria. He could not even get the kindness which he had learned to expect from his own clanspeople. People who understood the difficulties and losses he has suffered said that he should not have come back, and he, too, has come to realize this. However, the northern Chinese peasants have, through generations, developed a deep-rooted passion for the place of their ancestors. They cannot resist the idea of coming back home, unless a whole family or group of families have moved out simultaneously and sold all their properties, so that they would have nothing to live on if they should come back.[5]

The ties to home are as powerful today as they have ever been. Since the opening of China in the late 1970s, people who have done well overseas have been encouraged to pour money into their native places. A suitable donation is found for each person: a university for the super rich, a major investment for the business man, a school or a clinic for someone of modest means. The pressure to donate is not subtle, but it does not have to be. The emigrant plays a role he understands well, and his native place usually has a sufficiently clear idea of how much he can afford to be quite specific about what he should contribute. Refusal to make a donation is seen as antisocial and un-Chinese. The only major difference between present-day local benefactors and those of fifty years ago is that today most do not return permanently. In the past, return meant not only benefiting one's native place, but actually going back there to live. Shandong has done less well in terms of donations from former natives than Guangdong or Fujian, probably because so many potential donors live in Taiwan, and until the recent thawing of relations, it was very difficult for people to get back to Shandong for visits.

Roots of Local Attachment

Where does this strong sense of local identity and attachment come from? Why does the supposed Western propensity to migrate easily and permanently seem not to have a parallel in China? The most obvious answer would be that it has to do with stages of development, that Westerners did not move easily either until the industrial revolution and urbanization were well under way. This is true but simplistic. It obscures the fact that when movement did become possible in the West, how far people went and how long they stayed away were determined by careful family deliberations. The association of migration with development also downplays the profound and intense attachment of Chinese to their native places and the institutional underpinning buttressing that attachment. The migrant's attachment to home, and his longing for it when away, was extensively mythologized in traditional China. This emotional link served many purposes, some instrumental and even quite cynical. Family and village elders, local authorities, defenders of traditional values such as school teachers all instilled in the young the idea that they must be devoted to home, that they must never believe they could separate themselves from it. To a great extent these efforts persuaded most migrants that they were sojourners (*qiao*), who must return home sometime. Whether the migrants actually did or not was conditioned by a host of other factors: circumstances at home, the relative success of the migration, opportunities elsewhere, and personal proclivities. But few migrants felt comfortable severing their ties with home completely. In part this was because home did offer comfort and security, but it also exerted a pull on migrants in other ways.

First, home provided a link to the ancestors. Confucian values required descendants to stay close to the graves of their ancestors, to maintain them and sweep them once a year These attentions demonstrated that the ancestors were not forgotten and that descendants were trying, through their lives, to please them. A Baptist missionary noted this devotion in the early 1920s.

> The villagers of Shantung cling to their wretched homes with a passionate love we can hardly understand, and nothing but sheer

starvation staring them in the face could make them leave their ancestral farms and their fathers' graves . . .[6]

Moving away permanently and abandoning the ancestors would be like deliberately tearing oneself up by the roots, a painful and possibly fatal process.

Linked closely to the ancestors was the inheritance system, which required that one be at home to inherit one's rightful share. In his monumental study of Chinese agriculture, Wilhelm Wagner remarked that although the inheritance system was based on partible inheritance, it was complex enough and flexible enough that heirs might do poorly unless they stood up for their rights.[7] They had to be at home to make sure they got everything they deserved when property was being divided.

The state also had major interests in making sure that people stayed where they were supposed to be. It needed to foster local identities as a practical means of organizing and controlling a vast country—a place for everyone, and everyone in their place. Allowing people to move around freely was a recipe for trouble and turbulence; keeping them at home kept them quiet. The state tied people to their localities through systems of registration and control. The *baojia* registration system, practiced more or less efficiently by the Ming and Qing governments, and less so by the Guomindang, made it difficult for people to move without official permission. If people did move, it was either because the government ordered them to, in an officially sponsored migration such as the movement into Yunnan in the eighteenth century, or because the government was too weak to prevent movement. After 1949 the Communist government pursued the same policies of population control, but more effectively than had earlier governments. Its *hukou* system, introduced in the early 1950s, made migration without prior approval almost impossible until it started to break down under the market-based economic reforms of the mid-1980s.

The authoritarian harshness of these population control systems was softened by extolling the virtues and joys of each locality, so that people could be proud of where they were rather than frustrated by their inability to move. Pride in local history was instilled officially. It was the responsibility of the gentry of each county to edit the local gazetteer periodically. Although the format varied little from one county to another, with each county described in essentially the same terms, these gazetteers made a point of extolling the special virtues of each locality. They served the same purpose from place to place: to make the inhabitants proud of their own county. In the mid-1980s a new flood of gazetteers was commissioned, the first since the 1940s, with the clear intention of bolstering local loyalty as a substitute for the moribund ideology of socialism.

Because of their sense of local identity and their family ties, few migrants believed that they were leaving permanently or going to a place that might be an improvement over their native place. The expressions used to describe migration to Manchuria were bleak. Some spoke of poverty: *chuang guandong* carries the connotation of straggling off to Manchuria, driven by poverty at home, to struggle for a miserable existence beyond the boundary of the civilized world. Others spoke of the powerlessness and isolation of a migrant: *dang huangyu*, "to be a yellow fish," meaning to expose oneself to the horrors of the world with no protection. Some were simply bald geographical references: *shang haibei*, "to go north beyond the sea," that is, from the Peninsula.

Manchuria was usually considered to be a barbarous place; it was harsh, cold, and dangerous. If it was not full of wild animals, giant mosquitoes, and brazen bandits, then it was overrun by Japanese soldiers. The gazetteer of Deping, a major migrant-producing area, gives a sense of how life in Manchuria was seen: "Buffeted by the wind, drenched by the rain, thousands of miles away from home, the laborers go without proper food or clothing, yet endure with fortitude."[8]

Some people, usually those who were trying to lure migrants, had glowing things to say about Manchuria. There was the occasional flight of fancy about creating a new race, combining the physical characteristics of the Manchus with the culture of the Han to produce "a healthy, perfect new people."[9] But most potential migrants feared the cold, went in horror of the food, and loathed the mosquitoes.

Some migrants tried to improve the odds by starting their journeys only on what were considered locally to be lucky days. They had some latitude, because a lucky day was any day with a three, a six, or a nine in it, or a number divisible by three.[10] This belief still persists in much of Shandong: three, six, and nine days are good for departures (*sanliujiu wang wai zou*), and the railway authorities put extra carriages on trains on those days; two, five, and eight days are good to come home on (*erwuba hao hui jia*).[11]

The informants were unrelenting in their criticism of the Manchurian food—sorghum, maize, and beans—as compared to the culinary delights of Shandong. (They also remarked again and again that Beijing food was really Shandong food, hijacked by the shameless people of Beijing.) Although going from Shandong to Manchuria at that time might have seemed like moving from an area of shortage to one of surplus, migrants spoke more in terms of leaving good food for horrible food, moving from fine Shandong wheat to coarse Manchurian sorghum. The benchmark of prosperity for many, the demarcation between the old days and the happier present, was that now they could afford to eat fine grain and avoid coarse grain altogether.

Migration and Morality

Popular antipathy to migration meant that migrants had to cope with a widely held view that they were doing something unnatural by going away. One critique of migration had this to say about people who left home:

> Among people given to migrating, their morality, customs, faith, habits, moral outlook and behaviour are all unstable and change frequently. Migration destroys morality and fosters crime and evil.[12]

Behind this kind of statement was the assumption that people "adhere" (*nianzhuo*) to their native place naturally, that they belong to a specific patch of land as much as the land belongs to them. It is a visceral, physical connection, expressed in self-congratulatory sayings about people who have never left home, such as *laosi bu quxiang* (to grow old and die without leaving home), or *antu zhongqian* (attached to the soil, one hates to leave it).

Mallory pointed to another fact of life that made it easier for people to remain devoted to their native place — they did not expect much from it. A culture of poverty and hardship had inured people to the harshness of the natural surroundings of north China:

> . . . a cause of the lack of initiative which might induce the residents of the over-crowded, famine-threatened northern provinces to seek better opportunities may be traceable to the effects on the race of former oft-repeated starvation conditions. . . . These northern families . . . have developed habits of thrift and economy until the acquisitive instinct has become second nature, for the wasteful and extravagant have long since been eliminated during the many years of want. These characteristics are the natural counter-part of conservatism, a desire to keep at all costs what has been acquired, and they tend to make abhorrent the thought of leaving home and giving up a plot of land, however meager and inadequate to support a family.[13]

Mallory's views may be generalized, but they at least provide cultural background — not for the specific social and economic climates in which the migrants lived, but for the patient endurance of hardship so characteristic of people in North China. Such behavior was not stupid or apathetic, but a willing and dignified acceptance of a heavy burden. To stay home and endure hardship was admirable, to leave was not. Although migration was a routine part of life in much of Shandong, it could not be recognized as proper or admirable.

With these kinds of deep-seated cultural proclivities, migrants could admit to themselves, their families, and their *laoxiang* only that they were migrating to earn money and that they planned to return as soon as possible, if not in life then in death:

> Grim evidence of this very consequential attachment to the ancestral soil may be seen in the slow-moving stream of wooden carts, drawn by horses, mules and oxen in tandem and abreast, southward bound through the Great Wall at Shanhaikwan [Shanhaiguan] from Manchuria, each cart piled high with plain wooden coffins lashed together. These are the remains of the pioneers who have died in the "foreign land" of Manchuria.[14]

Laoxiang and Migration

Given the prevailing negative attitudes toward migration, few potential migrants had the courage or enthusiasm to strike out on their own. In making the painful decision to leave home, they needed reliable information about where they were going and advice and help from someone in whom they had confidence. Since no objective sources of information existed, they turned to the network that would reduce risks and provide some comfort, their *laoxiang* connections. The *laoxiang* relationship was the principal mechanism for migration.

Migration statistics usually describe movement from one large place (a country or province) to another. Recent work on Chinese labor, for example Elizabeth Perry's *Shanghai on Strike*, discusses regional recruitment patterns for a province or a large city (Canton, Ningbo, Yancheng, Hubei, Shandong).[15] But this is still too large a pool. Most migrants moved from one small place to another equally small place. Their movement may have been from one village to another or from their village to a specific factory or mine. The references to larger areas are not false because they do describe the actual movement; but they do not reflect how migrants saw the transition: They were moving from people they knew to other people they knew. The distance traveled might be enormous, but in terms of emotional comfort and social connections, it was very short. Owen Lattimore, who knew Manchuria better than any other foreign observer, had this to say in the 1930s:

The long-established practice of migrating to Manchuria to work for a season, in order to get funds for going back to China to stay, is one of the evidences of the negative style of Chinese migration, and illustrates its characteristic form of drift. On the other hand, it has played a large part in the establishment of the Shantung [Shandong] element in the Chinese population of Manchuria, and is also responsible for the fact— which might at first seem paradoxical—that the Shantung settlers are, by general recognition, the soundest and most successful of all immigrants. There is no adequate explanation other than the fact that the settler who derives from the old system of seasonal migration has behind him a solid tradition. To him Manchuria means something definite before he ever goes there, and when he sets out he has before him a known course of action. This, more than any question of facility of transport, similarity of agricultural methods, or any other factor whatever, explains the extraordinary predominance of Shantung men in Manchuria. A living social tradition has more validity than the most pressing economic necessity.[16]

Few people from Shandong who migrated outside the compass of organized recruitment went off into uncharted territory; they went to places where they knew people. Relationships were a natural conduit taking people from one place to another with a minimum of anxiety and insecurity. For example, many of the migrants from Puchengxiang, Binzhou, went to Xinjing (Changchun). Almost all the migrants from Chenhuzhen in Boxing moved to Fuyu, a district just north of the Songhua River in Jilin. A group of about twenty-five men left Yingjiacun, Zouping every year after the Spring Festival to go to Fengcheng in Liaoning; the group's membership varied from year to year, but the destination never changed.

The pattern of recruitment for migration was familiar to Shandong people for it resembled the method generally used to recruit men for the army. Senior soldiers or junior officers would go home to their native place, pick up a certain number of young men who were willing to enlist, pay a recruitment bonus to their families, and take them off to the army. This arrangement had benefits for both sides—the underemployed got jobs, and the army got relatively reliable men who had at least some personal connection to keep them loyal to their commander.[17]

Laoxiang ties were by nature flexible and convenient. They did not carry the obligations of family ties, but involved a clear sense of accounting, that there had to be some recompense for services rendered.

Liaoxiang ties made the great migration to Manchuria possible; they amplified existing ties to meet new needs and opportunities. Below are some of the roles that *laoxiang* played in the migration.

Recruiting

Usually the *laoxiang* connection first came into play as the means by which migrants left home. Local ties were often involved in labor recruitment. Being recruited by a *laoxiang* was less risky than going through one of the large Japanese companies, such as the Fuxun Mines, which ran permanent recruitment offices in most of the large centers in Shandong. This was generally considered to be the worst way to migrate. Zheng Fulin and Zhang Shuyun both left Ling County in 1943 for Dezhou and signed on with the Fuxun office there. They got no recruitment bonuses, earned almost no money while they were in Manchuria, lived in appalling conditions, and had to borrow their fares home — one from a *laoxiang* and the other from a relative.[18]

Some companies used *laoxiang* connections for indirect recruitment. Local agents out in the countryside would canvass their *laoxiang* networks each spring to find men willing to migrate. The periodic markets were ideal places to look for recruits. The five-day markets in Shandong, known as *ji*, or collections, attracted a good portion of the people living within a one to two-hour walk from the market. One of the market's key functions was to spread information — about job opportunities and about the dangers or opportunities of the political situation.[19]

In the 1980s the recommercialization of agriculture produced a resurgence of local markets. Lary observed a great throng at the market in Huimin. The crowd was relaxed and slow-moving; people had come to town not only to do a bit of shopping, but to chat, make arrangements, and generally visit. Like markets in years past, this was a setting for people to informally exchange information and seek out opportunities.

But *laoxiang* did not necessarily look out for the best interests of their fellows drafted to work in Manchuria. The local man who recruited Hou Shangrui and one hundred others from Fenghuangxiang, Ling County, in 1941 was a local "bad egg," whose only occupation was recruiting labor for Japanese enterprises in Manchuria. Hou's group was recruited for a brick kiln in Harbin. Although Hou did better than many people from Ling County, and came back with a small amount of money, he got no recruitment bonus and reported with some relish that his recruiter had been executed by the local Communist authorities after they took over.[20] In Huimin professional local recruiters, labeled "landlords" and "merchants of flesh" by the Communist county authorities, worked for Tianjin companies, which maintained extensive networks through the Shandong countryside.[21]

These full-time local recruiters were generally unpopular with the people they recruited. Zhang Wenjie from Caohuli, Huimin, reported with some pleasure that the man from a neighboring village who had recruited him in 1943, one Shi Dahu (Big Tiger), who lived by recruiting labor for the Japanese, had been punished after the arrival of the Communists.[22] Another man whose sordid activities in the recruitment line caught up with him was Zhang Zhixin, a tailor from Boxing. In 1939 he took Wu Yuzhen and two other *laoxiang* from a neighboring village to Jinan, with the promise that they would get jobs paying 5 yuan per day as tailors in Manchuria. Instead they were locked up in Jinan and taken off to a gold mine in northern Heilongjiang. When Wu finally got back six years later, he went and complained to Zhang about what had happened. Zhang gave him 30 yuan, which seemed to settle the matter.[23]

Although there were bad recruiters who passed recruits on virtually as commodities, there was much less lingering animosity toward men who recruited *laoxiang* to be part of a labor gang that they themselves headed as *batou* (labor contractor) or *gongtou* (labor boss). Neither term is very precise, nor is it clear what the distinction was between a professional recruiter and a *batou* or *gongtou*, except that the informants assumed that a *batou* or *gongtou* would stay with his men, act as their foreman at their destination, and generally have some concern for them beyond the purely mercenary.

But even this arrangement did not always work out. In 1940, several Huimin migrants were recruited by a man they referred to as their *gongtou*. Chen Dechang, a local carpenter, recruited twenty other carpenters and took them to Mishan, Heilongjiang, where he was to be their foreman. The migration was a disaster. The men had to work as farmhands because there were no carpentry tools at their destination, and they returned home with no money, though they had been paid a recruitment bonus before they left. Chen had not been very scrupulous about this payment: Some of his recruits got 20 yuan, others only 15. The money had come from a stake provided to Chen by a Tianjin company, the Qingshuizu. But Chen was just as much of a nuisance to the company as he was to the people he recruited. He took about 30 percent of the company's commission, but did not deliver the equipped carpenters they expected. The migrants, however, had no hard feelings toward him, and he was not punished when the Communists arrived.[24]

Some men who recruited their *laoxiang* were regarded with gratitude. When Ceng Zhaolin came home in 1940 to his township in

Linqu to recruit workers, his Japanese employers, who ran a mine in Changling, Jilin, paid for his journey. Ceng's arrival coincided with the beginning of the great drought in Linqu and many people were desperate to leave. Ceng arranged for not only workers, but whole families to move north and was regarded as something of a savior.[25] This form of migration, where a man came home specifically to recruit local people for his employers, was common. In a closely related form, *laoxiang* assisted with the journey only. In 1937 Hou Shangyu and eight others from his village in Ling County were taken to Manchuria by a *laoxiang* who had come home and was returning north. The *laoxiang* only escorted Hou and company on their journey; he had no jobs lined up at the other end. Hou moved around, doing odd jobs wherever he could find them, and eventually was quite successful. He sent money home regularly and brought money with him on each visit home during the eleven years he was away.[26]

Finding Jobs

A major challenge for first-time migrants who had not been recruited was finding a job. There was usually plenty of work available, but it was widely dispersed. The distances between places were enormous, and the cost of extensive rail travel was out of reach for poor migrants. Timing was also a critical issue. The work season for outdoor jobs in Manchuria was short—roughly April to October—so unless a migrant started work early in the season, his chances of covering his costs were limited. An equally important issue was the type of work. Migrants had the lowest opinion of jobs where they worked directly for Japanese employers in the mines or on the railways. They preferred jobs in factories that did not close down for the winter or in stores—usually Chinese-run—or on farms or in the forests, where the living conditions tended to be better.

Laoxiang connections were important in finding work. The connection in Puchengxiang, Binzhou, was Li Dingjie's father, a foreman in a flour mill in Xinjing. He lived in Xinjing for twenty years, beginning in 1925, and was a magnet for people from his home area. He did not arrange their migration or come home to recruit them, but when they showed up he acted as guarantor to get them jobs. With the jobs came accommodation in the mill's dormitories. Anyone from Puchengxiang and the surrounding villages could move to Xinjing and find work.[27]

In the same way, Zhang Xuefu was able to find jobs in Fenghuang (now Fengcheng), near Dandong, for anyone from Yingjiacun and the surrounding villages in Zouping. Each year a group of about twenty-five men from the village of 200 people, plus a number of people from neighboring villages, left for Fenghuang. There was no prearrangement; it was a locally understood pattern that lasted from the mid-1920s to the Japanese defeat. It did not originate with Zhang because he did not move north until 1939; he must simply have taken over the activity from another job-finder. Zhang himself never came home; he could hardly have done so since he had abandoned his family in Zouping and set up another in Fenghuang. It was not clear whether he made money finding jobs for others. While he had two families, which normally suggests affluence, he did not send remittances to his family at home, so he was not supporting both of them. Nevertheless there seemed to be nothing but warm feelings toward him, and when his Manchuria-born children wanted to move into his village in the early 1980s—Zhang had been long dead—they were welcomed.[28]

Some *laoxiang* migrations were quite casual. Hou Xiaolun, from Fenghuangxiang, Linqu, went off in 1936 with a group of seven *laoxiang,* one of whom had a friend who might be able to find them work in Mishan, Heilongjiang. There must have been a fairly high degree of certainty that the connection would work, given the distance to Mishan—nearly on the Soviet border in southeastern Heilongjiang. And the connection did work, though not in a very coherent way. Each of the men was found a job, but in different places. Hou managed to earn 100 yuan (Manchurian) in the first year he was there.[29]

Arranging Accommodations

One of the commonest forms of assistance provided through *laoxiang* relationships was finding accommodations. *Laoxiang* were not expected to provide free accommodation or cover living expenses except in emergencies, but they were expected to give newcomers a fair deal. Most single male migrants wanted to live as cheaply as possible. This usually meant sharing living quarters with large numbers of people. Sharing created major security problems. Migrants had few possessions, and the ones they did have became by consequence more important. They could not afford to be robbed. If one had no relatives, living with *laoxiang* was the obvious solution. The preexisting relationship reduced the risk of being cheated in rent or having possessions stolen.

Many informants reported that they had lived with *laoxiang* in Manchuria, sometimes in rooming houses run by *laoxiang,* sometimes in dormitories run by their employers. Zhang Hongbao of Sunzhenxiang, Zouping, was recruited in 1938 with a group of a dozen or so from his village and shipped to Dalian. While there he worked as a docker and lived in a dormitory whose inhabitants were all *laoxiang*. He earned enough and lived cheaply enough to send money home each year and to marry as soon as he returned in 1943.[30] His was a classic example of temporary migration, where the migrant's whole focus is to spend as little money as possible, go through no acculturation at all, and get home.

Providing Emergency Help

The *laoxiang* relationship was not normally a charitable one. People expected only a fair deal and some emotional warmth from their *laoxiang*. But there was usually an understanding that in emergency situations charity would come into play. This might mean a good deed done in the expectation of future considerations, or an interest-free loan, or help that would not be given to a stranger. In 1934, when Li Yunsheng of Sunzhenxiang, Zouping, had to flee from creditors at home, he went unannounced to a *laoxiang* in Hunjiang, Jilin, on the border with Korea. He knew that when he got to Jilin, he would not be completely on his own. And in fact, the man did find him a carpentry job, although that was the extent of his help.[31]

Victims of disasters needed more extensive help. They tended to arrive destitute, in family groups. They were not particularly welcome arrivals, especially in places where local people were not doing well themselves. But there was an understanding that they should be helped. Xiao Lianhe's family, from Chenhuzhen, Boxing, moved to Fuyu in 1941 after several of its members had died of cholera. The family had fled, pawning their house to pay their fares as far as Tianjin. A relative there gave them enough money to go on to Fuyu. They moved into what seemed a remote, inhospitable area, but was not because it was heavily settled with *laoxiang*. Although no one took overall responsibility for the family, they were able to move from one household to another and get odd jobs on the land or fishing in the Songhua.[32] Their case illustrates the difference between relatives and *laoxiang*—relatives had to help with money, *laoxiang* only with shelter and work opportunities.

Another common form of help was lending people the money to get home. Those whose migrations had failed had little choice but to go home. To do this, they needed to borrow the fare—unless they were willing to walk, which some did. Zheng Fulin of Zhangxilou, Ling County, went to work in the Fuxun coal mines in 1943. He earned almost no money, and at the end of two years he was so desperate that he borrowed 80 yuan from a *laoxiang* to get home. His action coincided with the closing of the mines after the Japanese defeat, but that was not the reason he gave for wanting to return to Shandong.[33] No one but a relative or a *laoxiang* would be willing to make such a loan.

The harshness of the Manchurian climate made the need to help newcomers more compelling than it would have been in warmer regions. Failure to shelter people in Manchuria might condemn them to death. In northern countries hospitality has a special flavor, because in winter offering or refusing hospitality is a life-and-death matter. Migrants from Shandong had to adjust their long-established habits of assistance to accommodate a new physical climate. This generally meant that they had to do more than they would have at home, even if they lacked the extra resources.

In the course of migration, increased demands on personal ties are common. Sometimes a formal means is found to deal with the challenges, such as the migrant associations developed in North America to provide business contacts, lodging, health care, emergency aid, education, and protection. China had long had such associations, the *huiguan*, generally translated into German as *Landsmannschaften*.[34] These existed in Manchuria, in the provincial capitals, and almost always represented provinces, not cities or counties.[35] They tended to serve only a restricted clientele, principally merchants, and would not have been places to which rural migrants could turn for help. Rural migrants set up few formal organizations for mutual aid. They seem to have relied much more on informal connections and meeting places, such as restaurants or stores run by *laoxiang* or railway stations, which still serve as important informal meeting places today.

Communicating

Laoxiang connections also performed the key function of transmitting news and money. People heading home would carry letters, report on how well or badly things were going, and convey news of the activities of any locals in their area in the north. Some people also asked *laoxiang* to carry money for them. Lan Runde, from Beigouzhen in Penglai, sent money home every year from 1934 to 1944 through *laoxiang*. He found them cheaper and more reliable than either the Post Office or a bank.[36]

The streams of communication home made it difficult for people to disappear unless they went to an area where they had no *laoxiang*. Home villages had a remarkably precise knowledge of where their permanent migrants were, if they were still alive, how many descendants they had, and what jobs they were doing. This knowledge did not come from any formal system of reporting, but from the extended network of *laoxiang*.

The apparent anonymity of the migrants in the great movement from Shandong to Manchuria does not tally with the facts. Almost all of the migrants moved along paths trodden before them by people they knew. Although far from home, they could spend their time with people from their home areas, bound together by the same bonds that at home tied them to their native place.

5

RETURN MIGRATION

The official term Chinese authorities use to refer to people living abroad is *qiao*, sojourners. Migrants are implicitly assumed to be people who in their hearts never leave home, for whom migration is only a temporary expedient to get through hard times. Return migration is then the inevitable outcome of migration. The majority of the migrants who went to Manchuria did in fact return promptly to their homes in North China (see Figure 5.1). The timing of their returns, however, was often as complex as the original decision to migrate and depended on their intentions before they migrated, their successes or failures in Manchuria, and circumstances at home.

REASONS FOR RETURN

Very few data were collected in the course of the migration to determine who left Manchuria and why. However, one source that deals with a small sample of people returning to Shandong and Hebei in 1934 and 1935 only points to some of the reasons people did return. Although the author intended to show that people were driven out of Manchuria by Japanese brutality, the answers he got did not fit this supposition.

The figures in Table 5.1 give an indication of the range of possible causes for return migration, but with an "other" category that accounts for more than 50 percent of the responses, they hardly seem complete. Another claim, made in late 1934, that an economic downturn was driving migrants out of Manchuria, with a thousand people a day coming home through Qingdao, was weakened by the fact that it was based on activity at the beginning of the normal return season, late autumn, as the winter begins to take hold in Manchuria.[1]

Table 5.1 Reasons for Migrants' Return

Reason for return	1934	1935
Visit family	793	469
Disasters (natural/manmade)	456	770
Unemployed	77	230
Japanese oppression	651	746
New Year	105	265
Unable to make ends meet	269	192
Other	2856	2893
Total	5207	5465

Source: Huang Jinyan, "Jiuyiba hou Shandong Hebei liang-sheng laiwang Dongbei sansheng zhi nonggong shuzi tongji," *Zhongguo shiye zazhi* 1.9 (1935): 1662.

The informants for the present study were quite precise about why they had come home; usually they gave a specific reason, and it was always colored by their attachment to home. Although travel between Manchuria and Shandong was easy, only rarely interrupted by disturbances, it was always expensive and time-consuming, since the travelers often had to walk long distances to or from the nearest port or railway station at either end of their journey. Moreover, their relatives would expect them to bring something back with them, either money, gifts, or both, so the idea of a casual return was not realistic.

Returning Laborers

The most common reason for return migration, and the one that kept the figures high, was the seasonal return as the Manchurian winter started and preparations for celebrating the New Year at home got under way. On the Shandong Peninsula, annual migration by the swallows was a long-established tradition. In Ye County, going to Manchuria in the spring and returning in the autumn was a normal routine for young men. The same pattern was common in Huang County.[2] A 1929 SMR study found that almost half (47.5 percent) of the migrants landing at Dalian in 1927, 1928, and 1929 arrived in the first four months of the year, while 45 percent of departures took place in October, November, December, and January.[3]

The "swallows" frequently moved in gangs, either formally recruited through a labor company or traveling with their own boss (see page 111). In some villages boys learned a specific skill that would help them earn money when they went north. Guo Baomeng, like many young men from his village in Zouping, was a tinker (*xiaolujiang*), skilled in repairing metal utensils. He went to Manchuria every year

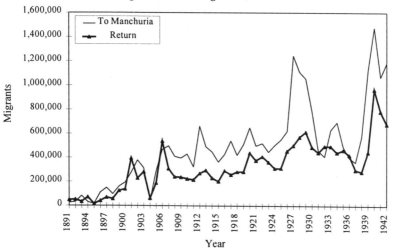

Fig. 5.1 Return Migration, 1891–1942

for five years, from the time he was twenty-one until he was twenty-five, always with a small group from his village, quite often his brothers. He married after his fourth trip, went out one more time, and then came home permanently. He managed to bring back about 50 yuan each time.[4]

Other villages specialized in training carpenters, men who could easily get casual work outside the village. Some went to Manchuria, others worked closer to home. They followed established routes and specialized in particular forms of carpentry: some made marriage furniture, others worked in construction. The older carpenters from Yangji Village, Boxing, for example, often took their apprentices with them. The young men thus got their first experience of migration very early and had little choice about going if they wanted to finish their apprenticeship. They were not paid as apprentices, which must have made taking them along an attractive proposition for the master.[5]

Those men who worked on short contracts in roving labor bands usually returned to spend the New Year at home. Other men hired on site in Manchuria where they worked outdoors would often be let go sometime in the fall. Their employer would not want to keep them idle through the winter. Of almost 2,000 men recruited in Huimin in the spring of 1940, eighty-seven came back within six months. The men were recruited by a local labor contractor and worked through the summer on the railway in Heilongjiang. They were then jammed into box cars, shipped as far as Cangzhou on the Hebei border, and walked the rest of the way home.[6]

Many of the swallows went to Manchuria only once. Poor wages and maltreatment from their employers or their *batou* deterred them from making repeat trips. Some, on the other hand, made all the money they needed in one trip. SMR statistics on northbound migrants in 1930 showed very few repeat migrants. Of 2,571 groups (11,284 people), only 735 included repeat migrants.[7] In 1925 a report on Shandong migrants described men who worked 250 days straight through, without any breaks, to earn as much as they could before they returned for the winter.[8] Most, however, stayed longer than a year, since one season in Manchuria was usually not long enough to make a sum of money sufficient for their purposes, whether getting married or buying land. In 1927 SMR researchers found that among the migrants they surveyed only 10 percent returned home within a year, while 20 percent remained for two years, 40 percent for three years, 15 percent for four years, and 15 percent for five years or longer.[9] A typical example was Zhang Hongbao of Zouping, who worked in Dalian as a docker for five years and then returned home to get married. One of four brothers, he had no choice but to earn the bride price himself. By living in a dormitory he was eventually able to send home the needed amount.[10]

Martin Yang's report on his native village described a pattern of return that was characteristic of many poorer areas of Shandong:

> Almost all the single men who went to Manchuria, or elsewhere, have come back sooner or later, after they have made some money. They come back to marry, to buy land, and to settle down. More than a dozen men have come home from Manchuria in the last ten or fifteen years. But not all of them came back with fortunes. Unlike emigrants from Hwanghsien [Huang County], Penglai and other counties on the eastern Shantung Peninsula, who, by and large, went to Manchuria as merchants, people of Taitou went there as farmers, vegetable gardeners, or other kinds of laborers. Therefore, this village has not been conspicuously benefited by those dozen adventurers, except in the case of two or three families.[11]

Migrants might not come home if they failed to make the money they had hoped for. Failure was such a humiliation that it had to be avoided, even if that meant staying longer than intended in Manchuria. The Ling County gazetteer reported in 1935 that almost all young men went out (mostly to Manchuria) intending to stay for only a short period, but that, like the yellow cranes, many did not come home after they left.[12] The inability to make money might mean staying on forever. Liu Zhangtai's father migrated from Penglai to Yingkou in 1894. At first he sent money home regularly and came home every few years for a visit, but as he sank deeper and deeper into opium addiction, the remittances dried up, and he no longer came home for visits. He eventually died alone in Yingkou.[13]

Migrants Fleeing Disaster

Refugees from disaster usually returned home as soon as possible. Destitute people were seldom welcome in neighboring counties, and their state of debilitation made it difficult for them to move elsewhere unless they received assistance. Such migrations were arranged from time to time by national and provincial authorities,[14] but the confusion of Republican China made this an infrequent scenario. As a result of the 1935 Yellow River and Grand Canal floods, the provincial flood relief committee moved 451,000 victims in southwestern Shandong into camps, but the vast majority (1,876,000) had to fend for themselves. All were expected to go home as soon as possible, and those who survived did.[15]

Some disasters lasted too long for a quick return. Beginning in 1940, Linqu was gripped by a terrible drought; this mountain county saw no rain for four years. Villages had to be abandoned; many people died of starvation, while others fled. Forty-nine percent of the population (168,000), left during the drought; most went to Manchuria, to wait out the disaster with relatives there. Over 100,000 of those who stayed in the county died. By the end of the drought only 80,000 people remained. Almost all the people who had left returned by the end of 1945, and by 1949 the population was almost back to predrought levels.[16]

Sometimes disasters occurred at the other end of the migration. In 1934 Liu Guangpu of Gaomi and his family returned from Tonghua, Jilin, where they had led a tough life as pioneer settlers. After cholera swept through the area, taking the lives of all the women in the family—Liu's mother, two sisters, and his wife—the men fled home, anxious to leave a place haunted by grief.[17] Some unlucky people encountered disaster at both ends. Gao Puchun's family fled from Linqu to relatives in Jilin in 1942 because of the drought at home, only to flee the other way the next year when plague, endemic in parts of Manchuria, broke out and killed two people they knew.[18]

Some disasters that forced people to move were manmade. Many families who settled on the land in Manchuria were terrorized by gangs of bandits known as *honghuzi*. Wang Yuxiang of Laiyang and his family had homesteaded in Laipigou, in the mountains of eastern Jilin. They were quite successful, but through the early 1920s the demands of the *honghuzi* became more and more onerous. Finally, in 1927 they abandoned their farm and returned to Shandong.[19] Jiang Xiuxiang, whose parents had come from Gaomi, was born on her parents' homestead in the mountains of Tonghua, Jilin. After her parents were killed by *honghuzi*, she and her new husband hung on for a few years, but in 1934 they gave up under the incessant harassment and returned to Gaomi.[20] The *honghuzi* were not strangers to the farmers. Most of them came from the same background as the families they harassed, the Shandong countryside, but they saw in the "wild west" atmosphere of Manchuria a chance to make money without the tedium of cultivating the land.

In 1931 came the Japanese conquest of Manchuria and the beginning of all-out hostility between Japan and China. An international border was drawn within China, and Chinese living in Manchuria found themselves under alien rule. One might expect this to have precipitated massive return migration, but in fact only two informants gave this as a reason for their return. Wang Duxian of Gaomi and his family rushed home as soon as the Japanese took over, giving up a successful business selling sheepskins for a miserable one selling fish at home.[21] Liu Zhangtai of Penglai, who had made five trips to various places in Manchuria, decided not to go again in 1933 because life under the Japanese was too precarious, and he was afraid of being arrested or press-ganged.[22]

Personal or family disasters sometimes provided the reason for return. The loss of a key family member might make it impossible to continue in Manchuria. Gao Honghuang and his family returned to Boxing from a village in the wilderness of the Heilongjiang and Inner Mongolia border after his father died. Gao was still an infant, and his mother could not farm on her own. She had no choice but to return to her husband's family. She never got over the thought of her husband buried so far away from home and was constantly looking for an opportunity to bring his bones back. It came during the Cultural Revolution. As a rather elderly Red Guard, Gao seized the chance to travel for free, "exchanging revolutionary experiences." He surreptitiously dug up his father's bones and brought them home hidden beneath his jacket, always fearing that other Red Guards might discover his feudal mission.[23]

The same fear of being buried alone in an alien land prompted the family of Zhang Xuelun to return to Zouping. His grandfather, son of the original migrant, was suddenly seized in his late sixties with the fear that he was going to die. He felt a great need to die at home, and so he uprooted his family and took them south in 1947.[24] The fear of dying away from home was frequently cited as a reason for return to Gaomi.[25]

In the case of Kang Guangwen, it was the death of his first wife in childbirth in Tonghua, Jilin, that brought him home. Initially he returned just to look for a second wife, and he succeeded in finding one. But his new wife would not go with him to Tonghua, so he had to settle down at home. The marriage enhanced their local prestige: He was respected for having managed to find a second wife, and she was respected for having taken such a strong stand.[26]

RETURN RATES

Return Rate Variations

The firm intention to return home at the earliest possible date expressed by virtually all of the informants is consistent with the data on return migration. Two-thirds of all migrants who went to Manchuria between 1891 and 1942 ultimately returned to their homes, and in most years the ratio of returnees to out-migrants hovered near or below this rate (see Figure 5.2). Most sharp deviations in the return ratio were related to specific events or changes in conditions in the home areas of North China, Manchuria, or both.

The beginning of the Sino-Japanese War in 1894 caused a wave of return migration to escape the fighting. In 1896, 1897, and 1898, however, construction of the Chinese Eastern and South Manchuria railway lines drew an influx of workers and pushed the return ratio down once more. Higher return rates between 1901 and 1906 were caused first by a harsh Russian military response to the Boxer Uprising in 1901 and then by the Russo-Japanese War in 1904–1905, most of which was fought in southern Manchuria.

A long period of relatively low annual return rates from 1907 to 1920 reflected steady economic growth in Manchuria and a series of disruptions in North China. The year 1911 was marked by the turmoil of the Republican Revolution, and 1914 saw the landing of Japanese forces at Longkou to launch an attack on the German holdings in Shandong at the beginning of the First World War. Both events precipitated waves of banditry and unrest, which were exacerbated by the attempt of Yuan Shikai to restore the Manchu monarchy in 1915 and 1916. Yuan's bid for power failed and accelerated the deterioration of the central government and its ability to deal with the banditry, disease, and drought that afflicted much of Shandong and Hebei in 1917 and 1918.

Fig. 5.2 Total Return Ratio, 1891–1942

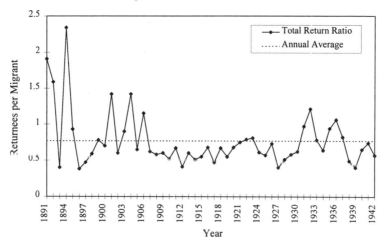

Year

From 1921 to 1923 the annual return ratios were near the long-term average, as banditry, famine, disease, and recurring warlord conflict in North China were largely balanced in Manchuria by a major plague epidemic in Heilongjiang in 1921 and extensive bandit activity of the kind that caused Wang Yuxiang and his family to abandon their Jilin farm a few years later.

Low return ratios in the late 1920s were caused mainly by negative developments in North China: civil war between Nationalist and warlord forces, conflict at Jinan in 1928 between Nationalist and Japanese troops (the "Jinan Incident"), and extensive drought and famine in Hebei and western Shandong. The numbers of migrants arriving in Manchuria peaked at over a million each year in 1927, 1928, and 1929, and far fewer migrants opted to return home.

Return ratios shot up between 1931 and 1937 after the seizure of Manchuria by the Japanese military. As the number of migrants entering Manchuria fell to less than half the level of peak years, the average rate of return rose to over 90 percent. The Japanese officials who controlled the new puppet state of Manchukuo first discouraged immigration of "foreign" (Chinese) laborers, then actively enforced tight immigration restrictions beginning in 1935.

Out-migration rose and return ratios fell again after 1938 when the Japanese authorities realized they would have to reverse their stand and encourage immigration to meet the labor requirements of the Manchurian economy as it strained to satisfy Japan's wartime demands. At the same time the economies of Hebei and Shandong were devastated by the effects of the Japanese invasion.

Home Area Return Rate Differences

Return rates varied from district to district across Shandong. Rates seem to have been high for the province as a whole. One recent source cites a return rate of 56 percent for the whole Republican period, 10.4 million of 18.4 million migrants.[27] This overall rate disguises local variations. In Linqu, where the only large-scale migration was caused by a single disaster, the return rate was almost 100 percent, whereas at the other end of the spectrum only about 30 percent of the 23,000 migrants from Laiyang returned. Most Laiyang migrants went in search of land in Manchuria, settled down, and did not think of coming back to an overcrowded place where there was little chance of acquiring land.[28] The local authorities in Huimin and Boxing reported return rates of more than 50 percent, but it is difficult in each case to distinguish short-term migrants from longer-term ones.[29] Gaomi had a much lower return rate. The local authorities estimated that of the 28,000 who migrated during the Republican period only 7,000, or 25 percent, had returned. This figure is misleading because it excludes the swallows, who migrated annually for the work season; it looked only at people who had migrated intending not to return.[30] In Penglai the situation changed over time. Between 1911 and 1942 departures and returns balanced each other; the rate was quite steady, about 31,000 in each direction per annum. After 1942 there was a mass migration when over 120,000 people left, either grabbed as forced labor or in flight from the fighting between the puppet government and Communist forces; only 41,000 returned, or about 30 percent.[31]

On a larger scale the migrant data indicate broad regional differences in return ratios between migrants from the Shandong Peninsula, most of whom traveled to Manchuria by way of the ports of Longkou and Yantai, and those from Hebei and other parts of Shandong, most of whom either took ships from Qingdao or Tianjin or else followed the land route. The highest average annual rate of return over the entire period between 1891 and 1942 occurred at Longkou and Yantai, where the annual number of returnees typically reached 85 percent of the number of migrants leaving for Manchuria. Longkou and Yantai served most of the Shandong Peninsula, including Penglai and Laiyang. Most migrants who did not travel through Longkou or Yantai came from areas of Shandong and Hebei located on or near the North China Plain, including Ling County, Huimin, Binzhou, Boxing, Zouping, Linqu, and Gaomi. The long-term average annual return ratio for the routes that served the North China Plain regions was 67 percent (see Figure 5.3).

Fig. 5.3 Annual Return Migration Rates by Home Area, 1891–1942

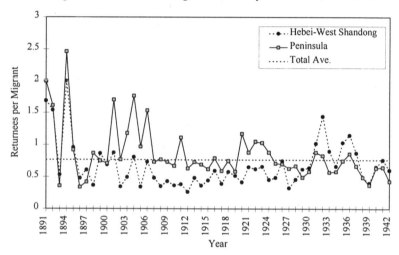

The higher return rates for migrants from the Shandong Peninsula compared to those from areas on or near the North China Plain reflect their relative distance from Manchuria. A shorter trip meant lower travel costs and a higher likelihood of meeting a migrant's financial goal. The 1927 SMR study of the migration found the migrant travel costs listed in Table 5.2. These were special discount fares for migrants that were 35 to 40 percent of normal fares.

The lowest cost—except for migrants who walked all the way—was the 1.59 yuan steamer fare paid by the small portion of ship passengers from Yantai who went no further than Dalian.[32] The shortest journeys also involved the smallest expenses for food and lodging. At the upper end of the cost range was the trip from Western Shandong: by rail from Jinan to Tianjin (3.90 yuan), by steamer from Tianjin to Dalian (3.50 yuan), by rail from Dalian to Changchun (5.15 yuan), and by rail from Changchun to Harbin (1.92 yuan), a total of 14.47 yuan in fares alone. These migrants also faced higher expenses for food and lodging because of their longer time on the road, as well as transportation to Jinan at the beginning of the trip, and the expense of traveling beyond Harbin for those headed to remote areas in northern Heilongjiang.[33]

Table 5.2. Migrant Fares between North China and Manchuria

Steamship Fares in 1927 (in yuan)				
To	From Tianjin	From Longkou	From Yantai	From Qingdao
Dalian	3.50	1.78	1.59	2.00
Yingkou	2.60	2.70	-	4.00

Migrant Fares on the South Manchuria Railway in 1925 (in yuan)

	From Dalian		From Yingkou	
To	Fares	% of Passengers	Fares	% of Passengers
Changchun	5.15	48.5	3.55	60.2
Gongzhuling	4.71	1.2	3.12	1.7
Sipingkai	4.35	2.5	2.76	3.5
Kaiyuan	3.70	7.2	2.10	4.6
Tieling	3.48	1.4	1.89	1.5
Shenyang	2.72	21.3	1.27	23.1
Anshan	2.14	3.0	-	-
Fushun	2.97	14.9	1.60	5.4
Average fare:	4.06		2.79	

Other Important Railway Fares in 1925 (in yuan)

Tianjin to Shenyang:	4.00	Changchun to Harbin:	1.92
Jinan to Qingdao:	2.20	Jinan to Tianjin:	3.90

Sources: MMTKK, *Minkoku jurokunen no manshu dekasegi sha*, 19–29, 171–76; and F. L. Ho, *Population Movement,* 5–6. *Note:* The steamship fares to Dalian are the average of the fares charged by the major companies on each run; two companies ran from Tianjin, three each from Longkou and Yantai, four from Qingdao. Some of the steamship fares are given in "small coin" (*xiao yang*) denominations, they have been converted to "big coin" (*da yang*) yuan at the rate of 1.14 "small coin" yuan = 1.00 full value yuan (see Sakatani, *Manchuria, A Survey*, 22). The fares were given in yen and have been converted here to yuan at the exchange rate implied by the haiguan tael exchange rates for yuan and yen in 1925: 0.7255 yuan = 1.00 yen (see Sakatani, *Manchuria, A Survey*, 295). "Average fare" is the weighted average of the fares with the percentages of passengers as the weights.

Migrants from the north coast of the Shandong Peninsula enjoyed a travel cost advantage of 0.41 yuan over people from Qingdao, if they were headed for the Dalian region. Travelers from the Jinan area destined north of Shenyang faced costs higher than those incurred by people from Yantai by 2.61 yuan each way if they took the Qingdao route, or by 3.59 yuan each way if they went by land. They also had to cover food and lodging expenses for several additional days en route. Thus migrants who wished to return home to western Hebei, western Shandong, and southern Shandong faced a financial barrier over twice as high as migrants returning to homes on the Peninsula.

POSTWAR RETURNS

No aggregate data exist on annual migration levels after 1942, but individual county records and interview accounts indicate that two major waves of return migration took place after the end of the Second World War. The first came in the years immediately following the Japanese surrender in 1945, and the second occurred in the 1980s.

1940s Returns

Several Shandong county histories report very high levels of return migration in the middle 1940s. In some areas the 1940s returns coincided with the end of major natural disasters—in Ling County, Huimin, and Linqu the terrible drought finally broke in 1944. But for many migrants the reason for return was quite different—the economy in Manchuria collapsed after the Japanese defeat in 1945. The people most affected were those working in the cities of Manchuria; people settled on the land had a better chance at surviving. Migrants flooded back to Shandong as factories and businesses in Manchuria closed and their livelihoods disappeared. The defeat was particularly disastrous for Penglai. Between 1944 and 1949, 41,000 people returned, 30 percent of the migrants from that county. Most of them were destitute.[34]

The collapse coincided, in some places, with the Communist takeover in Shandong. A few areas were liberated as early as 1945. Some informants came home at that time and in the years that followed, not so much to participate in glorious revolution as to be present when the land was divided during land reform. It was important to be physically on hand to get one's fair share. There was another great attraction of the Communist takeover—the forgiving of debts. People who had stayed away from home because they owed money and feared their creditors could now safely return.

People who tried to return after 1945 were sometimes stymied. By 1947 the Guomindang held the cities and ports of Shandong and the Communists the countryside. People trying to get back to Shandong could find themselves trapped in the ports. Some people returning to Linqu got stuck in Qingdao and found themselves in refugee camps, where inhabitants were a mix of poor migrants back from Manchuria and more prosperous people fleeing from the Communist occupation of the countryside.[35]

Post-1949 returns

Migration and return migration continued long after 1949. Many young people were sent up to Manchuria in the middle and late 1950s to "open up the wilderness." Other people went north in hard times, especially the early 1960s, to seek shelter with relatives. Some people went during the Cultural Revolution to escape political trouble at home. Whatever the scale of migration, return migration also continued, and this delayed state plans for the rapid growth of the Manchurian population.

Return migration followed several patterns. Many of the young people sent north during the Cultural Revolution came back as soon as it was over and return became possible. Others came back to retire, some from Manchuria, but some from the south, where many Shandong cadres had been sent in the early 1950s. The return migration most closely related to Manchuria followed a different pattern and was directly connected to the agricultural reforms begun in 1978. Shandong entered an economic boom period, which gradually transformed it from a very poor province into a much more affluent one. Word of the new prosperity made its way to Manchuria and aroused a great deal of interest among migrants and their descendants. Their desire to return was flattering to people in Shandong—what better proof of the innate superiority of the province—but it also caused problems.

The spring of 1984, when many of the interviews for this study took place, was a time of change in the Shandong countryside. Local government organization was in transition. Some counties still had communes, while in others communes had already been replaced by *xiang* (townships). Much more important to the farmers, fifteen-year land leases were being handed out, and to get land, one had to be at home.

News of the land distribution reached Manchuria rapidly, and, together with the general economic improvement, triggered a major return movement. The return movement to Ling County started in 1981; three years later 8,900 people had already come back, and many more were expected.[36] In some communities the return rate was very high indeed: The village of Zhangxilou in Ling County had already grown by 30 families—with another 10 to 20 expected—beyond the existing population of 132 households.[37] Return migration on this scale required careful thought and planning—profound decisions had to be made on who had the right to come back. Many villages actually began to define what it meant to "belong," and to decide whether there was a scale of rights. Most concluded that the right of return was not universal, and different places defined who belonged differently. Although the decisions seem to have been made at the village level, there were clear local patterns that took into account factors such as land supply as well as family ties.

Gaomi took a generous view of who could return—former inhabitants and their descendants up to the second or third generation. They could afford to do so because very few people had applied to come back.[38] Laiyang took the same view: Descendants up to the third generation could come back, but few wanted to. In fact Laiyang was having to recruit former locals with special skills to work in their many new enterprises, especially the canning of the famous Laiyang pears. The local authorities had been out to look for skilled former Laiyang natives, offering them substantially higher wages than would be paid to locals.[39] Ling County, under great pressure from would-be return migrants, was fairly restrictive about who could come back. Bianjianzhen would accept only people born there; Fenghuangxiang would accept both people born there and their first-generation descendants, provided they still had relatives there. A number of descendants without living relatives had been refused. Those who were allowed to returned only after formally contacting the village officials; people willing to work in the new enterprises rather than as farmers were the most welcome.[40] Huimin was even more restrictive; only people born in the county could return, and they had to be willing to live with relatives. Farmers were discouraged from coming home, given the land shortage, and only people with useful skills were welcomed.[41] Boxing, with its surplus of agricultural labor, was equally discouraging, though in some cases county officials would consider letting descendants come back.[42]

In other parts of Shandong return migration went quite poorly. One village in Juye, in the southwest of the province, had to expand by about 50 percent, building houses and infrastructure, to accommodate all the people who came back. Both there and elsewhere major anxieties surrounded the return of so many people, and the fact that they arrived without warning, expecting to be assigned land. A survey conducted in 1984–1985 in various parts of the province found that very few of the returnees were doing well.[43]

Individuals were reluctant to admit that return was not a pleasure; all the informants maintained they were glad they had come home. None spoke of Manchuria with any affection. Besides the obvious things they disliked— the food, the climate, and the mosquitoes—they also felt the place had let them down—not one of them had returned a rich man. The only person who came home in glory (*dang hongren*—"to be the fair-haired boy") was Li Chuanzhen, who returned to his village in Ling County as a soldier in the People's Liberation Army.[44] The game had changed—coming home in glory no longer meant wearing brocade, but a cotton army uniform.

6

NOT FOR POLITICS OR GLORY

The migration to Manchuria took place in the midst of tremendous political turmoil, as both Russia and Japan repeatedly tried to gain control over Manchuria, while Japan relentlessly encroached on Chinese territory. After the establishment of the People's Republic in 1949, the migration continued in the midst of a politically charged atmosphere, first during the nation-building drive of the 1950s, then during the ultra-socialist frenzy of the Cultural Revolution. Yet, as was true twenty years earlier, the migrants were moved neither by political fervor, nor by any sense of excitement or destiny. They were driven overwhelmingly by the narrow concerns of the family economy, and Manchuria just happened to be the place that best met their needs.

In its essence the modern history of Manchuria has revolved around imbalances in the classical economic trilogy of land, labor, and capital. At the end of the nineteenth century Manchuria had one of the richest endowments of natural resources in all of East Asia, but it lacked the labor force and capital equipment required to convert these raw materials into a thriving economy. Labor was abundantly available in the villages of North China, but there was little incentive for workers to move north until railways, steamships, roads, and factories created new jobs and made the products of Manchuria accessible to Chinese and world markets. Once the shipping lines and railways were in place, the irresistible force of family interests combined with Manchuria's hungry labor market drove the migration through all political vicissitudes except for interludes of active warfare. The fact that much of the investment and technology came from Russia and Japan made little difference to the migrants and their families.

The importance to the migration of economic conditions in Manchuria is best illustrated by three instances. First, the commitment of North Chinese workers to pursue family interests regardless of political concerns was dramatically demonstrated by the extraordinarily high level of migration that occurred in the late 1930s and early 1940s, despite the fact that China was at war with Japan, and Manchuria was dominated by the Japanese army. The second instance came in the 1950s when the socialist government of the People's Republic, which rejected market-driven economic forces, promptly resumed the transfer of population to Manchuria on a very large scale as soon as it began to rebuild China's national economy. Exploitation of Manchuria's natural resources was just as important to the planned economy of the PRC as it had been to the capitalist system of the Republic, and labor was still in short supply. The third instance was the remarkable reverse flow of migrants from the Northeast to their families' home villages in Shandong in the 1980s, when economic reform suddenly caused prospects at home to look more promising than conditions in Manchuria, where the supply of labor was finally sufficient for the region's needs.

MIGRATION AND POLITICS

China's most wrenching political issue during the Republican period was Japanese encroachment and then invasion. Slowly at first, then with gathering speed and intensity, the Japanese Empire swallowed up one piece of China after another. Japan merely suffered an early setback after the Sino-Japanese War (1885), when the intervention of Russia, France, and Germany forced the return of territory won from China. After defeating Russia in 1905, Japan accelerated economic activities in various parts of China. During the First World War it tried to seize Germany's holdings in Shandong and to consolidate a strong position on the coast. This move eventually failed because of public protest in China and heavy pressure from the remaining Powers, especially at the Washington Conference in 1922. These rebuffs did not, however, prevent Japan from intervening again in Shandong in 1927 during the Northern Expedition, Chiang Kai-shek's effort to unify China militarily.

Shandong was important to Japan, but the real focus of interest was always Manchuria. Japanese pressure there grew and grew, culminating in 1931 with outright takeover. Manchuria became the symbol of Japanese aggression. The League of Nations faltered, and the question of China's appeasement or resistance to Japan was the most emotional and potent political topic in China during the 1930s.[1] It was the issue over which the first significant mass movements developed in China, among students, merchants, and workers. The progressive Japanese encroachment through the 1930s was covered exhaustively in the press, and the heroes of the day were Chinese military leaders like Ma Zhanshan and Cai Tingkai who put up resistance.

The migrants from Shandong seem to have been little touched by this political turbulence; they were for the most part politically passive. This seems strange, given that they were moving into the crucible of Japanese expansion and economic development. Indeed, they were the true foot soldiers of imperialism. Without their labor the Japanese would have been able to do very little, since plans to settle large numbers of Japanese and Koreans in Manchuria had failed. The migrants were also victims of persistent abuse from the Japanese; the conditions in which they worked, in mines or on the railways, guaranteed physical maltreatment. They were often cheated, routinely humiliated, and treated as *Untermenschen* by a society riding a wave of racial supremacy.

One might expect the migrants to have stood at the forefront of anti-Japanese activity, and in fact there were displays of anti-Japanese hostility in Manchuria. After the surrender of Manchuria to Japan in 1931, a number of the Manchurian soldiers became irregulars (or guerrillas) and continued to fight the Japanese, especially in the far north. The urban Chinese population had little chance to resist, though some rural migrants did. The world of anti-Japanese resistance was captured by Xiao Jun in *Village in August*. Troops evicted from Manchuria played an important role in anti-Japanese activities in North China, notably in the Xian Incident (1936), when troops under Zhang Xueliang kidnapped Chiang Kai-shek and forced him to finally face the Japanese rather than pursue the Chinese Communists.

Among the civilian inhabitants of Manchuria, however, there was little resistance. Few universities and colleges in the region meant few students to demonstrate, a role students played powerfully elsewhere in China. There was no free press. Most of the Chinese elite who stayed in Manchuria after 1931 collaborated with the Japanese, as did the substantial White Russian population. Surviving Manchus became the mainstay of the puppet state set up in 1932, Manchukuo. But most ordinary people, including migrants from North China, seem to have been inert. Why did those who suffered most from the Japanese not fight them?

One reason might have been that the migrants did not actually know what was going on, that they were unaware of the bigger political picture and of being exploited. This seems impossible. It is true that the Japanese did not penetrate as deeply into local society as other nations did,[2] but they were highly visible. Shandong was the site of some of Japan's earliest shows of aggression. The Twenty-one Demands of 1915 were intended to entrench Japan in Shandong, and there were major clashes in Shandong between Chinese and Japanese forces in 1927 and 1928. Japanese encroachment in Manchuria was aggressive and obvious, at least in the cities and along the railway lines. Someone in a remote village might be unaware of the conflict, but a migrant who left a Shandong village and traveled to Manchuria would have to be aware that China was under assault. By the 1930s the anti-Japanese movement in China was vociferous and highly visible, with trade boycotts and the wide distribution of cigarette brands named after the heroes of anti-Japanese resistance, Ma Zhanshan and Cai Tingkai. Ignorance cannot explain the migrants' noninvolvement in anti-Japanese activity.

A more plausible explanation is that whatever the migrants felt about Japanese aggression, they could do very little to oppose it. For workers living in prison-like barracks, any kind of political organization would have been almost impossible. Even if one group of workers had been bold enough, organizing resistance in a single factory or mine would not have made much difference. Significant resistance would have required leadership and coordination, and this was not forthcoming from the Manchurian side. Much of the political and military elite had left with the "Young Marshall" Zhang Xueliang, putting up no resistance at all. Some who stayed became guerrillas, but others collaborated. The Chinese Communist Party was not much in evidence in Manchuria until the civil war after the Japanese defeat. How could poor, illiterate labor migrants organize themselves against tough, well-organized occupiers who had an excellent intelligence system and a modern army?

Another logical source of resistance, trade unions, did not exist in China at the time. The failure of the trade union movement has often been put down to ferocious Guomindang attacks on the Communist-led unions, especially in 1927. But Elizabeth Perry has shown that class-based unions stood little chance because other elements were so much more important in worker organization, especially regional and local associations.[3] This would certainly seem to be the case with the Shandong migrants to Manchuria, whose organizations were informal, based on *laoxiang* ties, and inward-looking to provide mutual protection; they were not geared to external activity.

Fear also played a role in discouraging migrants from anti-Japanese activities. The Japanese could act against opponents either directly, using their army or police, or indirectly, through bands of thugs (*ronin*) who acted as unofficial enforcers in Manchuria. Any visible resistance would almost certainly lead to an unpleasant death. The Japanese demonstrated their willingness to crush opposition even before they took over Manchuria. The "Old Marshall" Zhang Zuolin, chief warlord of Manchuria and loyal ally of the Japanese, met a nasty end after he was seen becoming friendly with the Guomindang; he and his train were blown up in 1928.

Another concern that deterred migrants from political activity was their obligation to family at home. Most migrants had a specific duty to perform: to earn money they could send back to the family. Getting involved in dangerous activities that risked their lives would compromise their ability to fulfill this primary duty. As long as their mindset was short-term, even if they actually stayed in Manchuria for a long time, resistance on any level was counterproductive. Migrants simply wanted to go home, and so they could put up with a great deal of hardship in the short run.

A final explanation was that the migrants saw no reason to rebel. They had grown up with abuse from landlords, soldiers, and bandits, in a world where there was little law or justice. The treatment they received in Manchuria from their Japanese employers was no worse. In this harsh world they learned to get through life by keeping to stoic, heads-down behavior (*chiku nailao*); they were not accustomed to political activism or the idea of fighting for their country. They were willing to put up with maltreatment so long as they could fulfill their own goal of improving the lives of their families.

The informants said little about Japanese aggression against China, though most recalled Japanese brutality toward themselves and other migrants. This was particularly true of those who went to Manchuria in the early 1940s, many of whom were treated as forced labor.[4] Perhaps they felt a sense of shame for having worked for the Japanese, but even if they blamed themselves, others did not seem to share that view. Although insulting terms (piglets, gold worshippers) are often used in Shandong for emigrants to southern provinces, and although there are epithets for people who directly collaborated with the foreign aggressors (*hanjian*), no one applied such terms to the Manchuria migrants. Rather, both the literature of that time and modern commentators tended to pity them for their poverty and the exploitation they suffered. In Shandong they are associated with the huge number of slave laborers who were taken to Japan and Korea during the war, never to return.

If the migrants did not take part in anti-Japanese activities in Manchuria, they might have been expected to do something when they returned to Shandong. Their direct experience of Japanese imperialism might have turned them into political activists. There were different reasons at different periods why this did not happen. In the 1920s Shandong was divided among warlords and bandits, and the situation was too chaotic for anti-Japanese action. By the 1930s, a Guomindang-allied governor, Han Fuju, brought order to the province, but he was not a loyal supporter of Nanjing. He pursued a friendly policy towards the Japanese and did not permit anti-Japanese activity.[5] By the late 1930s Shandong was under direct Japanese occupation. The experience of Japanese oppression in Manchuria does not seem to have led to enthusiasm for political action in Shandong, whether anti-Japanese, pro-Communist, or traditional; even the relatively recent Boxer tradition had disappeared. The Japanese occupation was harsh and long, extending from the end of 1937 to the middle of 1945. A mass grave where thousands of people were executed during the Japanese occupation is marked at Pipashan near Jinan. Such atrocities have been detailed since the 1980s in local publications.[6]

The Communist Party initially had only a tenuous existence in Shandong. Communist uprisings between 1928 and 1935 were minimal; of nine incidents listed, one was an attack on a German Catholic mission (Yanggu, 1928), and another (Yishui, 1933) is described as a Big Sword (secret society) uprising. The longest, at Richao in 1933, lasted thirteen days; the others all collapsed instantly.[7]

During the Japanese occupation, parts of Shandong became major base areas for guerrilla warfare against the Japanese, usually under direct control of the Eighth Route Army. Base areas dotted the Central Massif and the marshy land created when the Yellow River changed course in 1938. Shandong seemed to recover some of its reputation as a province of fighters, but the returned migrants seldom turned into guerrillas. One report from West Shandong about anti-Japanese guerrilla activity indicates that returnees from Manchuria were not identifiable participants in the activity.[8]

Once civil war started in 1946, parts of Shandong were liberated almost immediately, and the Communist movement developed quickly there. But again, there was no obvious connection between the fighting in Shandong and returning migrants; indeed, many migrants did not return until after the Communists had won, and then only to benefit from land reform. Several informants said they returned specifically because the

Communists had taken over their home district, the land was being divided, and they thought they should be there to get their share.

VIEWS ABOUT MIGRATION

Not the Promised Land

Manchuria in the 1920s and 1930s was a harsh, unromantic place. The northern region especially could be compared to the Wild West of North America — tough, testing, and lawless. In Manchuria, bandits took the place of outlaws, and opium was used instead of whiskey. But the Northeast lacked the glamour of the West — there were no cowboys, sheriffs, or Diamond Lils.[9] It was not a place that promised riches, except for the few who went after gold, ginseng, or furs. The common settler was guaranteed only hard labor. Settlers had to squeeze a growing season into the brief summer and harvest enough food and collect enough fuel to see them through the winter. Winter brought virtual hibernation when only the loggers and carters worked. Many of the swallows who worked for the factories, mines, and railroads, did not stay for the winter; to make their departure possible, they had to work straight through the spring, summer, and autumn without a single day of rest, for 250 days or more.[10] The physical harshness was compounded by political insecurity; many Chinese migrants lived at the mercy of arbitrary, brutal Japanese officials and their collaborators. The migrants had no official or legal protection; their only "protection" from political instability was to return home to Shandong, which they did in large numbers in bad years like 1931 and 1945.

Many migrants transcended the difficulties they encountered and settled down in both the countryside and in the cities, but those who encountered setbacks saw them as proof that Manchuria was not a good place to be. The timing of individual moves was critical to their outcome. The chances of permanent settlement were greater for those who moved before the mass migration in the 1920s and 1930s. The pioneer migrants who settled on the land in the late Qing did well; some of them got into lucrative pursuits such as opium growing or banditry in Jilin and Heilongjiang.[11] Later migrants were less likely to have these opportunities for "entrepreneurship."

But Manchuria's greatest drawback was the severity of its climate. Nowadays carnivals, ice carving, and sports put winter in a better light, but in the 1920s and 1930s there were no distracting activities to lessen the severity of the season.[12] Settlers in Manchuria did, however, enjoy that solace of many northern peoples—hard liquor. Manchuria is famous for a great range of potent home brews.

The Ideology of Sacrifice for the Family

The people who went to Manchuria did not do so to find a new world, nor were they stimulated by an ambition to make their fortune.[13] Migration had more to do with the lives of their families at home than with the pursuit of individual hopes. The central issue for migrants was the survival of the family in a tough world. They did not make decisions in their own individual interest, nor were they inspired by a political ideology; they went away under the instructions and moral pressure of their elders to make money and spare the family at home from having to feed them. This pressure was precisely balanced by pressure to return to the family at home. This made permanent departure and the long-term alienation of a migrant's income-earning capacity unlikely.[14]

The migrants moved within a very traditional world. They were not like some of Europe's pioneering migrants; they did not see their destination as an opportunity for liberty, riches, and modernity; they were not shaking the dust of the old world off their feet. They may more aptly be compared with migrants from another very traditional society, the people who moved from Quebec to the milltowns of Massachusetts in the late nineteenth century. Migrants from Quebec also operated within a tight familial structure, which managed their departure, their time away, and their eventual return. Their lives were governed by a powerful duty:

> The sense of duty was a manifestation of family culture—a set of values that entailed not only a commitment to the well-being and self-reliance or survival of the family but one that took priority over individual needs and personal happiness.[15]

This sense of family obligation involved sending money home to contribute to the family economy. In China it also involved financing key family rituals. Often an individual migrated to raise money for a marriage, or a funeral, or to pay off debts incurred by family rites. Only wealthy families could expect to generate a large enough surplus from farming to pay for the enormous costs associated with ceremonies.[16] Eventually the migration came to be a rite in itself, the rite of passage for young men, when they first began to make a major contribution to the family economy. Migration became a stage between childhood and marriage in a society that had no adolescence.

The Shandong migrants were not viewed critically as they once might have been—as people who had abandoned their familial duties. An ultraconservative description of migrants written in the 1930s referred to them as beggars, rascals, rogues, petty thieves, big thieves, soldiers, bandits, and toughs (*haohan*). But this description no longer applied in a region where migration had become fully integrated into the economic and social fabric.[17] The purpose of migration was not to achieve permanent change, but to support the family's traditional life in its traditional home. Often, as we have seen, the actual outcome was quite different, but preservation of the family remained the basic motivation.

POST-1949 MIGRATION

Migration to Manchuria broke off in the last stages of the war against Japan and did not resume during the civil war, which dragged on until 1949. The Manchurian economy was in ruins; much of the industry that had survived was dismantled and shipped off to the Soviet Union by the occupying forces. Some of the earliest and most ferocious fighting of the civil war took place in Manchuria and revolved especially around lines of communication. It was not a good time to migrate to Manchuria and the only people leaving Shandong were substantial numbers of Guomindang supporters and army units, who fled to Taiwan.

Policy and Migration in the People's Republic
    What happened to Shandong's long tradition of migration under the planned socialist economy of the People's Republic? Under Communist control migration patterns apparently changed dramatically. The official version holds that international movement was virtually outlawed, and spontaneous internal movement was increasingly restricted under the *hukou* registration system. Only after the reforms started in 1978 did migration cease to be a government-controlled exercise. In reality, however, migration actually continued throughout the Maoist era, often at very high levels.[18] What changed was that it had become less visible.
    State-Managed Migration. As soon as Manchuria was firmly under Communist control in late 1948, migration resumed, but in a different manner. Some of it was state-managed, with large groups of people recruited in Shandong to "open up the wilderness and settle the frontiers." Thousands of technicians, engineers, managers, cadres, and planners were sent to Manchuria from other liberated areas all over China to begin the task of rebuilding and expanding the infrastructure and industrial base that were so important for China's modernization.[19]

The PRC turned to Shandong for a ready supply of hardy, uncomplaining people.[20] In the second half of the first Five Year Plan, the Ministry of the Interior and the Ministry of Labor and Agricultural Settlement put together a huge project intended both to relieve overpopulation in the south and west of Shandong and to open up northern parts of Heilongjiang. Between 1955 and 1960 over a million people moved, 75 percent of them to Heilongjiang.[21] Although the aim of the project was to fill young people with a sense of adventure and revolutionary enthusiasm for developing the Great Northern Waste (*bei da huang*), there were major problems at every stage, and the state had great difficulty keeping people in Manchuria. The return rate sometimes went as high as 50 percent.[22] Organized migration looked uncomfortably like forced migration, and even revolutionary hyperbole could not make the Great Northern Waste more attractive than its god-forsaken name.

Specialized migrations, movements of experts and technicians to provide the skills needed on new projects, occurred in tandem with the mass movements. Although few of these skilled migrants came from Shandong, Shandong did provide one special export: reliable cadres. As the Communists established control over the recalcitrant provinces of the south and southwest, they found that they needed honest, hard-working, and committed cadres from outside those regions. These people came to be known as the southbound cadres (*nanxia ganbu*).

Within the province of Shandong the race for socialist construction created its own demands for migration, especially during the Great Leap Forward (1958–1960). The construction of roads, railways, and especially dams led to the massive displacement of people. Some were sent directly to the border regions, others were resituated close to their old homes, but almost always in undesirable places, given the shortage of good land. These were some of the most painful moves. Executed by authorities in the white heat of enthusiasm for the Leap, they forced families to leave ancestral homes that were about to be inundated. People's sense of loss was intense. Added anguish came later when it became clear that many of the dams had been poorly planned and were in fact of little use. The land and the villages were nonetheless lost forever.[23]

Voluntary Migration. Voluntary migration also continued throughout the thirty years from 1949 to 1978, on a much larger scale than was apparent to foreigners at the time. The PRC authorities introduced the *hukou* system in the mid-1950s largely to stem the flow of farmers into the cities and towns. They were much less concerned about people moving from one rural area to another, especially when the migrants did not try to use the heavily controlled trains. A tremendous amount of "self-starter" migration continued in Shandong after 1949, which meant that people moved without official sanction. Shandong farmers continued to circulate north to Manchuria and back again, using well-established channels of personal connections. This kind of movement reached its height with the huge migrations of the early 1960s to escape the ravages of famine in Shandong. Many of these were family migrations, though at other periods the practice of young men going off for short periods was probably the norm.

These voluntary movements were carefully observed by local officials, and the migrants seem to have been counted. According to one fairly authoritative source for Shandong, out-migration exceeded in-migration by about four million.[24] Most of the self-starter migration was by no means haphazard; it followed established personal patterns and involved people moving back and forth within well-known settings. Local authorities were probably even glad to see people leave during times of dire food shortage.

Of course, the Maoist era migrations were different in motivation from the earlier movements. To enrich the family or to provide cash for a bride price or wedding celebration was no longer appropriate, though a recent study from Jilin suggests that these practices did not disappear as absolutely as was once thought.[25] The idea of migrating to save money to buy land became irrelevant once land was no longer saleable. The fact that migration continued, however, suggests that it continued to serve as a way of easing the normal economic pressures on rural families, even in the context of the Communist economic system.

The Reform Era

Migration in the reform era after 1978 had its own special characteristics, though it resembled that of the Republican period much more closely than that of the Maoist era. The element of coercion disappeared, while the desire for remittances reemerged as a key issue, with the added twist that remittances not only helped support the family at home but also provided capital to start small businesses after the migrant returned home. The biggest change for Shandong was the reversed direction of the migration. In the early 1980s, almost for the first time in its history, Shandong experienced a boom economy, which made it a receiving rather than a sending province.

Domestic Movements. There were many return migrants from Manchuria in the late 1970s and 1980s, people coming back to their villages to take up land leases or to work at specialized jobs (see pp. 124–

126, chapter 5). Unskilled labor also flowed into the new boom towns of
Jinan, Qingdao, Zibo, and Yantai, much of it from within the province. In
addition, there was considerable movement within the rural areas of the
province, as township and village enterprises in the richer counties
looked for labor. A knitting factory in Penglai employed girls from the
nearby hill counties, who worked under tight controls and were specifically forbidden to marry young men from the village in which they
worked. Migrants with special skills moved into Shandong from other
provinces. A Yangzhou barber in Jinan was one of a large number of
young men who had fanned out over China, capitalizing on Yangzhou's
famed barbering tradition. Very few migrants were recruited outside
Shandong, but they came on their own, looking for work. Most were
neither appreciated or admired; their receiving communities considered
them a nuisance and—like the denizens of China's major cities—tended
to blame them for local disorders and crime.

The 1980s also brought a substantial return of cadres who had gone
to the south but had never acculturated. These were happy homecomings
for both migrants and their home communities; most of these returnees
received state pensions, a useful additional income in poor villages.

Overseas Ties. One group of anticipated return migrants seems not
to have come back—the people who either went abroad or to Taiwan in
1949. At various times the provincial government has tried to encourage
people to come home from abroad. New housing developments have
been built in the coastal cities to attract people home, notably in Yantai
and Qingdao, where settlements for overseas Chinese were started even
before the Cultural Revolution. The 1980s and 1990s have seen many
return visits from abroad, and the revival of travel from Taiwan in the
late 1980s has brought many Shandong natives back to the homes they
had to leave four decades ago. But few visits have led to permanent
returns. These visitors received mixed receptions: The joy of reunion
with long-lost family was often soured by the bitterness of relatives who
had suffered major persecution, especially during the Cultural Revolution,
simply because they had family members in Taiwan. This bitterness was
understandable. The nephews and nieces of a Maoming man who was
transported to Taiwan in 1949 as part of the defeated Guomindang army
were denied education because of their absent uncle.[26] The brother of a
man who had left Jinan in the 1930s and then moved to Taiwan was kept
under long-term surveillance by people who moved into his house after
1949, to make sure that he did not spy for Taiwan. The surveillance
lasted almost thirty years, far longer than the brothers had known each
other in their youth.[27]

Although they have not returned to settle, Shandong people in Taiwan and abroad have made substantial investments and business contracts with their native province. One Shandong native in Canada, Xie Peizhi, even managed to convince the government of Saskatchewan to establish a sister province relationship with Shandong.

The Shandong homeland lives on in the memories of the people who left it, but their children are much less likely to feel its pull. Migration beyond the mainland of China seems to result in permanent resettlement. The leaves no longer fall close to the roots.

Post-1949 Migration Data

There is no aggregate statistical record of interregional migration since 1949; no counterpart of the systematic SMR surveys has been carried out under the People's Republic. The PRC has, however, taken pains to track China's population through a series of censuses that have improved in quality and sophistication over time, particularly since the census of 1982.[28] With reasonably reliable data on birth rates, death rates, and population totals, a rough measurement of the overall size and distribution of migration can be gleaned from provincial population figures that reveal differences between natural increase (births minus deaths) and actual population change.

Table 6.1 shows that the scale of net migration to Manchuria between 1950 and 1989 was as large as in the early years of the twentieth century. For the entire forty-year period total net migration came to 8.2 million, nearly as many as the 8.8 million who arrived in the fifty-two years from 1891 through 1942. It is also apparent that by far the greatest part of this movement occurred in the 1950s and 1960s, when Manchuria received a total of nearly 6 million migrants in a twenty-year period.

Table 6.1 Net Migration by Decade in
Manchuria, 1950–1989 (in thousands)

Years	Liaoning	Jilin	Heilongjiang	Total
1950–59	+ 781	- 85	+ 2,874	+ 3,570
1960–69	- 940	+ 1,013	+ 2,137	+ 2,210
1970–79	- 494	+ 299	+ 1,965	+ 1,770
1980–89	+ 808	+ 57	- 150	+ 715
Total	+ 155	+ 1,284	+ 6,826	+ 8,265

Sources: Appendix Tables 12–19. *Note:* Migration is calculated as the difference between natural increase (births minus deaths) and total reported population growth. Figures for Liaoning and Heilongjiang do not include 1950–1953.

The table also reveals interesting distinctions between the three provinces of Manchuria in the timing of migration. Liaoning Province, which was already densely populated before 1949, apparently received around 781,000 migrants in the 1950s, but experienced net out-migration of well over a million in the 1960s and 1970s. In the 1980s the flow reversed and a gradual but steady stream of in-migration added 808,000 to the population. During the period between the censuses of 1953 and 1982, the province's average annual rate of population growth was 1.9 percent, only slightly above the national rate of 1.89 percent.[29] It is likely that much of the reduction in population growth was due to the high proportion of Liaoning's population that lived in urban and suburban areas. In 1980 about 42 percent of the province population lived in cities, and around two-thirds of the total lived in the massive urban-industrial complex of Shenyang, Fushun, Anshan, Benxi, and Liaoyang.[30]

Population growth in Jilin, on the other hand, was very close to the national average of 2.31 percent in the 1950s, when the province experienced a net outflow of 85,000 people. In the 1960s Jilin received a net inflow of over a million migrants, followed by almost 300,000 in the 1970s. The 1980s saw little significant net migration, with a ten-year balance of 57,000 in-migrants.

Heilongjiang was the destination of the majority of migrants entering Manchuria in the first three decades of the People's Republic. Between 1953 and 1982 the population of Heilongjiang grew at an average annual rate of 3.48 percent, almost twice the national rate.[31] In the 1950s Heilongjiang received nearly 3 million net in-migrants, in the 1960s over 2.1 million, and in the 1970s nearly 2 million. Only in the 1980s did the movement finally reverse, with a net outflow of 150,000, the majority undoubtedly "sent-down youth," returning to their homes in provinces like Liaoning, Hebei, and Shandong from the grim settlements of the Great Northern Waste.

The disparity between Liaoning's post-1949 record of little migration and the heavy flow of people into Heilongjiang up to the 1980s reflects the differences between the economic structures and development patterns in northern and southern Manchuria. In the early 1950s the area that is now Liaoning had roughly one-third the land area of Heilongjiang, but almost twice the population. It was already the site of China's premier iron and steel facility, Anshan, and was the nation's leading center of heavy industry. In 1982 Liaoning produced 8.5 percent of China's gross industrial output value, exceeded only by Shanghai (11.4 percent) and Jiangsu (9.0 percent). In heavy industry Liaoning accounted for 11.1 percent of the national total, more than any other province or municipality.[32]After an initial injection of new labor in the 1950s, the development of Liaoning was primarily based on technology improvements, capital construction, and rising labor productivity— "capital deepening"—rather than further exploitation of new sources of raw materials. In other words, by the 1960s Liaoning did not need additional workers.

Heilongjiang, on the other hand, followed a development path that was much more extensive in nature, relying heavily on additions to the labor force as well as large infusions of capital construction to tap vast reserves of natural resources, particularly land, oil, and lumber. Among the main destinations of migrants were the numerous state farms established in northern Heilongjiang as part of the effort to tame the Great Northern Waste, China's last large area of untilled arable land. In 1982 there were 872 state farms in Heilongjiang, farming two million hectares of land. This constituted 23 percent of the province's total cultivated land area, and 40 percent of the area under state farms in the entire country.[33] The other main focal points in the development of Heilongjiang were timber and petroleum. Although Harbin has become an important industrial center, the value of industrial output for the entire province as recently as the early 1990s was still dominated by the extraction and processing of primary products, particularly petroleum and natural gas (26.8 percent), as well as lumber (3.7 percent), coal (5.9 percent), and food, beverages, and tobacco (12.5 percent).[34]

By the early 1980s, however, the economy of Heilongjiang had also reached a point where further development required increased productivity rather than further expansion of the scope of economic activity. The need for capital investment was most evident in the transportation sector. Agriculture and coal mining, in particular, were capable of substantial increases in output through improved management and mechanization, but the capacities of the railways, highways, and waterways were already strained.[35] The cessation of net migration into Heilongjiang in the late 1970s signaled the transition from an era of extensive development to one of intensive development, a turning point that Liaoning had reached some twenty-five years earlier.

Migration has had some role to play in post-1949 changes in the size of the Shandong population, though nothing like the degree to which it has been influenced by natural growth. Migration, voluntary or involuntary, was spread unevenly over the years. Although 6.17 million people left the province between 1950 and 1984—most of them for Manchuria—

Table 6.2 Net Migration by Decade in
Shandong and Hebei, 1950–1989 (in thousands)

Years	Shandong	Hebei, Beijing, Tianjin
1950–59	- 1,142	+ 5,756
1960–69	- 3,188	- 1,561
1970–79	- 723	+ 445
1980–89	+ 1,467	+ 1,087
Total	- 3,586	+ 5,727

Sources: Appendix Tables 12–19. Note: Net migration is calculated as
the difference between natural increase (births minus deaths) and total
reported population growth.

1.63 million went in one year alone, 1960, the lowest point of the agricultural crisis caused by the Great Leap Forward. That year many people
fled in desperation from near starvation in Shandong to join relatives in
Manchuria, in a reprise of the famine migrations of the Republican
period (see Appendix Table 15). Over two-thirds of the migrants in that
year were the so-called self-starters.[36] There has also been a substantial
return movement since 1949, which gained in magnitude as Shandong's
economy has picked up with the post-1978 reforms. While 6.17 million
migrated out of the province between 1950 and 1985, over 3.8 million
moved in, a large portion returning from Manchuria.[37]

The effects of migration on the area within the province boundaries
of Hebei — including the municipalities of Beijing and Tianjin, which have
the status of separate provinces in the People's Republic — are considerably
less clear than those in Shandong. The largest difference from Shandong
occurred in the 1950s, when the Hebei region experienced in-migration
totaling 5.75 million. The largest part of this influx was to Beijing, the
national capital, which alone added nearly 4 million people (see
Appendix Table 18). In the 1960s Hebei-Beijing-Tianjin lost over 1.5
million out-migrants, largely as a result of the "sending down" of urban
youth to the countryside during the Cultural Revolution in the late 1960s
and early 1970s.[38] Net migration for the area in the next two decades
came to a total of 1.53 million in-migrants, almost exactly equal to the
outflow of the 1960s and in all likelihood made up to a considerable
degree of "sent-down youth" returning home. Thus migration did affect
the Hebei-Beijing-Tianjin population after 1949, but unlike Shandong this
region does not seem to have been a significant source of migrants to
Manchuria in this period.

MIGRATION IN THE 1990S

Population movement in China no longer focuses on Manchuria, but migration continues to be a vital element of economic and social change. As in the past, it continues to be driven by family-centered motivations to make the best of new opportunities in China's rapidly evolving markets.

The explosive growth and dramatic transformation of China's economy in the 1990s have produced the largest migrations in Chinese history, with as many as 120 million people at a time living away from their homes.[39] Much of this is short-term labor migration, often referred to by the term "blind flood" (*mangliu*). The migrants are primarily young rural workers who travel to the industrialized cities of the eastern coast. In some respects this movement is very different from the migration to Manchuria. The migrants of the 1990s are not moving from one geographic region to another, but from rural areas all over China, to the cities. The present migration shows age concentrations similar to the earlier movement into Manchuria. Most of the migrants are young people who send most of their earnings home to their families and put together a stake to marry or to set themselves up in a small business when they go home. Today, however, a large portion of the migrants are young women.

The migrations of the 1990s carry much the same risks as the migration to Manchuria: There is some possibility of becoming rich, some possibility of incurring major losses, and a probability that the migrants will simply do slightly better away from home than they would if they had not left.[40] The certain beneficiaries of their migration are their employers and the consumers of the goods they produce. Their employers may be unknown to them and are often foreigners or overseas Chinese. They may have as little contact with them as the Manchurian migrants had with the upper strata of Manchurian society. Their world is bounded, as was the world of the Manchuria migrants, by their *laoxiang*, fellow workers, and labor contractors.

Contract labor continues to satisfy an economic rationale. For the seasonal work that most migrants to Manchuria performed, labor contracting was for many the most practical way of meeting fluctuating employer and laborer needs. For young girls today going from the interior to the factories of the coast, contract labor has the attraction of security. It also comes with a long tradition: It has been a key means of organizing labor since at least the Song period (A.D. 960–1279).[41] Convenience and tradition, however, do not mitigate the exploitation involved in this arrangement. Contract labor remains a dream-come-true for low-wage employers.

In its underlying causes as well, migration in the 1990s resembles the migration to Manchuria in several respects. Now, as in the early part of the century, workers are moving—flowing—from an overcrowded rural labor pool into places where economic growth is more rapid, jobs more plentiful, and incomes higher. And as with the earlier migration, the shortage of urban labor is due in part to barriers created by previous government policies that hindered the ability of workers to move in response to economic opportunities. Finally, the motivation of today's migrants again comes not from an ambition to break new ground or make history, but simply from a desire to help their families get ahead.

NOTES

NOTES TO THE INTRODUCTION

[1] Unless otherwise noted, all migrant numbers come from Thomas R. Gottschang, "Migration from North China to Manchuria: An Economic History, 1891–1942" (Ph.D. diss., University of Michigan, 1982), 91–114.

[2] Henry S. Shryock, Jr., *Population Mobility Within the United States* (Chicago: Community and Family Study Center, University of Chicago, 1964), 82–83, Table 5.13. Barbara A. Anderson, *Internal Migration During Modernization in Late Nineteenth-Century Russia* (Princeton: Princeton University Press, 1980), 123. Donald W. Treadgold, *The Great Siberian Migration* (Princeton, 1957). Brinley Thomas, *Migration and Economic Growth: A Study of Great Britain and the Atlantic Economy* (Cambridge: Cambridge University Press, 1954), 72–74. Joseph J. Spengler and George C. Myers, "Migration and Socioeconomic Development: Today and Yesterday," in *Internal Migration: A Comparative Perspective*, ed. Alan A. Brown and Egon Newberger. (New York: Academic Press, 1977), 16.

[3] Shandongsheng difang shizhi bianzuan weiyuanhui, *Shandong shizhi ziliao*, vol. 2 (Jinan, 1982), 150.

[4] Gottschang, "Migration," 109–10.

[5] *Nankai tongji zhoubao* 2.30 (November 4, 1929): 4. A breakdown by province is given in Y. Sakatani, *Manchuria: A Survey of Its Economic Development* (New York: Garland, 1980; originally prepared for the Division of Economics and History of the Carnegie Endowment for International Peace, 1932), 98.

[6] Diana Lary, "Hidden Migrations: Movement of Shandong People, 1949 to 1978," *Chinese Environment and Development*, 7.1-2 (Spring/Summer 1996): 56–72.

[7] Ta Chen, *Chinese Migrations, with Special Reference to Labor Conditions* (Bulletin of the United States Bureau of Labor Statistics, No. 340. Washington: Government Printing Office, 1923; reprinted, Taipei: Ch'eng-wen Publishing Company, 1967).

145

[8] R. C. Forsyth, *Shantung: The Sacred Province of China* (Shanghai: Christian Literature Society, 1912), 393.

[9] John Lossing Buck, *Land Utilization in China* (Chicago: University of Chicago Press, 1937), 395–97. Buck's figures are drawn from the famous survey he coordinated of over 200,000 farm families.

[10] Wang Yaoyu, "Shandong nongmin licun de yige jiantao," in *Zhongguo jingji yanjiu*, ed. Fang Xianting (Changsha: Shangwu, 1938), 178–87.

[11] Henry Kinney, *Modern Manchuria and the South Manchurian Railway Company* (Dalian: Japanese Advertiser Press, 1928), 1.

[12] Buck, *Land Utilization*, 393–97.

[13] Ministry of Industry, National Agricultural Research Bureau, "Survey of the rural exodus," in *Nongqing baogao* 4.7 (July 1936): 171–75.

[14] For a concise overview of the history of Chinese migration, see Lloyd E. Eastman, *Family, Fields, and Ancestors* (New York: Oxford University Press, 1988), 8–12.

[15] See Oded Stark, *The Migration of Labor* (Cambridge, Mass.: Blackwell Publishers, 1991), especially 3–6.

[16] Ramon H. Myers, *The Chinese Peasant Economy, Agricultural Development in Hopei and Shantung, 1890–1949* (Cambridge, Mass.: Harvard University Press, 1970); Philip C. C. Huang, *The Peasant Economy and Social Change in North China* (Stanford: Stanford University Press, 1983).

[17] Huang, *The Peasant Economy*, 215, 272.

[18] Myers, *The Chinese Peasant Economy*, 151.

[19] Ibid., 277–78.

[20] Prasanjit Duara, *Culture, Power and the State: Rural North China, 1900–1942* (Stanford: Stanford University Press, 1988); Kenneth Pomeranz, *The Making of a Hinterland: State, Society, and Economy in Inland North China, 1853–1937* (Berkeley: University of California Press, 1993).

[21] Duara, *Culture, Power and the State*, 95, 116.

[22] Pomeranz, *Making of a Hinterland*, 154–73, 201–22.

[23] Ibid., 64.

[24] Elizabeth J. Perry, *Rebels and Revolutionaries in North China, 1845–1945* (Stanford: Stanford University Press, 1980).

[25] Joseph W. Esherick, *The Origins of the Boxer Uprising* (Berkeley: University of California Press, 1987).

NOTES TO CHAPTER 1

[1] Shan Man et al., *Shandong minsu* (Jinan: Shandongsheng xinhua shudian, 1988), 153.

[2] Ibid., 223.

[3] Huang Cecang, *Shandong* (Shanghai: Zhonghua shuju, 1936), 104.

[4] Interview with Dr. Chang Tsun-wu (a native of Linqu), Academia Sinica, Taipei, April 1992.

[5] Lin Qingshan, *Kang Sheng waizhuan* (Beijing: Zhongguo qingnian chubanshe, 1988), 2.

[6] E.W. Burt, *Fifty Years in China: the Story of the Baptist Mission in Shantung, Shansi and Shensi* (London: Carey Press, 1925), 21.

[7] Ferdinand von Richthofen, *Schantung und seine Eingangspforte Kiautschou* (Berlin: D. Reimer, 1898), 94.

[8] Wilhelm Berensmann, *Wirtschaftsgeographie Shantungs unter besondere Beruchsichtigung des Kiautchougebiet* (Berlin: Susserott, 1904), 599.

[9] See the account of the project written by Lu Yu, the population studies scholar from Shandong Academy of Social Sciences, in *Qingdai he minguo Shandong yimin dongbei shilue* (Shanghai: Shanghai shehui kexueyuan chubanshe, 1987), 68–136. Lary had specifically requested visits to five counties—Ling, Zouping, Linqu, Laiyang, and Penglai—for which she already had materials. The other counties were fitted in along the way.

[10] Ling County, Zhangxilou Production Brigade, introduction, 4/14/84. Zouping, Sunzhen township, introduction, 4/19/84.

[11] Interview with Zhao Qingfu, Gaomi County, Kangzhuang, 4/15/84.

[12] Interview with Hou Shangjian, Ling County, Fenghuang Township, 4/13/84.

[13] The poor brother had little joy from his ox. He came home with lung disease and died within a year. Interview with Hu Huiliang, Zouping County, Sunzhen Township, 4/19/84.

[14] Interview with Zhang Guangwen, Gaomi County, Kangzhuang, 4/25/84.

[15] Linqu County, Daxingzhong Production Brigade, introduction, 4/22/84.

[16] Lary, "Hidden Migrations," 56–72.

[17] Zou Yilin, "Huang He xiayou hedao bianyi ji qi yinxiang gaishu," in Tan Qixiang ed., *Huang He shi lunzong* (Shanghai: Fudan daxue chubansha, 1986), 231–32.

[18] For a slightly different description of the regions of Shandong, based more on official designations, see Joseph Esherick, *The Origins of the Boxer Uprising* (Berkeley: University of California Press, 1987), 7–14.

[19] Berensmann, *Wirtschaftsgeographie*, 619.

[20] *North China Herald*, June 24, 1926, 154.

[21] David D. Buck, *Urban Change in China: Politics and Development in Tsinan, Shantung, 1980–1949* (Madison: University of Wisconsin Press, 1978), 46–47.

[22] *Ling xianzhi* (1936), 470.

[23] Shandong nongye diaochahui, *Shandong zhi nongye gaikuang* (Jinan, 1922), 60.

[24] Kenneth Pomeranz describes the negative economic impact of the shift of commercial transportation away from the Grand Canal; see *Making of a Hinterland*, 2–17.

[25] Ling County, introduction, 4/11/84.

[26] Forsyth, *Shantung*, 353.

[27] Huimin County, introduction, 4/15/84.

[28] Pan Junguo, *Huimin diqu fengwu zonglan* (Jinan: Shandong youyi shushe, 1988), 11.

[29] Binzhoushi, introduction, 4/16/84.

[30] Pan, *Huimin diqu fengwu zonglan*, 43.

[31] Ibid., 43.

[32] Shandong nongye diaochahui, *Shandong zhi nongye gaikuang* (Jinan, 1922), 38–39.

[33] R. P. Bonaventure Peloquin, *Debuts d'un Missionaire* (Montreal, 1922), 59.

[34] Xiangcun jianshe yanjiuyuan, *Shandong xiangcun jianshe yanjiuyuan ji Zouping shiyan qu*, (Zouping: Shandong nongcun jianshe yanjiuyuan chubanshe, 1936), 52. See also Guy Alitto, *The last Confucian: Liang Shu-ming and the Chinese Dilemma of Modernity* (Berkeley: Unviersity of California Press, 1979).

[35] C. K. Yang, *A North China Local Market Economy*, (New York: Institute of Pacific Relations, 1944), 5.

[36] Linqu County, introduction, 4/21/84.

[37] Shandong nongye diaochahui, *Shandong*, 52–56.

[38] *Linqu xianzhi*, 5.

[39] Interview with Dr. Chang Tsun-wu, Taipei, April 1992.

[40] Shandong nongye diaochahui, *Shandong*, 29.

[41] Chen Hansheng, "Nanmin de Dongbei liuwang," in *Zhongguo nongcun jingji lun*, ed. Feng Hefa (Shanghai: Liming shuju, 1934), 333.

[42] Gaomi County, introduction, 4/24/84.

[43] Laiyang County, introduction, 4/27/84.

[44] *Penglai xianzhi*, vol. 2, 170.

[45] Ibid.

[46] Alex Armstrong, *Shantung* (Shanghai: Mercury, 1891), 62.

[47] Ibid., 61.

[48] Franklin L. Ho, "Reminiscences of Franklin Lien Ho," as told to Crystal Lorch, 113. Manuscript in the possession of Dr. Samuel Ho.

[49] Franklin L. Ho, *Population Movement to the North Eastern Frontier in China* (Shanghai: China Institute of Pacific Relations, 1931).

[50] Ho, *Population Movement*, 1.

[51] A firsthand account of the activities of the SMR Research Department is given by Ito Takeo in *Life Along the South Manchurian Railway: The Memoirs of Ito Takeo*, transl. Joshua A. Fogel (Armonk, New York: M.E. Sharpe, Inc., 1988).

[52] Huang, *The Peasant*, 34–43. See also John Young, *The Research Activities of the South Manchuria Railway Company, 1907–1945: A History and Bibliography* (New York: East Asian Institute, Columbia University, 1966); and Chao Chung-fu, "Jindai dongsansheng yimin wenti zhi yanjiu" (Research on the problem of migration to the Three Eastern Provinces in the modern period), in *Zhongyang yanjiuyuan, jindai shi yanjiusuo jikan* 4.2 (Dec. 1974): 654–55.

[53] Minami manshu tetsudo kabushiki kaisha (South Manchuria Railway Company, hereafter MMTKK) *Minkoku juroku nen no manshu dekasegi sha* (Migrant workers in Manchuria in 1927) by Nakashima Soichi (Dairen: Shomubu Chosaka, 1927).

[54] Ibid., 1–16, 26–31.

[5]5 Ibid., 4–5, 16–17.

[56] "Shi ichigatsu ita gogatsu dairen keiyo santo jikirei kuri ido soku tokei" (Statistics on migration of laborers from Shandong and Zhili through Dairen, from January to May 1928), *Mantetsu chosa geppo* 8.7 (July 1928): 174–99. "Showa san nendo kami hanki minami manshu ni okeru santo jikirei kuri ido soku tokei" (Statistics on migration of laborers from Shandong and Zhili in South Manchuria in the first half of 1928), *Mantetsu chosa geppo* 8.9 (Sept. 1928): 117–51 and 8.10 (Oct. 1928): 78–104. MMTKK, *Minkoku jushichinen no manshu dekasegi sha* (Migrant workers in Manchuria in 1928) by Kurimoto Yutaka (Dairen: Shomubu Chosaka, 1929). MMTKK, *Minkoku juhachinen manshu dekasegi imin ido jokyo* (Movement of migrant workers in Manchuria in 1929) by Kurimoto Yutaka (Dairen: Shomubu Chosaka, 1930). MMTKK, *Minkoku*

jukyunen manshu dekasegi imin ido jokyo (Movement of migrant workers in Manchuria in 1930) by Kurimoto Yutaka (Dairen: Shomubu Chosaka, 1931).

[57] MMTKK, *Manshu no kuri* (Laborers in Manchuria) (Dairen: Keizai Chosakai, 1934), 15–17.

[58] South Manchuria Railway Company, Fifth Report on Progress in Manchuria, to 1936 (Dalian: 1936), 122.

[59] Ibid., 123. The 1935 "Regulations Governing Foreign Laborers" (Departmental Order No. 1 of the Department of Civil Affairs, Promulgated March 21, 1935) are presented on 194–95.

[60] Ibid., 194.

[61] MMTKK, *Manshu kezai tokei nempo 1937–38* (Annual report on Manchurian economic statistics, 1937–1938) (Dalian, 1939) MMTKK, *Kita shina keizai tokei teiyo* (Summary of North China economic statistics) (Dalian, 1943).

[62] Hsiao Liang-lin, *China's Foreign Trade Statistics, 1864–1949.* (Cambridge, Mass.: Harvard University Press, 1974); Albert Feuerwerker, *The Foreign Establishment in China in the Early Twentieth Century* (Ann Arbor: Center for Chinese Studies, The University of Michigan, 1976), 59–72.

[63] China Maritime Customs (CMC), *Returns of Trade and Trade Reports* on Newchwang, Tientsin, and Chefoo for 1876 (Shanghai: Statistical Department of the Inspectorate General of Customs, 1877).

[64] Gottschang, "Migration," 91–100.

[65] CMC, *Returns of Trade and Trade Reports* for Newchwang, 1898, 1899, and 1901; also for Chefoo, 1908.

[66] MMTKK, *Minkoku jurokunen no manshu dekasegi sha*, 3.

[67] Ibid., 26; MMTKK, *Minkoku jushichinen no manshu dekasegi sha*, 34; MMTKK, *Minkoku juhachinen manshu dekasegi imin ido jokyo*, 32.

[68] Gottschang, "Migration," Table 3.1.

[69] Derivation of the series is explained in Gottschang, "Migration," 91–100.

[70] On circular migration, see Charles Tilly, "Migration in Modern World History," in *Human Migration, Patterns and Policies,* William H. McNeill and Ruth S. Adams (Bloomington: Indiana University Press, 1978), 51–57.

[71] CMC, *Returns of Trade and Trade Reports* for Longkou, 1916.

[72] Ida Pruitt, *A Daughter of Han, The Autobiography of a Chinese Working Woman* (Stanford: Stanford University Press, 1967), 7.

NOTES TO CHAPTER 2

[1] See Stark, *Migration of Labor.*

[2] "De xian zhi jingji gaikuang," in *Zhongguo jingji zhoukan* (July 23, 1927): 2.

[3] L. Richard, *Comprehensive Geography of the Chinese Empire and Dependencies* (Shanghai: T'usewei Press, 1908), 84.

[4] Sherman Cochran, *Big Business in China* (Cambridge, Mass.: Harvard University Press, 1980), 140–44.

[5] Harriet Rietveld, "Women and Children in Industry in Chefoo," in *Chinese Economic Monthly* 3.12 (Dec. 1926).

[6] The following are examples of the many articles and monographs dealing with incomes and living expenses in Manchuria: MMTKK, *Chugokujin rodosha no chingin* (Wages of Chinese laborers) (Dalian: Sosaishitsu Hitogotoka, 1933); MMTKK, *Mantetsu chugokujin seikeihi chosa* (Study of cost-of-living of South Manchuria Railway Company Chinese) (Dalian: Shachoshitsu Jinjika, 1926); MMTKK, *Dairen shichu ni okeru kaso chugokujin no inshokubutsu shirabe* (Study of the diet of lower class Chinese in the city of Dalian) (Dalian: Shachoshitsu Jinjika, 1927); MMTKK, *Dairen ni okeru chugokujin rodosha no seikatsu jotai* (Standard of living of Chinese workers in Dalian) (Dalian: Shachoshitsu Jinjika, 1928); MMTKK, *Manshu noka no seisan to shohi* (Production and consumption of Manchurian farmers) (Dalian: Shachoshitsu Chosaka, 1922). Estimated occupational distribution of the labor force in Manchuria appears in *The Manchoukuo Year Book, 1934* (Tokyo: Toa-keizai chosakyoku, 1934), 653.

[7] F L. Ho, *Population Movement*, 18.

[8] MMTKK, *Shina keizai nempo* (China economic yearbook) (Dalian: Chosabu, 1940), 253–54, Table 90.

[9] Kwang-chih Chang, *The Archaeology of Ancient China*, revised edition (New Haven: Yale University Press, 1968), 164–67, 351–54; Chao Chung-fu, "Jindai dongsansheng yimin wenti zhi yanjiu" (Research on the problem of migration to the Three Eastern Provinces in the modern period), in *Zhongyang yanjiuyuan, jindaishi yanjiusuo jikan* 4.2 (Dec. 1974): 617; Owen Lattimore, *Inner Asian Frontiers of China* (Boston: Beacon Press, 1962), 103.

[10] North China is one of the eight premodern macroregions identified by G. William Skinner, "Regional Urbanization in Nineteenth-Century China," in *The City in Late Imperial China*, ed. G. William Skinner (Stanford: Stanford University Press, 1977).

[11] Lattimore, *Inner Asian Frontiers*, 103-15; Robert H. G. Lee, *The Manchurian Frontier in Ch'ing History* (Cambridge, Mass.: Harvard University Press, 1970), 6-7, 14-16.

[12] See Charles O. Hucker, *China's Imperial Past: An Introduction to Chinese History and Culture* (Stanford: Stanford University Press, 1975), 148, 275-83, 293-95; R.H.G. Lee, *Manchurian Frontier*, 7-9.

[13] R.H.G. Lee, *Manchurian Frontier*, 19, 78; Waller Wynne, *The Population of Manchuria* (Washington, D.C.: Bureau of the Census, International Population Reports P-90, No. 7, 1958).

[14] R.H.G. Lee, *Manchurian Frontier*, 6-7, 66; Ho Ping-ti, *Studies on the Population of China, 1368-1953* (Cambridge, Mass.: Harvard University Press 1959), 78-79, 158-59; Lattimore, *Inner Asian Frontiers*, 103-39; Wang I-shou, "Chinese Migration and Population Change in Manchuria, 1900-1940" (Ph.D. dissertation, University of Minnesota, 1971), 38, 39.

[15] Jing Su and Luo Lun, *Landlord and Labor in Late Imperial China*, translated by Endymion Wilkinson (Cambridge, Mass.: Harvard University Press, 1978), 91.

[16] Ibid., 89.

[17] Liu Nanming, "Contribution à l'étude de la population chinoise," (Ph.D. dissertation, Faculté des letters de l'Université de Paris, Geneva: 1935), 197-99.

[18] Adachi Kinnosuke, *Manchuria: A Survey* (New York: R. M. McBride, 1925).

[19] R.H.G. Lee, *Manchurian Frontier*, 36-39, 112-14; Lattimore, *Inner Asian Frontiers*, 134-35.

[20] R.H.G. Lee, *Manchurian Frontier*, 102; P. T. Ho, *Studies on the Population*, 159; Wang I-Shou, "Chinese Migration," 39.

[21] P. T. Ho, *Studies on the Population*, 231-32.

[22] CMC, *Returns of Trade and Trade Reports* for Newchwang 1876, 8. See also CMC, *Decennial Reports, 1892-1901*, vol. 1, 3.

[23] For a study of the development of Manchuria from a Chinese perspective, see Gavin McCormack, *Chang Tso-lin in Northeast China, 1911-1928: China, Japan and the Manchurian Idea* (Stanford: Stanford University Press, 1977).

[24] Lu Yu, *Renkou wenti lun* (Jinan: Zhongguo guangbo dianshi chubanshe, 1989), 81.

[25] Alexander Hosie, *Manchuria, Its People, Resources, and Recent History* (Boston: J. B. Millet Company, 1910), 173.

[26] Immanuel C. Y. Hsu, *The Rise of Modern China* (New York: Oxford University Press, 1970), 404-16.

[27] Chao Chung-fu, "Jindai dongsansheng," 642, makes this point.

[28] See chapter 1.

[29] Lattimore, *Inner Asian Frontiers,* 17–18, 141 n. 60; R.H.G. Lee, M*anchurian Frontier,* 105–11; Chao Chung-fu, "Jindai dongsansheng," 615.

[30] See CMC, *Decennial Reports, 1902–1911,* Vol. 1, 37–38, on the effect of rail transportation on the economy of Jilin (Kirin); see 136–37 for a discussion of the growth of steam shipping.

[31] The founding and organization of the Japanese South Manchuria Railway Company are described in SMR, *Second Report on Progress in Manchuria to 1930* (Dairen: 1931), 97–101. The "Japanese Imperial Ordinance sanctioning Organization of South Manchuria Railway Company," the "Japanese Government Order regarding South Manchuria Railway Company," and the "Revised Articles of Association of the South Manchuria Railway Joint Stock Company" appear on 253–67.

[32] See McCormack, *Chang Tso-lin,* 247–248.

[33] See Huenemann, *Dragon and Iron Horse,* 235–36. Also CMC, *Decennial Reports 1902–1911,* vol. 1, 229–30.

[34] Sakatani, *Manchuria,* 107.

[35] G. William Skinner estimates that no more than 10 percent of the intermediate-level agricultural marketing systems had achieved "true modernization" in transportation and market structure by 1948. "Marketing and Social Structure in Rural China, Part II," *The Journal of Asian Studies* 24.2 (Feb. 1965): 211–28. See Thomas G. Rawski, *Economic Growth in Prewar China,* (Berkeley: University of California Press, 1989), 181–215.

[36] CMC, *Returns of Trade and Trade Reports* for Newchwang, 1900.

[37] Hosie, *Manchuria, Its People,* 142.

[38] CMC, *Decennial Reports 1922–1931,* vol. 1, 136–37.

[39] CMC, *Returns of Trade and Trade Reports* for Newchwang, 1899.

[40] SMR, *Fifth Report on Progress in Manchuria, to 1936* (Dalian: SMR, 1936), 70.

[41] Described by Huenemann, *Dragon and Iron Horse,* 44.

[42] CMC, *Returns of Trade and Trade Reports* for Newchwang, 1899.

[43] See John E. Schrecker, *Imperialism and Chinese Nationalism: Germany in Shantung* (Cambridge, Mass.: Harvard University Press, 1971).

[44] See Tim Wright, *Coal Mining in China's Economy and Society, 1895–1937* (Cambridge: Cambridge University Press, 1984).

[45] C. Walter Young, "Chinese Colonization and the Development of Manchuria," in Institute of Pacific Relations, *Problems of the Pacific, 1929;* proceedings, edited by J. B. Condliffe (Chicago: University of Chicago Press, 1930), 434.

[46] SMR, *Fifth Report,* 68.

[47] Ibid., 70. (The activities of the SMR are described in detail in the six "reports on progress in Manchuria.") The SMR's contributions to the "secondary expansion process" are discussed by Shun-hsin Chou, "Railway Development and Economic Growth in Manchuria," *China Quarterly* 45 (Jan.–Mar. 1971): 81–82.

[48] The population data is explained in Appendix Table 3.

[49] Thomas G. Rawski finds a 96 percent correlation between modern sector fixed investment and foreign trade volume between 1913 and 1936; "Economic Growth and Integration in Prewar China," Toronto: Joint Centre on Modern East Asia, Discussion Paper #5, 1982, Appendixes A,B,C,D.

[50] H. J. von Lochow, *China's National Railways: Historical Survey and Postwar Planning* (Peking, 1948), 48.

[51] Rawski, "Economic Growth," Appendices B and C.

[52] Albert Feuerwerker, *Economic Trends in the Republic of China, 1912–1949* (Ann Arbor: Center for Chinese Studies, The University of Michigan, 1977), 104–105, Table 28.

[53] Wang Yaoyu, "Shandong nongmin licun de yige jiantao," 180.

[54] Detailed descriptions of depredations are given in Feng Hefa, "Bingzhai yu nongmin," in *Zhongguo nongcun jingji lun,* ed. Feng Hefa (Shanghai, 1934).

[55] CMC, *Returns of Trade and Trade Reports* for Newchwang, 1904, 1905.

[56] See Feng Hefa, "Bingzhai yu nongmin."

[57] See Chao Chung-fu, , "1920–30 niandai de Dongsansheng yimin," *Jindaishi yanjiusuo jikan* 2 (1971): 336.

[58] James Sheridan, *Chinese Warlord* (Stanford: Stanford University Press, 1966), 256.

[59] Diana Lary, *Warlord Soldiers* (Cambridge: Cambridge University Press, 1985), 73–74.

[60] Huang Cecang, *Shandong,* 104.

[61] Shao Fujun, "Shandong Luxian Shaoquan xiang shehui zhuangkuang diaocha," in *Cunzhi* 2.1 (December 1930): 1.

[62] CMC, *Returns of Trade and Trade Reports* for Tientsin, 1925.

[63] CMC, *Returns of Trade and Trade Reports* for Kirin, Dairen, Newchwang, 1911.

[64] P. T. Ho, *Studies on the Population,* 233–36. Walter H. Mallory, *China: Land of Famine* (New York: American Geographical Society, 1926), 36–37, 45–58.

[65] P. T. Ho, *Studies on the Population,* makes this point on page 254. For accounts of the famine of 1920 and its causes, see *The China Yearbook,* 1921–1922 edition

(Tianjin: The Tientsin Press, Ltd., 1922), 820–21; CMC, *Returns of Trade and Trade Reports* for Tientsin, 1920.

[66] P. T. Ho, *Studies on the Population,* 231–33.

[67] See Peking United International Famine Relief Committee, *The Report of the Peking United International Famine Relief Committee: The North China Famine of 1920–1921, With Special Reference to the West Chihli Area* (Peking: 1922), 12–14.

[68] SMR, *Second Report,* 220–26.

[69] Ibid.; also CMC, *Returns of Trade and Trade Reports* for Chefoo, 1909, 1919; Kiaochow, 1919, 1926; Tientsin, 1919.

[70] CMC, *Returns of Trade and Trade Reports* for Chefoo, 1911.

[71] CMC, *Returns of Trade and Trade Reports* for Tientsin, Kiaochow, 1919.

[72] CMC, *Returns of Trade and Trade Reports* for Kiaochow, 1929, 1930.

[73] CMC, *Decennial Reports, 1902–1911,* vol. 1, 41–43, gives a brief history of banditry in Manchuria.

[74] Elsworth Carlson, *The Kaiping Mines, 1877–1912* (Cambridge, Mass.: Harvard University Press, 1971), 45–48.

[75] Lynda Shaffer, *Mao and the Workers: The Hunan Labor Movement* (Armonk, N.Y.: M. E. Sharpe, 1982), 207, describes in detail how the contract system worked for the Anyuan Mines in Hunan, where Mao Zedong cut his teeth as an organizer.

[76] Interview with Professor Chang Tsun-wu, Taipei, April 1992.

[77] Wang Kuixi et al., *Jindai Dongbeishi* (Haerbin: Heilongjiang renmin chubanshe, 1984), 199–200.

[78] Peter Richardson, "Chinese indentured labour in the Transvaal gold mining industry," in *Indentured Labour in the British Empire, 1834–1920,* ed. Kay Saunders (London: Croom Helm, 1984), 271.

[79] *China Weekly Review* (August 12, 1928), 48; *The China Yearbook,* 1931, 536.

[80] C. Walter Young, "Chinese Colonization," 434.

[81] Boris Torgasheff, "Mining labor in China," in *Chinese Economic Journal* 6.5 (April 1930): 533; and Lowe Chuan-hua, *Facing Labour Issues in China* (Shanghai: China Institute of Pacific Relations, 1933), 21–22.

[82] *Zhongguo nongcun* 1.4 (Jan. 1935): 92.

[83] Hitano Kenichiro, "The Japanese in Manchuria 1906–1931: A study of the historical background of Manchukuo" (Ph.D. dissertation, Harvard University, 1993), 164–65.

[84] C. Walter Young, "Chinese labor emigration to Manchuria," *Chinese Economic Journal* 1.7 (July 1927): 629.

[85] SMR figures cited in Chao Chung-fu, "1920-30 niandai di dongsansheng yimin" (Migrants to the Three Eastern Provinces, 1920-1930), in *Zhongyang yanjiuyuan, jindaishi yanjiusuo jikan* 2 (June 1971): 337.

[86] Hitano Kenichiro, "Japanese in Manchuria," 156-57.

[87] Yeh Ch'ing-kuang, *Coolies and Mandarins: China's Protection of Overseas Chinese During the Late Ch'ing Period (1851-1911)* (Singapore: Singapore University Press, 1985).

[88] C. Walter Young, "Chinese Colonization," 430.

[89] Burt, *Fifty Years in China*, 104.

[90] CMC, *Returns of Trade and Trade Reports* for Chefoo and Chingtao. See Gottschang, "Migration," 107.

[91] Richardson, "Chinese Indentured Labour," 271-72.

[92] Harley Farnsworth MacNair, *The Chinese Abroad* (Shanghai: Commercial Press, 1925), 234.

[93] See Persia Crawford Campbell, *Chinese Coolie Emigration to Countries within the British Empire* (London: S. King, 1923), 161-267, for a long and detailed account of the Transvaal migration, written from a liberal point of view.

[94] For a fuller discussion of recruitment bonuses, see chapter 3.

[95] *Jiaozhou zhi* (1931), 490-94. There are also extensive descriptions of recruitment for World War I in Huai Xi, "Zhongguo laodong yimin shigao," *Zhongguo laodong* 1.10 (1935), 275-77. See also Ta Chen, *Chinese Migrations*, 142-58.

[96] SMR, *Second Report*, 13.

[97] SMR, *Sixth Report*, 146.

[98] Ibid.

[99] Ibid., 116-29.

[100] A good example of this sort of program is MMTKK, *Man-mo nosei shian* (Private plan for administering agriculture in Manchuria and Mongolia) (Dairen: Chihobu Chihoka, 1918).

[101] SMR, *Sixth Report*, 135, 146.

[102] Ibid., 130.

[103] SMR, *Sixth Report*, "Chosenese [Korean] Immigration Map of Manchoukuo" (at front of volume), and 129-36.

[104] See Thomas R. Gottschang, "Economic Change, Disasters, and Migration: The Historical Case of Manchuria," *Economic Development and Cultural Change* 35.3 (Apr. 1987): 461–90.

NOTES TO CHAPTER 3

[1] Ling County, introduction, 4/11/84.

[2] Tamara Hareven, *Family Time and Industrial Time* (Cambridge, Mass.: Harvard University Press, 1982), 109.

[3] Ibid., 108.

[4] Cited in Wu Yulin, ed., *Zhongguo renkou Shandong fence* (Beijing: Zhongguo caizheng jingji chubanshi, 1986), 86.

[5] Reginald Johnston, *Lion and Dragon in Northern China.* (Oxford: Oxford University Press, 1987), 140.

[6] Interview with Wang Bingguang, Boxing County, Chenhu, 4/18/84.

[7] Interview with Meng Jingen, Ling County, Jiangxiqiao Township, 4/11/84.

[8] Interview with Jiang Lanqi, Laiyang County, Chengxiang, Wugezhuang, 4/29/84.

[9] Interview with Wang Yuxiang, Laiyang County, Chengxiang, 4/29/84.

[10] Interview with Gao Xuchang, Penglai County, Beigou, 4/30/84.

[11] Pamela Atwell, *British Mandarins and Chinese Reformers* (Oxford: Oxford University Press, 1985), 70.

[12] This contradiction between pride in having many sons and the anguish of marrying them all persists today. The person who arranged interviews in Gaomi, Zhao Fuan, was the father of four sons of marriageable age, each of whom had found his own bride-to-be. Mr. Zhao was struggling with the major contributions he had to make to each new household.

[13] Martin C. A. Yang, *A Chinese Village: Taitou, Shantung Province* (New York: Columbia University Press, 1945), 107.

[14] Wu Yulin, *Zhongguo renkou*, 78.

[15] Interview with Guo Baofu, Ling County, Fenghuang Township, 4/13/84.

[16] Interview with Zhao Guiqian, Laiyang County, Chengxiang, 4/28/84.

[17] "Gesheng nongcun jingji yu nongmin yundong," in *Cunzhi* 2.6 (Oct. 31, 1931): 9.

[18] Interview with Zhao Qingfu, Gaomi County, Kangzhuang, 4/25/91.

[19] Interview with Zhao Yongting, Linqu County, Damingzhong Production Brigade, 4/22/84.

[20] Interview with Zhang Xincheng, Ling County, Fenghuang Township, 4/13/84.

21 Chen Hansheng, "Nanmin de Dongbei liuwang," in *Zhongguo nongcun jingji lun*, ed. Feng Hefa (Shanghai: Liming shuju, 1934), 338.

22 "Gesheng nongcun jingji yu nongmin yundong," in *Cunzhi* 2.6 (Oct. 31, 1931): 9.

23 Owen Lattimore, *Manchuria: Cradle of Conflict* (New York: Macmillan, 1932), 272.

24 Interview with Gao Puchun, Linqu County, Chengguan, 4/23/84.

25 Interview with Wu Shutian about his cousin Wu Liantian, Laiyang County, Chengxiang, 4/28/84.

26 Interview with Wang Xibiao, Boxing County, Chenhu, 4/18/84.

27 MMTKK, *Manshu kezai tokei nempo 1937–38* (Dalian: Chosabu, 1939), 300–301; MMTKK, *Kita shina keizai tokei teiyo* (Dalian: Chosabu, 1943), 244–48. See Gottschang, "Migration," 99–100.

28 Xiao Wan, "Shandong Zhaoyuan xian nongcun gaikuang," in *Zhongguo nongcun jingji lunwenji*, ed. Qian Jiaju (Shanghai: Zhongguo shuju, 1935), 556.

29 Guo Yizhi, "Pochan sheng zhong di yige Jinan nongcun," in *Zhongguo nongcun jingji lunwenji*, 515.

30 Wu Gumin, *Zouping shiyan xian hukou diaocha baogao* (Shanghai: Zhonghua shuju, 1935), 217.

31 Interview with Gao Xuyuan, Penglai County, Beigou, 4/30/84.

32 Interviews with Sun Hongshan and Wei Xianxing, Laiyang County, Chengxiang, 4/28/84.

33 Interview with Yu Shulin, Boxing County, Pangjia Township, 4/12/84.

34 Interview with Guo Baomeng, Zouping County, Weiqiao Commune, Guoxing Village, 4/20/84.

35 Wang Pilian, "Zhang Congchang zhi si," in *Jinan wenshi ziliao* 1 (1984): 178–187

36 McCormack, *Chang Tso-lin*, 153–56.

37 Johnston, *Lion and Dragon*, 146.

38 Interview with Liu Zhengzhong, Binzhou, Pucheng Township, 4/16/84.

39 Boxing County, Pangjia Township, introduction, 4/17/84.

40 Interview with Jing Wenguang, Linqu County, Chengguan, 4/23/84.

41 *Jiaozhou zhi* (1931), 498.

42 Interview with Zhang Zhenbao, Laiyang County, Chengxiang, 4/28/84.

43 Interview with Zu Chengheng, Huimin County, Zaohuli Commune, 4/15/84.

44 Interview with Sun Zhiguo, Zouping County, Weiqiao Commune, 4/20/84.

45 *Linqu xianzhi* (1935), 38, 413.

[46] Linqu County, introduction, 4/21/84.

[47] Linqu County, Daxingzhong Village, introduction, 4/21/91.

[48] Interview with Jiang Lanqi, Laiyang County, Chengxiang, 4/29/84.

[49] Interview with Gong Wenxue, Laiyang County, Chengxiang, 4/28/84.

[50] Interview with Qu Rongyu, Laiyang County, Chengxiang, 4/29/84.

[51] Interview with Wang Guiqian, Zouping County, Weiqiao Commune, 4/20/84.

[52] Interview with Ma Xiuqing, Shandong Provincial Government, Foreign Affairs Office, April 18, 1984.

[53] Johnston, *Lion and Dragon,* 209.

[54] Interview with Li Yunpeng (Li Yunsheng's cousin), Zouping County, Sunzhen Township, 4/19/84.

[55] Boxing County, introduction, 4/17/84.

[56] Laiyang County, Chengxiang, introduction, 4/27/84.

[57] Yang, *Chinese Village,* 136.

[58] Johnston, *Lion and Dragon,* 244.

[59] Interview with Liu Huanwu, Binzhou, Pucheng Township, Fucheng Village, 4/16/84.

[60] Interview with Feng Yuexiu, Zouping County, Sunzhen Township, 4/19/91.

[61] Interview with Li Chuanzhen, Ling County, Zhangxiqiao Township, 4/11/84.

[62] Interview with Zhang Shuyun, Ling County, Zhangxilou Production Brigade, 4/14/84.

[63] Huang Puce, "Woguo nongmin licun wenti," in *Fuxing yuekan* 4.1 (Sept. 1935): 43.

[64] Zouping County, Weiqiao commune, introduction, 4/20/84.

[65] Interview with Yu Shulin, Boxing County, Pangjia Township, 4/17/84.

[66] Interview with Liu Zhengzhong and Liu Huanwu, Binzhou, Pucheng Township, 4/16/84.

[67] Interview with Liu Huanwu, Binzhou, Pucheng Township, 4/16/84.

[68] Interview with Cui Dengwen, Boxing County, Pangjia Township, 4/17/84.

[69] Interview with Wu Benzhi, Laiyang County, Chengxiang, 4/29/84.

[70] Boxing County, Panjia Township, introduction, 4/17/84.

[71] Gaomi County, introduction, 4/24/84.

[72] Laiyang County, introduction, 4/27/84.

[73] Chu Chia-hua, *China's Postal and Other Communications Services* (Shanghai: China United Press, 1937), 75.

[74] Liu Yanmian, "Jin shibanian Zhongguo youzheng zhi lianhuan zhishu," *Tongji yuebao* 1.5 (July 1929)

[75] *Ling xianzhi* (1936), 293.

[76] Interviews with Zhang Hongbao and Li Gongshui, Zouping County, Sunzhen Township, 4/19/84.

[77] Chu Chia-hua, *China's Postal and Other Communications Services*, 25.

[78] Traditional institutions that handled remittances were also called *piaozhuang* (note shops) and *huiduizhuang* (remittance shops). Sakatani, *Manchuria: A Survey*, 36–37.

[79] Penglai County, Yujiagou, introduction, 5/1/84.

[80] Penglai County, Beigou, introduction, 4/30/84.

[81] Laiyang County, Chengxiang, introduction, 4/29/84.

[82] Hosie, *Manchuria, Its People*, 190.

[83] Interview with Liu Zhengzhong, Binzhou, Pucheng Township, 4/16/84.

[84] Interview with Zhao Yonghu, Linqu County, Xingzhong Production Brigade, 4/23/84.

[85] Interview with Hou Shangjian, Ling County, Fenghuang Township, 4/13/84.

[86] Interview with Guo Baomeng, Zouping County, Weiqiao Commune, 4/20/84.

[87] Interview with Sun Hongshan, Laiyang County, Chengxiang, 4/28/84.

[88] Pomeranz, *Making of a Hinterland*, 40–45.

[89] CMC, *Returns of Trade and Trade Reports for* Lungkow, 1917.

[90] C. K. Yang, *North China Local Market Economy*, 9.

[91] F. L. Ho, *The Reminiscences of Franklin Lien Ho*, vol. 2, 153.

[92] Interview with Hou Xiaolun, Ling County, Fenghuang Township, 4/13/84.

[93] Liu Yanwan, "Jin shibanian Zhongguo."

[94] *Deping xian xuzhi* (1935), 322.

[95] MMTKK, *Manshu no kuri* (Coolies in Manchuria) (Dalian: Keizai Chosakai, 1934), 68–70. See also "Nyu-ri man hokushi rodosha no ketai kin oyobi so kingaku" (Money carried along and remitted by North Chinese laborers entering and leaving Manchuria), *Mantetsu chosa geppo* 21.2 (Feb. 1941): 205–14.

[96] Charles Robert Roll, Jr., *The Distribution of Rural Incomes in China: A Comparison of the 1930s and the 1950s* (New York: Garland, 1980), 13.

[97] Interviews with Liu Huanwu and Li Dingjie, Binzhou, Pucheng Township, 4/16/84.

[98] Interview with Qu Rongyu, Laiyang County, Chengxiang, 4/29/84.

NOTES TO CHAPTER 4

[1] Interview with Liu Changxin, Dalian Institute of Demography, 5/4/84.

[2] Yang, *Chinese Village*, 116.

[3] Mallory, *China: Land of Famine*, 19–20.

[4] Lattimore, *Manchuria: Cradle of Conflict*, 200.

[5] Yang, *Chinese Village*, 200.

[6] Burt, *Fifty Years in China*, 104.

[7] Wilhelm Wagner, *Die chinesische Landwirtschaft* (Berlin: P. Parey, 1926), 142.

[8] *Deping xian xuzhi* (1935), 322.

[9] See Zhang Zhenyi, "Renhuo tiancai xia zhi Shandong renmin yu Dongbei yimin," *Xin Yaxiya* 2.3 (June 1931): 43.

[10] I.e., the 3rd, 6th, 9th, 12th, 13th, 15th, 16th, 18th, 19th, 21st, 23rd, 24th, 26th, 27th, 29th, 30th, or 31st. Gaomi County, introduction, 4/24/84

[11] Shan Man et al., *Shandong minsu*, 145.

[12] Fei Xiaotong, "Chengxiang lianxi de you yimian," *Zhongguo jianshe* 7.1 (1948): 33.

[13] Mallory, *China: Land of Famine*, 83.

[14] C. Walter Young, "Chinese Colonization," 442.

[15] Elizabeth Perry, *Shanghai on Strike* (Stanford: Stanford University Press, 1993), 26.

[16] Lattimore, *Manchuria: Cradle of Conflict*, 197.

[17] Diana Lary, *Warlord Soldiers* (Cambridge: Cambridge University Press, 1985), 25.

[18] Interviews with Zheng Fulin and Zhang Shuyun, Ling County, Zhangxilou Production Brigade, 4/14/84.

[19] C.K. Yang, *North China*, 9.

[20] Interview with Hou Shangrui, Ling County, Fenghuang Township, 4/13/84.

[21] Huimin County, introduction, 4/15/84.

[22] Interview with Zhang Wenjie, Huimin County, Zaohuli Commune, 4/15/84.

[23] Interview with Wu Yuzhen, Boxing County, Pangjia Township, 4/17/84.

[24] Interviews with Zu Chengheng, Huimin County, Zaohuli Commune, 4/15/84.

[25] Interview with Zhao Yonghu, Linqu County, Xingzhong Production Brigade, 4/23/84.

[26] Interview with Hou Shangyu, Ling County, Fenghuang Township, 4/13/84.

[27] Interview with Li Dingjie, Binzhou, Pucheng Township, 4/16/84.

[28] Zouping County,Weiqiao Commune, introduction, and interview with Guo Baomeng, same place, 4/20/84.

[29] Interview with Hou Xiaolun, Ling County, Fenghuang Township, 4/13/84.

[30] Interview with Zhang Hongbao, Zouping County, Sunzhen Township, 4/19/84.

[31] Interview with Li Yunpeng, Zouping County, Sunzhen Township, 4/19/84.

[32] Interview with Xiao Lianhe, Boxing County, Chenhu, 4/18/84.

[33] Interview with Zheng Fulin, Ling County, Zhangxilou Production Brigade, 4/14/84.

[34] Ho Ping-ti, *Zhongguo huiguan shilun* (On the History of *Landsmannschaften* in China) (Taipei: Taiwan xuesheng shuju, 1966).

[35] Dalian, Institute of Demography, Introduction, 5/4/84.

[36] Interview with Lan Runde, Penglai County, Beigou, 4/30/84.

NOTES TO CHAPTER 5

[1] See *Zhongguo nongcun* 1.4 (Jan. 1935): 92.

[2] Huang Cecang, *Shandong*, 136, 140.

[3] MMTKK, *Minkoku juhachinen manshu dekasegi imin ido jokyo*, 15–18, 87–89.

[4] Interview with Guo Baomeng, Zouping County, Weiqiao Commune, Guoxing Village, 4/20/84.

[5] Interview with Yu Shulian, Boxing County, Yangji Village, 4/17/84.

[6] Interview at Huimin County, Caohuli, 4/15/84.

[7] Chao Chung-fu, "1920–30," 337.

[8] Xu Hengyao, "Manmeng de laodong zhuangkuang yu yimin," *Dongfang zazhi* 22.21 (Nov. 1925): 31.

[9] MMTKK, *Minkoku jurokunen no manshu dekasegi sha*, 147–48.

[10] Interview with Zhang Hongbao, Zouping County, Sunzhen Township, 4/19/84.

[11] Yang, *Chinese Village*, 200.

[12] *Lingxian xuzhi* (1935), 350.

[13] Interview with Liu Zhangtai, Penglai County, Liujiagou, 5/1/84.

[14] In 1929, 117,000 famine refugees from Henan came to Manchuria with government assistance. MMTKK, *Minkoku juhachinen manshu dekasegi imin ido jokyo*, 14–15.

[15] Lillian Li, "Life and Death in a Chinese Famine: Infanticide as a Demographic Consequence of the 1935 Yellow River Flood," *Comparative Studies in Society and History* 33.3 (July 1991): 466–510.

[16] Linqu County, introduction, 4/21/84.

[17] Interview with Liu Guangpu, Gaomi County, Kangzhuang, 4/25/84.

[18] Interview with Gao Puchun, Linqu County, Chengxiang, 4/23/84.

[19] Interview with Wang Yuxiang, Laiyang County, Chengxiang, 4/29/84.

[20] Interview with Jiang Xiuxiang, Gaomi County, Kangzhuang, 4/25/84.

[21] Interview with Wang Duxian, Gaomi County, Chengguan, 4/26/84.

[22] Interview with Liu Zhangtai, Penglai County, Liujiagou, 5/1/84.

[23] Interview with Guo Honghuang, Boxing County, Chenhu, 4/18/84.

[24] Interview with Zhang Xuelun, Zouping County, Weiqiao Commune, 4/20/84.

[25] Gaomi County, introduction, 4/24/84.

[26] Interview with Kang Guangwen, Gaomi County, Kangzhuang, 4/25/84.

[27] Lu Yu, *Shandong renkou qianyi he chengzhenhua yanjiu* (Jinan: Shandong daxue chubanshe, 1988), 1.

[28] Linqu County, introduction, 4/20/84, and Laiyang County, introduction, 4/27/84.

[29] Huimin County, introduction, 15/4/84, and Boxing County, introduction, 4/17/84.

[30] Gaomi County, introduction, 4/23/84.

[31] Penglai County, introduction, 4/30/84.

[32] The SMR researchers believed that at least 95 percent of the migrants who landed at Dalian moved on to other destinations. MMTKK, *Minkoku jurokunen no manshu dekasegi sha*, 14.

[33] *The Manchoukuo Year Book 1934* (Tokyo: Toa-keizai chosakyoku, 1934), 676.

[34] Penglai County, Beigou, introduction, 4/30/84.

[35] Linqu County, Chengguan, introduction, 4/23/84.

[36] Ling County, introduction, 4/11/84.

[37] Ling County, Zhangxilou Production Brigade, introduction, 4/14/84.

[38] Gaomi County, introduction, 4/24/84.

[39] Laiyang County, introduction, 4/27/84.

[40] Ling County, Bianjian, introduction, 4/12/84, Fenghuang Township, introduction, 4/13/84, and Zhangxilou Production Brigade, introduction, 4/14/84.

[41] Huimin County, introduction, 4/15/84.

[42] Boxing County, introduction, 4/17/84.

[43] Tian Fang, and Zhang Donghao, *Zhongguo renkou qianyi xintan* (Beijing: Zhishi chubanshe, 1989), 347–49.

[44] Interview with Li Chuanzhen, Ling County, Zhangxiqiao Township, 4/11/84. Li was recruited by the PLA in Manchuria

NOTES TO CHAPTER 6

[1] For a detailed discussion of Chiang Kai-shek's appeasement efforts, see Parks Coble, *Facing Japan* (Cambridge, Mass.: Harvard University Press, 1991).

[2] German, British, and American missionaries, business people, and mercenaries were much more invasive of local society than the Japanese. For an excellent description of the bellicose activities of German missionaries, for example, see Joseph Esherick, *The Origins of the Boxer Uprising* (Berkeley: University of California Press, 1987), 79–83.

[3] Elizabeth Perry, *Shanghai on Strike.*

[4] People who migrated during this period were referred to as *huagong,* a term that suggests they were treated even worse than regular migrants.

[5] Han Fuju eventually paid with his life for his appeasement of the Japanese. He was executed by the Guomindang in January 1938 for failing to resist during the Japanese invasion of Shandong.

[6] *Jinan wenshi ziliao* 6 (1985): 1–12.

[7] Tian Keshen, and Wang Yaoliang, *Guanghui de bainian licheng* (Jinan: Shandong renmin chubanshe, 1984), 235–51.

[8] Gao Jiong, "Women senyang gaicao tufei?" in *Kangzhan zhong di Zhongguo nongcun dong tai,* ed. Qian Jiaju (Guilin: Xinzhi shuju, 1939), 100.

[9] Ren Meixi, "Hanren yizhi Dongbei yanjiu," *Xin Yaxiya,* 4.5 (September 1932): 76.

[10] Xu Hengyao, "Manmeng de laodong zhuangkuang yu yimin," 31.

[11] Ren Meixi, "Hanren yizhi Dongbei yanjiu," 72; Tsao Lien-en, *Chinese Migration and the Three Eastern Provinces* (Shanghai: Bureau of Industrial and Commercial Information, 1931), 838.

[12] One of the most beloved songs in Quebec starts: "Mon pays ce n'est pas un pays, c'est l'hiver" (My country is not a country; it is winter).

[13] Xu Shilian (Leonard Hsu), *Zhongguo renkou wenti* (Shanghai: Shangwu, 1930), 97.

[14] The central and complex role of the family as the decision-making unit in migrant behavior is explored from a variety of angles by Oded Stark in *Migration of Labor*.

[15] Hareven, *Family Time and Industrial Time*, 108.

[16] Liu Sufen, *Yantai maoyi yanjiu, 1867-1919* (Taibei: Zhongguo lishi xiehui, 1990), 99.

[17] Tong Zhang, "Zhongguo nongmin licun de yanzhongxing," *Jianshe pinglun* 2.2-4 (May-July 1936): 1.

[18] Lary, "Hidden Migrations," 56-72.

[19] Discussion with officials of the Ministry of Shipping, Harbin, May 1984.

[20] Lary, "Hidden Migrations," 60-61.

[21] Sun Qingji, *Shandongsheng dili* (Jinan: Shandongsheng xinhua shudian, 1987), 268; Tian and Zhang, *Zhongguo renkou*, 339-41.

[22] Tian and Zhang, *Zhongguo renkou*, 341.

[23] In 1984 Lary observed a huge reservoir bed near Linqu that seldom held any water, but whose bottom was derelict land.

[24] Sun Qingji, *Shandongsheng dili*, 268.

[25] Yan Yunxiang, *The Flow of Gifts: Reciprocity and Social Networks in a Chinese Village.* (Stanford: Stanford University Press, 1996).

[26] Interview, Yantai, 1988.

[27] Interview, Taipei, April 1997.

[28] For a detailed analysis of Chinese population data, see Judith Banister, *China's Changing Population* (Stanford: Stanford University Press, 1987), 12-49.

[29] Ibid., 302-3.

[30] *Statistical Yearbook of China 1983*, compiled by the State Statistical Bureau, People's Republic of China (Hong Kong: Economic Information and Agency, 1983), 106. *Almanac of China's Economy, 1981*, compiled by the Economic Research Center, the State Council of the People's Republic of China and the State Statistical Bureau (New York and Hong Kong: Modern Cultural Company Limited, 1981), 30, 866. In the 1964-1978 period the three autonomous municipalities—Beijing, Tianjin, and Shanghai—all had population growth rates below one percent. John S. Aird, "Recent Demographic Data from China: Problems and Prospects," U.S. Congress, Joint Economic Committee, *China Under the Four Modernizations*, Part 1 (Washington, D.C.: U.S. Government Printing Office, 1982), 197. Also see Banister, *China's Changing Population*, 261.

[31] Banister, *China's Changing Population*, 302-3.

[32] *Statistical Yearbook of China 1983*, 234; Table 5.

[33] *Almanac of China's Economy* 1981, 822.

[34] *1993 Zhongguo jingji nianjian* (1993 almanac of China's economy) (Beijing: Jingji guanli chubanshe, 1993), 397.

[35] Interviews in Harbin with officials of the Ministries of Railways, Shipping, and Communications, May 1984.

[36] Wu Yulin, ed., *Zhongguo renkou Shandong fence*, 95.

[37] Ibid., 108.

[38] See Banister, *China's Changing Population*, 308.

[39] Elizabeth Croll and Huang Ping, "Migration For and Against Agriculture in Eight Chinese Villages," *China Quarterly* 149 (March 1997): 128 n.

[40] Lincoln Day and Ma Xia, eds., *Migration and Urbanization in China* (Armonk, NY: M.E. Sharpe, 1994), 4–5.

[41] Lynda Shaffer, *Mao and the Workers*, 79.

GLOSSARY

anjiafei 安家費
antu chongqian 安土重遷

batou 把頭
biaoge 表哥
biaoshu 表叔

chiku nailao 吃苦耐勞
chuang guandong 闖關東

dang hongren 當紅人
dang huangyu 當黃魚
diduo renshao 地多人少
Dongbei 東北
Dongsansheng 東三省

erwuba hao hui jia 二五八好
　回家

fenjia 分家

gangshi 港式
gongtou 工頭

haiwaicun 海外村
hanbing 寒病
honghuzi 紅胡子
hukou 戶口
huagong 華工
huidui 匯兌

ji 集

jiating guannian 家庭觀念

kunsi zai benxiang 困死在本鄉

laosi bu quxiang 老死不去鄉
laoxiang 老鄉
lihai 厲害

mu 畝

nansia ganbu 南下干部
nian 年
nianzhe 粘著

qiao 橋
qiaowuju 橋務句

renduo dishao 人多地少
renhuo 人禍

sanliujiu wang wai zou 三六九
　往外走
shang haibei 上海北
shuboshu 叔伯叔
shugao qianzhang, ye luo gui gen
　樹高千丈葉落歸根
Shuihu zhuan 水滸傳
sui 歲

tangxiong 堂兄
tawang 他往
tongxin 通信

167

xiantong 現銅
xianyang 現洋
xiang 鄉
xiao jiating 小家庭

yan 燕
yijin huanxiang 衣錦還鄉
yuan 元
yuanji 元藉

zaxingcun 雜姓村
zifa 自發

STATISTICAL APPENDIX

Table A.1
Estimated Migration between North China and
Manchuria, 1891–1942 (in thousands)

Year	To Man-churia	Return	Net	Year	To Man-churia	Return	Net
1891	24.7	47.2	-22.5	1917	540.9	256.7	284.2
1892	32.4	51.4	-19.0	1918	422.0	281.0	141.0
1893	81.8	32.8	49.0	1919	511.0	281.7	229.3
1894	30.7	71.8	-41.1	1920	650.1	439.8	210.3
1895	16.4	15.2	1.2	1921	499.7	377.1	122.6
1896	109.6	41.2	68.4	1922	519.0	408.4	110.6
1897	149.1	69.6	79.5	1923	446.7	363.9	82.8
1898	96.7	57.1	39.6	1924	504.1	310.2	193.9
1899	159.2	124.8	34.4	1925	548.2	311.3	236.9
1900	193.3	136.3	57.0	1926	621.4	454.9	166.5
1901	277.4	394.9	-117.5	1927	1,243.4	501.3	742.1
1902	379.7	227.9	151.8	1928	1,109.5	571.8	537.7
1903	313.4	281.6	31.8	1929	1,054.2	614.9	439.3
1904	44.2	62.7	- 18.5	1930	779.9	486.8	293.1
1905	285.6	187.0	98.6	1931	459.1	443.6	15.5
1906	466.8	536.8	- 70.0	1932	410.0	496.4	- 86.4
1907	496.7	307.9	188.8	1933	630.3	495.1	135.2
1908	410.9	238.6	172.3	1934	695.2	442.9	252.3
1909	395.4	236.5	158.9	1935	491.8	463.4	28.4
1910	430.1	223.4	206.7	1936	399.3	422.6	-23.3
1911	322.8	215.0	107.8	1937	362.2	296.8	65.4
1912	661.9	268.7	393.2	1938	573.8	282.7	291.1
1913	491.8	295.4	196.4	1939	1,123.7	445.7	678.0
1914	449.1	228.9	220.2	1940	1,475.1	965.1	510.0
1915	364.4	201.4	163.0	1941	1,066.3	784.5	281.8
1916	428.0	291.3	136.7	1942	1,183.9	679.1	504.8

Sources: MMTKK, *Minkoku juroku nen no manshu dekasegi sha*; "Shi ichigatsu ita gogatsu dairen keiyo santo jikirei kuri ido soku tokei" (Statistics on migration of laborers from Shandong and Zhili through Dairen, from January to May 1928) in *Mantetsu chosa geppo* 8.7 (July 1928): 174–99; "Showa san nendo kami hanki minami manshu ni okeru santo jikirei kuri ido soku tokei" (Statistics on migration of laborers from Shandong and Zhili in South Manchuria in the first half of 1928) in *Mantetsu chosa geppo* 8.9 (Sept. 1928): 117–51 and 8, 10 (Oct. 1928): 78–104; MMTKK, *Minkoku jushichinen no manshu dekasegi sha*; MMTKK, *Minkoku kuhachinen manshu dekasegi imin ido jokyo*; MMTKK, *Minkoku jukyunen manshu dekasegi imin ido jokyo*; MMTKK, *Manshu no kuri*, 15–17; *Manshu kezai tokei nempo 1937–38* (Annual Report on Manchurian Economic Statistics, 1937–1938) (Dairen, 1939); *Kita shina keizai tokei teiyo* (Summary of North China Economic Statistics) (Dairen, 1943); CMC, *Returns of Trade and Trade Reports*, annual reports on Qingdao, Chefoo, Longkou, Tientsin, Newchwang, Dairen, and Andong.

Notes: Derivation of the series is explained above in chapter 1. It is presented in full detail in Gottschang, "Migration," 91–100.

Table A.2
Estimated Migration to Manchuria by
Area of Origin, 1891–1942 (in thousands)

Year	Shan-dong Pen-insula	Hebei/ West Shan-dong	Hebei/ Shandong Total	Year	Shan-dong Pen-insula	Hebei/ West Shan-dong	Hebei/ Shandong Total
1891	17.8	6.8	24.6	1917	222.2	318.7	540.9
1892	24.2	8.1	32.3	1918	211.8	210.2	422.0
1893	62.5	19.3	81.8	1919	284.4	226.6	511.0
1894	22.6	8.1	30.7	1920	223.5	426.6	650.1
1895	12.4	4.0	16.4	1921	223.0	276.6	499.6
1896	79.2	30.4	109.6	1922	200.5	318.4	518.9
1897	112.9	36.2	149.1	1923	185.7	261.0	446.7
1898	42.8	53.9	96.7	1924	188.0	316.0	504.0
1899	108.9	50.4	159.3	1925	200.8	347.4	548.2
1900	145.1	48.1	193.2	1926	215.9	405.5	621.4
1901	184.8	92.6	277.4	1927	319.6	923.8	1,243.4
1902	226.6	153.1	379.7	1928	288.2	821.4	1,109.6
1903	185.7	127.7	313.4	1929	295.0	759.2	1,054.2
1904	28.4	15.7	44.1	1930	250.0	529.9	779.9
1905	142.5	143.1	285.6	1931	170.8	288.3	459.1
1906	243.1	223.7	466.8	1932	153.2	256.7	409.9
1907	280.0	216.7	496.7	1933	219.7	410.6	630.3
1908	223.7	187.2	410.9	1934	240.1	455.1	695.2
1909	218.0	177.3	395.3	1935	156.1	335.6	491.7
1910	219.1	210.9	430.0	1936	122.8	276.5	399.3
1911	125.7	197.2	322.9	1937	91.2	270.9	362.1
1912	253.2	408.7	661.9	1938	162.3	411.4	573.7
1913	232.5	259.3	491.8	1939	227.3	896.3	1,123.6
1914	201.5	247.6	449.1	1940	253.3	1,221.9	1,475.2
1915	224.9	139.5	364.4	1941	259.1	807.1	1,066.2
1916	191.4	236.6	428.0	1942	236.7	947.2	1,183.9

Sources: See Table A.1, and Gottschang, "Migration," 101. *Note:* The Shandong Peninsula refers to Jiaodong District of Shandong Province. West Shandong refers to Shandong Province minus Jiaodong District.

Table A.3
Estimated Population, 1891–1942 (in millions)

Year	Hebei and Shandong Total	Shandong Peninsula	Hebei/West Shandong	Manchuria
1891	64.71	12.60	52.11	22.58
1892	64.90	12.65	52.25	22.64
1893	65.09	12.70	52.39	22.71
1894	65.21	12.69	52.52	22.85
1895	65.42	12.76	52.66	22.90
1896	65.59	12.79	52.80	22.99
1897	65.68	12.77	52.91	23.14
1898	65.77	12.71	53.03	23.31
1899	66.07	12.80	53.27	23.53
1900	66.37	12.84	53.53	23.74
1901	66.64	12.86	53.78	23.98
1902	67.09	13.05	54.04	24.04
1903	67.28	13.06	54.22	24.37
1904	67.58	13.16	54.42	24.59
1905	67.95	13.25	54.70	24.76
1906	68.19	13.31	54.88	25.05
1907	68.60	13.51	55.09	25.17
1908	68.75	13.50	55.25	25.55
1909	68.92	13.52	55.40	25.91
1910	69.11	13.53	55.58	26.27
1911	69.25	13.53	55.72	26.68
1912	69.49	13.61	55.88	26.99
1913	69.44	13.58	55.86	27.59
1914	69.59	13.59	56.00	27.99
1915	69.71	13.59	56.12	28.42
1916	69.89	13.57	56.32	28.80
1917	70.10	13.60	56.50	29.15
1918	70.16	13.58	56.58	29.66
1919	70.55	13.63	56.92	30.14
1920	70.92	13.61	57.31	30.71
1921	71.24	13.75	57.49	31.27
1922	71.65	13.83	57.82	31.75
1923	72.07	13.94	58.13	32.22
1924	72.52	14.05	58.47	32.67

Table A.3— *Continued*

Year	Hebei and Shandong Total	Shandong Peninsula	Hebei/West Shandong	Manchuria
1925	72.86	14.13	58.73	33.23
1926	73.17	14.18	58.99	33.84
1927	73.55	14.22	59.33	34.39
1928	73.35	14.21	59.14	35.53
1929	73.36	14.22	59.14	36.47
1930	73.47	14.18	59.29	37.33
1931	73.72	14.18	59.54	38.05
1932	74.26	14.27	59.99	38.49
1933	74.90	14.35	60.55	38.84
1934	75.51	14.40	61.11	39.56
1935	76.00	14.44	61.56	40.41
1936	76.73	14.54	62.19	41.05
1937	77.53	14.67	62.86	41.64
1938	78.24	14.79	63.45	42.33
1939	78.72	14.85	63.87	43.26
1940	78.82	14.85	63.97	44.60
1941	79.09	14.91	64.18	45.79
1942	79.60	14.97	64.63	46.76

Source: Gottschang, "Migration," 81–84, 109–112.

Table A.4
Migrants per Thousand Population, 1891–1942

Year	Shan-dong Pen-insula	Hebei/ West Shan-dong	Hebei/ Shan-dong Total	Year	Shan-dong Pen-insula	Hebei/ West Shan-dong	Hebei/ Shan-dong Total
1891	1.414	.131	.381	1917	16.335	5.641	7.716
1892	1.916	.155	.499	1918	15.596	3.715	6.014
1893	4.919	.368	1.256	1919	20.865	3.981	7.243
1894	1.784	.154	.471	1920	16.421	7.444	9.167
1895	.973	.076	.251	1921	16.219	4.812	7.014
1896	6.194	.575	1.671	1922	14.501	5.507	7.243
1897	8.842	.685	2.271	1923	13.325	4.489	6.199
1898	3.361	1.016	1.470	1924	13.386	5.405	6.951
1899	8.506	.946	2.410	1925	14.213	5.916	7.525
1900	11.303	.899	2.912	1926	15.225	6.874	8.493
1901	14.368	1.722	4.162	1927	22.479	15.570	16.906
1902	17.366	2.833	5.660	1928	20.279	13.889	15.127
1903	14.217	2.356	4.658	1929	20.742	12.838	14.370
1904	2.159	.289	.653	1930	17.633	8.937	10.615
1905	10.758	2.616	4.203	1931	12.047	4.842	6.227
1906	18.267	4.076	6.846	1932	10.740	4.279	5.521
1907	20.729	3.933	7.241	1933	15.309	6.781	8.415
1908	16.570	3.389	5.977	1934	16.675	7.447	9.207
1909	16.126	3.201	5.737	1935	10.814	5.452	6.471
1910	16.196	3.795	6.223	1936	8.445	4.446	5.203
1911	9.288	3.539	4.662	1937	6.219	4.310	4.671
1912	18.604	7.313	9.525	1938	10.977	6.484	7.334
1913	17.124	4.641	7.083	1939	15.309	14.034	14.274
1914	14.828	4.421	6.454	1940	17.057	19.101	18.715
1915	16.547	2.486	5.227	1941	17.380	12.576	13.482
1916	14.104	4.201	6.124	1942	15.811	14.655	14.873

Sources: Tables A.1 and A.3.

Averages: Shandong Peninsula: 13.085　　Hebei and West Shandong: 5.178
　　　　Hebei and Shandong Total: 6.711

Table A.5
Railway Freight Tonnage, 1891–1931 (in million tons)

Year	Hebei and West Shandong	Manchuria	Year	Hebei and West Shandong	Manchuria
1891	.413	–	1912	8.205	9.079
1892	.413	–	1913	10.489	10.528
1893	.688	–	1914	9.973	11.404
1894	.688	–	1915	11.473	13.431
1895	.688	–	1916	11.181	13.507
1896	.688	–	1917	11.590	13.845
1897	.917	–	1918	12.892	14.850
1898	.917	–	1919	15.046	17.167
1899	.917	–	1920	15.595	18.808
1900	.459	–	1921	18.130	21.051
1901	1.221	2.144	1922	14.289	21.263
1902	1.422	2.144	1923	18.819	24.775
1903	1.759	2.260	1924	16.875	24.871
1904	2.863	2.912	1925	15.924	26.581
1905	5.235	6.240	1926	11.198	29.098
1906	6.018	4.736	1927	15.159	35.020
1907	5.300	4.249	1928	11.643	33.702
1908	5.974	5.957	1929	13.370	37.036
1909	6.252	7.255	1930	14.511	35.327
1910	6.231	7.485	1931	17.257	36.185
1911	6.444	9.011	–	–	–

Sources: David D. Buck, Urban Change in China (Madison: University of Wisconsin, 1978), 44–7; Cheng, Lin [H. Lin Cheng], The Chinese Railways, A Historical Survey (Shanghai: China United Press, 1935), PAGES?; CMC, Decennial Reports 1922–1931, 153; CMC, Returns of Trade and Trade Reports for Kiaochow, each year; Newchwang, 1901, 1903; Tianjin, 1892, 1893, 1897, 1901, 1903, 1904, 1905, 1910; China, Ministry of Railways, Bureau of Railway Statistics, Statistics of Chinese National Railways 1915–1929 (Nanking, 1931), 158–173; The China Yearbook, 1912, 1913, 1914, 1916, 1921–1922, 1923, 1924–1925, 1932 editions; Chi-ming Hou, Foreign Investment and Economic Development in China 1840–1937 (Cambridge, Mass.: Harvard University Press, 1965), 62; "Ko-sai tetsu do" (The Jiao-Ji Railway), Mantetsu chosa geppo 16, 3 (March 1936): 144; The Manchoukuo Year Book, 1934 (Tokyo: Toa-keizai Chosakyoku, 1934), 486–522; Sakatani, Manchuria, 48–80; Schrecker, Imperialism and Chinese Nationalism, 104–24; Yan Zhongping, comp., Zhongguo jindai jingji shi tongji zhiliao shuanji (Selected statistics on China's modern economic history) (Beijing: Kexue, 1955), 207.
Notes: Railways serving Hebei and West Shandong. The Beijing-Hankou (Bei-Han) Railway: 1,317 kilometers. Construction begun 1897, completed 1906. The Beijing-Liaoning (Bei-Ning) Railway: 1,538 kilometers. Construction begun 1878, completed 1907. Also known as the Peking-Mukden Line and the Beijing-Shenyang Line. The Tianjin-Pukou (Tian-Pu) Railway: 1,106 kilometers. Construction begun 1908, opened to traffic 1910,

completed 1912. The Shandong (Jiao-Ji or Kiao-Tsi) Railway. 446 kilometers. Construction begun 1899, opened to traffic 1901, completed 1904.

Railways serving Manchuria. The South Manchuria Railway (SMR): 1,075 kilometers. Construction begun by Russia in 1896, completed in 1901, reconstructed by Japan, with the addition of a branch to Andong, completed in 1907; the Chinese Eastern Railway (CER). 1,727 kilometers. Construction begun 1897, completed 1901. The Jilin-Changchun (Ji-Chang) Railway: 171 kilometers. Completed 1912. The Jilin-Tunhua (Ji-Tun) Railway: 266 kilometers. Completed 1928. The Sipingkai-Taonan (Si-Tao) Railway: 502 kilometers. Completed 1918. The Taoan-Ananji (Tao-An) Railway: 259 kilometers. Completed 1927. The Shenyang-Hailongzheng (Shen-Hai) Railway: 415 kilometers. Completed 1928. Also known as the Fenghai line. The Hulan-Hailun (Hu-Hai) Railway: 298 kilometers. Completed 1928. The Dahushan-Dongliao (Da-Dong) Railway, 256 kilometers. Completed 1927.

    Freight tonnage carried on the Beijing-Liaoning Railway is counted in both totals because it reflects economic activity in both areas. In some cases tonnage of railways in Manchuria was estimated on the basis of the lines' revenues, which are reported in the *Manchoukuo Year Book, 1934*. The revenue figures were converted to a constant price basis using an index of wholesale prices in Dalian, from the *Manchuria Year Book, 1931*, p. 186.

Table A.6
Railway Freight Tons Per Capita of Population, 1891–1931

Year	Hebei and West Shandong	Manchuria	Year	Hebei and West Shandong	Manchuria
1891	.008	–	1912	.147	.336
1892	.008	–	1913	.188	.381
1893	.013	–	1914	.178	.407
1894	.013	–	1915	.204	.473
1895	.013	–	1916	.199	.469
1896	.013	–	1917	.205	.475
1897	.017	–	1918	.228	.501
1898	.017	–	1919	.264	.569
1899	.017	–	1920	.272	.612
1900	.009	-	1921	.315	.673
1901	.023	.089	1922	.247	.670
1902	.026	.089	1923	.324	.769
1903	.032	.093	1924	.289	.761
1904	.053	.118	1925	.271	.800
1905	.096	.252	1926	.190	.860
1906	.110	.189	1927	.256	1.018
1907	.096	.169	1928	.197	.949
1908	.108	.233	1929	.226	1.015
1909	.113	.280	1930	.245	.946
1910	.112	.285	1931	.290	.951
1911	.116	.338	–	–	–

Sources: Tables A.3 and A.5.

Table A.7
Total Net Trade, 1891–1931
(in million 1913 Haiguan Taels)

Year	Shan- dong Pen- insula	Hebei/ West Shan- dong	Man- churia	Year	Shan dong Penin sula	Hebei/ West Shan- dong	Man- churia
1891	32.627	103.303	40.391	1912	35.838	181.955	194.152
1892	32.488	94.769	36.648	1913	37.230	210.053	198.308
1893	29.110	95.323	37.992	1914	29.047	165.198	178.412
1894	26.206	80.583	28.915	1915	41.533	135.932	182.654
1895	29.799	86.228	15.827	1916	36.719	161.606	192.399
1896	32.243	85.945	36.978	1917	34.153	178.654	225.762
1897	33.253	84.901	44.521	1918	30.099	177.936	220.917
1898	40.387	97.948	56.160	1919	36.264	214.965	283.680
1899	41.939	125.577	81.065	1920	34.071	180.781	268.357
1900	38.261	51.974	40.816	1921	49.224	231.219	295.027
1901	52.665	82.253	98.320	1922	42.677	263.543	316.992
1902	45.588	136.249	90.081	1923	41.806	261.866	322.319
1903	43.179	106.048	90.164	1924	31.250	282.311	300.249
1904	38.420	110.714	79.099	1925	32.434	295.326	348.594
1905	46.693	170.191	126.032	1926	34.089	291.508	398.175
1906	43.413	194.308	94.179	1927	33.333	327.844	409.220
1907	32.766	172.323	81.480	1928	29.665	336.420	438.271
1908	29.496	123.830	101.086	1929	24.339	333.653	424.710
1909	41.376	154.086	152.349	1930	24.149	307.698	378.674
1910	39.561	161.004	173.947	1931	33.250	335.066	380.651
1911	39.631	182.225	201.722	–	–	–	–

Sources: CMC, Returns of Trade and Trade Reports, annual. Nankai Institute of Economics, Nankai Index Numbers, 1936 (Tientsin: Nankai University 1937), Table VII. Chi-ming Hou, Foreign Investment and Economic Development in China 1840–1937 (Cambridge, Mass.: Harvard, 1965), 232. Gottschang, "Migration," 183–94.

Note: Shandong Peninsula: Trade at the ports of Longkou and Yantai (Chefoo). Hebei and West Shandong: Trade at the Hebei ports of Qinhuangdao and Tianjin, plus the Shandong port of Qingdao. Manchuria: The total of trade at all Manchuria ports, including Andong, Dalian, and Yingkou on the southern coast, and in the north the border crossing points at Manzhouli, Aihe (Aigun), and Suifenhe, and the river ports of Sanxing and Harbin. 1897–1907: There were no Customs reports from Dalian or the northern Manchuria border and river ports until 1908. Trade values for these years are estimated on the basis of reported rail traffic and trade at other ports.

Table A.8
Total Net Trade Per Capita of Population, 1891–1931 (in 1913 Haiguan Taels)

Year	Shan-dong Pen-insula	Hebei/ West Shan-dong	Man-churia	Year	Shan-dong Pen-insula	Hebei/ West Shan-dong	Man-churia
1891	2.589	1.982	1.789	1912	2.633	3.256	7.193
1892	2.568	1.814	1.619	1913	2.741	3.760	7.188
1893	2.292	1.819	1.673	1914	2.137	2.950	6.374
1894	2.065	1.534	1.265	1915	3.056	2.422	6.427
1895	2.335	1.637	.691	1916	2.706	2.869	6.681
1896	2.521	1.628	1.608	1917	2.511	3.162	7.745
1897	2.604	1.605	1.924	1918	2.216	3.145	7.448
1898	3.170	1.847	2.409	1919	2.661	3.777	9.412
1899	3.277	2.357	3.445	1920	2.503	3.154	8.738
1900	2.980	.971	1.719	1921	3.580	4.022	9.435
1901	4.095	1.529	4.100	1922	3.086	4.558	9.984
1902	3.493	2.521	3.747	1923	2.999	4.505	10.004
1903	3.306	1.956	3.700	1924	2.224	4.828	9.190
1904	2.919	2.034	3.217	1925	2.295	5.029	10.490
1905	3.524	3.111	5.090	1926	2.404	4.942	11.766
1906	3.262	3.541	3.760	1927	2.344	5.526	11.899
1907	2.425	3.128	3.237	1928	2.088	5.689	12.335
1908	2.185	2.241	3.956	1929	1.712	5.642	11.645
1909	3.060	2.781	5.880	1930	1.703	5.190	10.144
1910	2.924	2.897	6.621	1931	2.345	5.627	10.004
1911	2.929	3.270	7.561	–	–	–	–

Sources: Appendix Tables 3 and 7.

Table A.9
Total Migration from North China to Manchuria,
Return Migration, and Return Ratio, 1891–1942 (in thousands)

Year	To Man-churia	Return	Return Ratio	Year	To Man-churia	Return	Return Ratio
1891	24.7	47.2	1.91	1917	540.9	256.7	0.47
1892	32.4	51.4	1.59	1918	422.0	281.0	0.67
1893	81.8	32.8	0.40	1919	511.0	281.7	0.55
1894	30.7	71.8	2.34	1920	650.1	439.8	0.68
1895	16.4	15.2	0.93	1921	499.7	377.1	0.75
1896	109.6	41.2	0.38	1922	519.0	408.4	0.79
1897	149.1	69.6	0.47	1923	446.7	363.9	0.81
1898	96.7	57.1	0.59	1924	504.1	310.2	0.61
1899	159.2	124.8	0.78	1925	548.2	311.3	0.57
1900	193.3	136.3	0.70	1926	621.4	454.9	0.73
1901	277.4	394.9	1.42	1927	1,243.4	501.3	0.40
1902	379.7	227.9	0.60	1928	1,109.5	571.8	0.51
1903	313.4	281.6	0.90	1929	1,054.2	614.9	0.58
1904	44.2	62.7	1.42	1930	779.9	486.8	0.62
1905	285.6	187.0	0.65	1931	459.1	443.6	0.97
1906	466.8	536.8	1.15	1932	410.0	496.4	1.21
1907	496.7	307.9	0.62	1933	630.3	495.1	0.78
1908	410.9	238.6	0.58	1934	695.2	442.9	0.64
1909	395.4	236.5	0.60	1935	491.8	463.4	0.94
1910	430.1	223.4	0.52	1936	399.3	422.6	1.06
1911	322.8	215.0	0.67	1937	362.2	296.8	0.82
1912	661.9	268.7	0.41	1938	573.8	282.7	0.49
1913	491.8	295.4	0.60	1939	1,123.7	445.7	0.40
1914	449.1	228.9	0.51	1940	1,475.1	965.1	0.65
1915	364.4	201.4	0.55	1941	1,066.3	784.5	0.74
1916	428.0	291.3	0.68	1942	1,183.9	679.1	0.57

Source: Table A.1

Total to Manchuria: 25,432.9
Total Returned: 16,723.1
Total Return Ratio: 0.66
Average Annual Return Ratio: 0.77

Table A.10
Migration from Hebei and West Shandong to
Manchuria and Return, 1891–1942 (in thousands)

Year	To Man-churia	Return	Return Ratio	Year	To Man-churia	Return	Return Ratio
1891	6.8	11.5	1.69	1917	318.7	124.9	0.39
1892	8.1	12.5	1.54	1918	210.2	121.7	0.58
1893	19.3	10.3	0.53	1919	226.6	117.1	0.52
1894	8.1	16.1	1.99	1920	426.6	178.7	0.42
1895	4.0	3.8	0.95	1921	276.6	180.8	0.65
1896	30.4	14.6	0.48	1922	318.4	198.1	0.62
1897	36.2	22.0	0.61	1923	261.0	172.1	0.66
1898	53.9	19.9	0.37	1924	316.0	143.8	0.45
1899	50.4	43.6	0.86	1925	347.4	169.7	0.49
1900	48.1	33.1	0.69	1926	405.5	304.1	0.75
1901	92.6	81.2	0.88	1927	923.8	300.2	0.33
1902	153.1	53.3	0.35	1928	821.4	377.8	0.46
1903	127.7	63.2	0.49	1929	759.2	469.3	0.62
1904	15.7	12.7	0.81	1930	529.9	340.9	0.64
1905	143.1	49.2	0.34	1931	288.3	293.9	1.02
1906	223.7	164.2	0.73	1932	256.7	369.1	1.44
1907	216.7	104.5	0.48	1933	410.6	369.9	0.90
1908	187.3	66.0	0.35	1934	455.1	303.5	0.67
1909	177.3	76.7	0.43	1935	335.6	346.9	1.03
1910	210.9	77.0	0.36	1936	276.5	317.2	1.15
1911	197.2	75.6	0.38	1937	270.9	235.9	0.87
1912	408.7	108.3	0.27	1938	411.4	203.7	0.49
1913	259.3	125.2	0.48	1939	896.3	362.4	0.40
1914	247.6	90.1	0.36	1940	1,221.9	803.6	0.66
1915	139.5	61.7	0.44	1941	807.1	616.0	0.76
1916	236.6	140.6	0.59	1942	947.2	577.0	0.61

Source: Gottschang, "Migration," 94–104.

Total to Manchuria: 16,021.4
Total Returned: 9,535.5
Total Return Ratio: 0.59
Average Annual Return Ratio: 0.67

Table A.11
Migration from the Shandong Peninsula to
Manchuria and Return, 1891–1942 (in thousands)

Year	To Manchuria	Return	Return Ratio	Year	To Manchuria	Return	Return Ratio
1891	17.8	35.6	2.00	1917	222.2	131.8	0.59
1892	24.2	38.9	1.61	1918	211.8	159.4	0.75
1893	62.5	22.6	0.36	1919	284.4	164.6	0.58
1894	22.6	55.6	2.46	1920	223.5	261.1	1.17
1895	12.4	11.4	0.92	1921	223.0	196.4	0.88
1896	79.2	26.6	0.34	1922	200.5	210.3	1.05
1897	112.9	47.6	0.42	1923	185.7	191.8	1.03
1898	42.8	37.1	0.87	1924	188.1	166.3	0.88
1899	108.9	81.2	0.75	1925	200.8	141.7	0.71
1900	145.1	103.2	0.71	1926	215.9	150.8	0.70
1901	184.8	313.6	1.70	1927	319.6	201.1	0.63
1902	226.6	174.6	0.77	1928	288.2	194.0	0.67
1903	185.7	218.4	1.18	1929	295.0	145.5	0.49
1904	28.4	50.0	1.76	1930	250.0	145.9	0.58
1905	142.5	137.8	0.97	1931	170.8	149.7	0.88
1906	243.1	372.6	1.53	1932	153.2	127.3	0.83
1907	280.0	203.4	0.73	1933	219.7	125.2	0.57
1908	223.7	172.6	0.77	1934	240.1	139.4	0.58
1909	218.0	159.8	0.73	1935	156.1	116.5	0.75
1910	219.1	146.3	0.67	1936	122.8	105.4	0.86
1911	125.7	139.5	1.11	1937	91.2	60.8	0.67
1912	253.2	160.4	0.63	1938	162.3	78.9	0.49
1913	232.5	170.1	0.73	1939	227.3	83.3	0.37
1914	201.5	138.8	0.69	1940	253.3	161.5	0.64
1915	224.9	139.7	0.62	1941	259.1	168.5	0.65
1916	191.4	150.7	0.79	1942	236.7	102.1	0.43

Source: Gottschang, "Migration," 94–104.

Total to Manchuria: 9,410.8
Total Returned: 7,187.4
Total Return Ratio: 0.76
Average Annual Return Ratio: 0.85

Table A.12
Population Changes in Liaoning, 1950–1989 (in thousands)

Year	Population	Increase	Natural Growth	Migration
1950	18,760	450	–	–
1951	18,890	130	–	–
1952	19,320	430	–	–
1953	20,390	1,070	–	–
1954	21,530	1,140	+ 734	+ 406
1955	22,170	640	+ 646	- 6
1956	23,070	900	+ 599	+ 301
1957	23,950	880	+ 761	+ 119
1958	24,450	500	+ 718	- 218
1959	25,020	570	+ 391	+ 179
1960	25,600	580	+ 500	+ 80
1961	25,190	-410	- 26	- 384
1962	25,490	300	+ 630	- 330
1963	26,530	1,040	+ 1,045	- 5
1964	27,340	810	+ 822	- 12
1965	28,080	740	+ 793	- 53
1966	28,700	620	+ 646	- 26
1967	29,180	480	+ 603	- 123
1968	29,820	640	+ 671	- 31
1969	30,450	630	+ 686	- 56
1970	30,840	390	+ 670	- 280
1971	31,340	500	+ 586	- 86
1972	31,710	370	+ 564	- 194
1973	32,210	500	+ 539	- 39
1974	32,570	360	+ 386	- 26
1975	32,820	250	+ 326	- 76
1976	33,110	290	+ 263	+ 27
1977	33,450	340	+ 298	+ 42
1978	33,940	490	+ 435	+ 55
1979	34,430	490	+ 407	+ 83
1980	34,870	440	+ 310	+ 130
1981	35,350	480	+ 418	+ 62
1982	35,920	570	+ 495	+ 75
1983	36,290	370	+ 287	+ 83
1984	36,550	260	+ 218	+ 42
1985	36,860	310	+ 256	+ 54

Table A.12— *Continued*

Year	Population	Increase	Natural Growth	Migration
1986	37,260	400	+ 369	+ 31
1987	37,770	510	+ 447	+ 63
1988	38,260	490	+ 378	+ 112
1989	38,760	500	+ 344	+ 156

Source: Hsueh Tien-tung, Li Qiang, Liu Shucheng, eds., *China's Provincial Statistics, 1949-1989* (Boulder: Westview Press, 1993), 100.

Note: Population figures are year-end. Natural growth is calculated as the rate of natural increase (birth rate minus death rate) times the previous year's population. Migration is calculated as total increase minus natural growth. The data have been adjusted to exclude the portions of Liaoning that were added to Inner Mongolia in 1979. See Hsueh et al., xii.

Table A.13
Population Changes in Jilin, 1950–1989 (in thousands)

Year	Population	Increase	Natural Growth	Migration
1950	10,295	210	+ 295	- 85
1951	10,398	103	+ 296	- 193
1952	10,646	248	+ 342	- 94
1953	11,332	686	+ 329	+ 357
1954	11,647	315	+ 431	- 116
1955	12,021	374	+ 323	+ 51
1956	12,245	224	+ 302	- 78
1957	12,481	236	+ 323	- 87
1958	12,809	328	+ 302	+ 26
1959	13,130	321	+ 187	+ 134
1960	13,971	841	+ 294	+ 547
1961	14,143	172	+ 203	- 31
1962	14,764	621	+ 434	+ 187
1963	15,371	967	+ 555	+ 412
1964	15,951	580	+ 486	+ 94
1965	16,391	440	+ 491	- 51
1966	16,793	402	+ 426	- 24
1967	17,221	428	+ 477	- 49
1968	17,663	442	+ 491	- 49
1969	18,082	419	+ 442	- 23
1970	18,604	522	+ 485	+ 37
1971	19,152	548	+ 484	+ 64
1972	19,627	475	+ 458	+ 17
1973	20,079	452	+ 391	+ 61
1974	20,345	266	+ 281	- 15
1975	20,639	294	+ 262	+ 32
1976	20,926	287	+ 256	+ 31
1977	21,179	253	+ 255	- 2
1978	21,493	314	+ 294	+ 20
1979	21,846	353	+ 299	+ 54
1980	22,107	261	+ 218	+ 43
1981	22,309	202	+ 274	- 72
1982	22,576	267	+ 245	+ 22
1983	22,695	119	+ 158	- 39
1984	22,845	150	+ 147	+ 3
1985	22,980	135	+ 151	- 16

Table A.13 — *Continued*

Year	Population	Increase	Natural Growth	Migration
1986	23,153	173	+ 191	- 18
1987	23,364	211	+ 229	- 18
1988	23,574	210	+ 208	+ 2
1989	24,030	456	+ 306	+ 150

Source: Hsueh et al., *China's Provincial Statistics,* 118. *Note:* See Table A.12.

Table A.14
Population Changes in Heilongjiang, 1950–1989 (in thousands)

Year	Population	Increase	Natural Growth	Migration
1950	10,370	251	--	--
1951	10,728	358	--	--
1952	11,105	377	--	--
1953	11,897	792	--	--
1954	12,502	605	+ 383	+ 222
1955	13,212	710	+ 364	+ 346
1956	14,182	970	+ 304	+ 666
1957	14,785	603	+ 371	+ 232
1958	15,637	852	+ 352	+ 500
1959	16,820	1,183	+ 275	+ 908
1960	18,071	1,251	+ 370	+ 881
1961	18,971	900	+ 291	+ 609
1962	18,935	- 36	+ 471	- 507
1963	19,720	785	+ 691	+ 94
1964	20,533	813	+ 611	+ 202
1965	21,339	806	+ 665	+ 141
1966	21,886	547	+ 575	- 28
1967	22,589	703	+ 580	+ 123
1968	23,434	845	+ 654	+ 191
1969	24,408	974	+ 543	+ 431
1970	25,226	818	+ 708	+ 110
1971	26,272	1,046	+ 683	+ 363
1972	27,234	962	+ 704	+ 258
1973	28,186	952	+ 680	+ 272
1974	28,940	754	+ 571	+ 183
1975	29,581	641	+ 477	+ 164
1976	30,194	613	+ 403	+ 210
1977	30,725	531	+ 368	+ 163
1978	31,296	571	+ 374	+ 197
1979	31,687	391	+ 346	+ 45
1980	32,038	351	+ 273	+ 78
1981	32,393	355	+ 264	+ 91
1982	32,811	418	+ 345	+ 73
1983	32,782	- 29	+ 241	- 270
1984	32,954	172	+ 216	- 44
1985	33,114	160	+ 212	- 52

Table A.14 — *Continued*

Year	Population	Increase	Natural Growth	Migration
1986	33,315	201	+ 253	- 52
1987	33,640	325	+ 307	+ 18
1988	34,015	375	+ 321	+ 54
1989	34,424	409	+ 455	- 46

Source: Hsueh et al., *China's Provincial Statistics*, 136. *Note:* See Table A.12.

Table A.15
Population Changes in Shandong, 1950–1989 (in thousands)

Year	Population	Increase	Natural Growth	Migration
1950	45,490	910	+ 830	+ 80
1951	47,320	920	+ 980	- 60
1952	48,270	950	+ 930	+ 20
1953	49,240	970	+ 1,003	- 33
1954	50,520	1,280	+ 1,294	- 14
1955	51,740	1,220	+ 1,204	+ 16
1956	52,560	820	+ 1,073	- 253
1957	53,730	1,170	+ 1,261	- 91
1958	54,220	490	+ 661	- 171
1959	53,730	- 490	+ 1,460	- 636
1960	51,880	- 1,850	- 217	- 1,633
1961	52,650	770	+ 160	+ 610
1962	54,260	1,610	+ 1,379	+ 231
1963	55,850	1,590	+ 1,786	- 196
1964	56,060	210	+ 1,386	- 1,176
1965	57,110	1,050	+ 1,429	- 379
1966	58,510	1,400	+ 1,424	- 240
1967	59,680	1,170	+ 1,241	- 71
1968	60,860	1,180	+ 1,808	- 628
1969	62,650	1,790	+ 1,496	+ 294
1970	64,410	1,760	+ 1,687	+ 73
1971	65,680	1,270	+ 1,379	- 109
1972	66,830	1,150	+ 1,321	- 171
1973	67,930	1,100	+ 1,143	- 44
1974	68,760	830	+ 937	- 107
1975	69,710	950	+ 971	- 21
1976	70,380	670	+ 758	- 88
1977	70,990	610	+ 687	- 77
1978	71,600	610	+ 732	- 122
1979	72,320	720	+ 777	- 57
1980	72,960	640	+ 545	+ 95
1981	73,950	990	+ 740	+ 250
1982	74,940	990	+ 815	+ 175
1983	75,640	700	+ 519	+ 181
1984	76,370	730	+ 529	+ 201
1985	76,950	580	+ 449	+ 131

Table A.15 — *Continued*

Year	Population	Increase	Natural Growth	Migration
1986	77,760	810	+ 677	+ 133
1987	78,890	1,130	+ 1,695	- 565
1988	80,090	1,200	+ 947	+ 253
1989	81,600	1,510	+ 897	+ 613

Source: 1950–1985: Wu Yulin, *Zhongguo renkou: Shandong fence* (Beijing, 1989), 95-6; 1986–1989: Hsueh et al., *China's Provincial Statistics*, 262. *Note:* See Table A.12.

Table A.16
Population Changes in Hebei, Beijing, and Tianjin, 1950–1989
(in thousands)

Year	Population	Increase	Natural Growth	Migration
1950	37,583	662	+ 630	+ 32
1951	38,510	927	+ 652	+ 275
1952	39,598	1,088	+ 692	+ 396
1953	40,816	1,218	+ 763	+ 455
1954	42,314	1,498	+ 904	+ 594
1955	43,361	1,047	+ 936	+ 111
1956	44,792	1,431	+ 861	+ 570
1957	46,011	1,219	+ 929	+ 290
1958	49,118	3,107	+ 749	+ 2,358
1959	50,431	1,313	+ 638	+ 675
1960	50,951	520	+ 437	+ 83
1961	51,000	49	+ 227	- 178
1962	52,036	1,036	+ 1,095	- 59
1963	53,184	1,148	+ 1,518	- 370
1964	53,920	736	+ 1,193	- 457
1965	55,009	1,089	+ 1,204	- 115
1966	55,941	932	+ 1,023	- 91
1967	56,860	919	+ 956	- 37
1968	57,837	977	+ 1,108	- 131
1969	58,636	799	+ 1,005	- 206
1970	59,742	1,106	+ 1,113	- 7
1971	60,855	1,113	+ 1,031	+ 82
1972	61,957	1,102	+ 1,007	+ 95
1973	62,928	971	+ 872	+ 99
1974	63,680	752	+ 643	+ 109
1975	64,383	703	+ 591	+ 112
1976	64,785	402	+ 422	- 20
1977	65,491	706	+ 733	- 27
1978	66,307	816	+ 842	- 26
1979	67,146	839	+ 811	+ 28
1980	68,027	881	+ 850	+ 31
1981	69,168	1,141	+ 1,113	+ 28
1982	70,488	1,320	+ 944	+ 376
1983	71,382	894	+ 790	+ 104
1984	72,282	900	+ 773	+ 127

Table A.16 — *Continued*

Year	Population	Increase	Natural Growth	Migration
1985	73,109	827	+ 777	+ 50
1986	74,130	1,021	+ 945	+ 76
1987	75,270	1,140	+ 1,133	+ 7
1988	76,352	1,082	+ 1,020	+ 62
1989	77,581	1,229	+ 1,003	+ 226

Source: Hsueh et al., *China's Provincial Statistics,* 10 (Beijing), 28 (Tianjin), 46 (Hebei). *Note:* See Table A.12.

Table A.17
Population Changes in Hebei, 1950–1989 (in thousands)

Year	Population	Increase	Natural Growth	Migration
1950	31,470	610	+ 495	+ 115
1951	32,050	580	+ 517	+ 63
1952	32,720	670	+ 547	+ 123
1953	33,430	710	+ 589	+ 121
1954	34,430	1,000	+ 686	+ 314
1955	35,290	860	+ 711	+ 149
1956	35,890	600	+ 633	- 33
1957	36,700	810	+ 657	+ 153
1958	37,320	620	+ 496	+ 124
1959	37,910	590	+ 403	+ 187
1960	37,790	- 120	+ 177	- 297
1961	37,950	160	+ 57	+ 103
1962	38,840	890	+ 745	+ 145
1963	39,560	720	+ 1,065	- 345
1964	39,970	410	+ 899	- 489
1965	40,870	900	+ 966	- 66
1966	41,830	960	+ 839	+ 121
1967	42,540	710	+ 777	- 67
1968	43,470	930	+ 865	+ 65
1969	44,450	980	+ 792	+ 188
1970	45,500	1,050	+ 900	+ 150
1971	46,400	900	+ 845	+ 55
1972	47,280	880	+ 837	+ 43
1973	48,040	760	+ 724	+ 36
1974	48,620	580	+ 547	+ 33
1975	49,130	510	+ 513	- 3
1976	49,430	300	+ 346	- 46
1977	49,980	550	+ 635	- 85
1978	50,570	590	+ 719	- 129
1979	51,050	480	+ 683	- 203
1980	51,680	630	+ 715	- 85
1981	52,560	880	+ 927	- 47
1982	53,560	1,000	+ 705	+ 295
1983	54,200	640	+ 606	+ 34
1984	54,870	670	+ 613	+ 57
1985	55,480	610	+ 647	- 37

Table A.17 — *Continued*

Year	Population	Increase	Natural Growth	Migration
1986	56,270	790	+ 793	- 3
1987	57,100	830	+ 928	- 98
1988	57,950	850	+ 848	+ 2
1989	58,810	860	+ 855	+ 5

Source: Hsueh et al., *China's Provincial Statistics*, 46. *Note:* See Table A.12.

Table A.18
Population Changes in Beijing, 1950–1989 (in thousands)

Year	Population	Increase	Natural Growth	Migration
1950	2,043	12	+ 44	- 32
1951	2,220	177	+ 44	+ 133
1952	2,488	268	+ 52	+ 216
1953	2,766	278	+ 67	+ 211
1954	3,104	338	+ 89	+ 249
1955	3,201	97	+ 95	+ 2
1956	3,832	631	+ 103	+ 528
1957	4,011	179	+ 130	+ 49
1958	6,318	2,307	+ 116	+ 2,191
1959	6,841	523	+ 133	+ 390
1960	7,321	480	+ 163	+ 317
1961	7,210	- 111	+ 109	- 220
1962	7,236	26	+ 196	- 170
1963	7,474	238	+ 255	- 17
1964	7,650	176	+ 165	+ 11
1965	7,759	109	+ 124	- 15
1966	7,701	- 58	+ 94	- 152
1967	7,820	119	+ 101	+ 18
1968	7,817	- 3	+ 133	- 136
1969	7,676	- 141	+ 117	- 258
1970	7,712	36	+ 110	- 74
1971	7,825	113	+ 96	+ 17
1972	7,927	102	+ 87	+ 15
1973	8,058	131	+ 76	+ 55
1974	8,140	82	+ 43	+ 39
1975	8,223	83	+ 28	+ 55
1976	8,285	62	+ 21	+ 41
1977	8,381	96	+ 50	+ 46
1978	8,497	116	+ 57	+ 59
1979	8,706	209	+ 66	+ 143
1980	8,857	151	+ 81	+ 70
1981	9,008	151	+ 97	+ 54
1982	9,178	170	+ 129	+ 41
1983	9,332	154	+ 93	+ 61
1984	9,452	120	+ 80	+ 40
1985	9,579	127	+ 65	+ 62

Table A.18 — *Continued*

Year	Population	Increase	Natural Growth	Migration
1986	9,710	131	+ 77	+ 54
1987	9,880	170	+ 115	+ 55
1988	10,012	132	+ 87	+ 45
1989	10,211	199	+ 72	+ 127

Source: Hsueh et al., *China's Provincial Statistics,* 10. *Note:* See Table A.12.

Table A.19
Population Changes in Tianjin, 1950–1989 (in thousands)

Year	Population	Increase	Natural Growth	Migration
1950	4,070	40	+ 91	- 51
1951	4,240	170	+ 91	+ 79
1952	4,390	150	+ 93	+ 57
1953	4,620	230	+ 107	+ 123
1954	4,780	160	+ 129	+ 31
1955	4,870	90	+ 130	- 40
1956	5,070	200	+ 125	+ 75
1957	5,300	230	+ 142	+ 88
1958	5,480	180	+ 137	+ 43
1959	5,680	200	+ 102	+ 98
1960	5,840	160	+ 97	+ 63
1961	5,840	0	+ 61	- 61
1962	5,960	120	+ 154	- 34
1963	6,150	190	+ 198	- 8
1964	6,300	150	+ 129	+ 21
1965	6,380	80	+ 114	- 34
1966	6,410	30	+ 90	- 60
1967	6,500	90	+ 78	+ 12
1968	6,550	50	+ 110	- 60
1969	6,510	- 40	+ 96	- 136
1970	6,530	20	+ 103	- 83
1971	6,630	100	+ 90	+ 10
1972	6,750	120	+ 83	+ 37
1973	6,830	80	+ 72	+ 8
1974	6,920	90	+ 53	+ 37
1975	7,030	110	+ 50	+ 60
1976	7,070	40	+ 55	- 15
1977	7,130	60	+ 48	+ 12
1978	7,240	110	+ 66	+ 44
1979	7,390	150	+ 62	+ 88
1980	7,490	100	+ 54	+ 46
1981	7,600	110	+ 89	+ 21
1982	7,750	150	+ 110	+ 40
1983	7,850	100	+ 91	+ 9
1984	7,960	110	+ 80	+ 30
1985	8,050	90	+ 65	+ 25

Table A.19— *Continued*

Year	Population	Increase	Natural Growth	Migration
1986	8,150	100	+ 75	+ 25
1987	8,290	140	+ 90	+ 50
1988	8,390	100	+ 85	+ 15
1989	8,560	170	+ 76	+ 94

Source: Hsueh et al., *China's Provincial Statistics*, 28. *Note:* See Table A.12.

Bibliography

County Gazetteers for Shandong

Changle xianzhi 昌樂縣志. 1934.

De xianzhi 德縣志. 1935.

Deping xian xuzhi 德平縣續志. 1935.

Fan xianzhi 範縣志. 1935.

Guangrao xianzhi 廣饒縣志. 1935.

Guantao xianzhi 館陶縣志. 1936.

Guan xianzhi 冠縣志. 1933.

Jiaozhou zhi 膠州志. 1931.

Lijin xianzhi 利津縣志. 1935.

Lingxian xiangtu zhi 陵縣鄉土志. 1907.

Lingxian xuzhi 陵縣續志. 1935.

Ling xianzhi 陵縣續志. 1936.

Linqu xianzhi 臨朐縣志. 1935.

Penglai xianzhi 蓬萊縣志. 2 vols. 1963.

Pingdu xianzhi 平度縣志. 1936.

Qingcheng xianzhi 青城縣志. 1936.

Shen xianzhi 莘縣志. 1937.

Wei xianzhi 濰縣志. 1941.

Weihaiwei xianzhi 威海縣志. 1929.

Xiajin xianzhi 夏津縣志. 1934.

Periodicals

China Yearbook. Tianjin and Shanghai, 1912–1939.

Chinese Economic Journal. Shanghai: Bureau of Industrial and Commercial Information, 1927.

Chinese Economic Monthly. Beijing: Bureau of Economic Information, 1923–1926.

Cunzhi 村治. Beiping, 1930–1932.

Dongfang zazhi 東方雜誌. Shanghai, 1925.

Fuxing yuekan 復興月刊. Nanjing: Xin Zhongguo jianshe xuehui, 1932–1935.

Jianshe pinglun 建設評論. 1936.

Jinan wenshi ziliao 濟南文史資料. No. 6, 1985.

Jindaishi yanjiusuo jikan 近代史研究所季刊. Taipei, 1971–1974.

Jingji yanjiu 經濟研究. Beiping, 1938

Mantetsu chosa geppo 滿鐵調查月報 (Research monthly of the South Manchuria Railway Company). 1919–1942. Title varies: 1.1 (Dec. 1919) to 10.1 (January 1930): *Chosa jiho* 調查時報 (Research review); 10.2 (February 1930) to 11.8 (August 1931): *Manmo jijo* 滿蒙事情 (Manchuria-Mongolia Affairs).

Minjian banyuekan 民間半月刊. Beiping: Minjian she, 1934–1936.

Nankai tongji zhoubao 南開統計周報 (Nankai Weekly Statistical Service). Tianjin: Nankai jingji yanjiusuo, 1929–.

Nongcun jingji 農村經濟. Zhenjiang: Nongcun jingji yuekan she, 1934–1935.

Nongqing baogao 農情報兒. Nanjing: Shiye bu, 1935–1937.

North China Herald. 1926.

Shandongsheng jianshe yuekan 山東省建設月刊. Jinan: Shandongsheng jianshe ting, 1931.

Tongji yuebao 統計月報. Nanjing: Lifa bu, 1929–1931.

Xiangcun jianshe 鄉村建設. Zouping, 1935.

Xin Zhonghua 新中華. Shanghai, 1934.

Zhongguo jianshe 中國建設. Shanghai, 1948.

Zhongguo jingji yanjiu 中國經濟研究. Nanjing: Zhongguo jingji yanjiu hui. 1938.

Zhongguo jingji zhoukan 中國經濟周刊. Beijing: Jingji taolun qu, 1923–1927.

Zhongguo laodong 中國勞動. 1935.

Zhongguo nongcun 中國農村. Guangzhou: Zhongguo nongcun jingji yanjiu hui, 1934–1937.

Zhongguo shiye zazhi 中國實業雜誌. Nanjing, 1935.

Interviews

Chang Tsun-wu 張存武, Taipei 台北市, April 1992.

Cui Dengwen 崔鄧文, Boxing County 博興縣, Pangjia Township 龐家鄉, 4/17/84.

Feng Yuexiu 馮月修, Zouping County 鄒平縣, Sunzhen Township 孫鎮鄉, 4/19/91.

Gao Baofu 高寶福, Ling County 陵縣, Fenghuang Township 鳳凰鄉, 4/13/84.

Gao Puchun 高普春, Linqu County 臨朐縣, Chengguan 城關鎮, 4/23/84.

Gao Xuzhang 高緒章, Penglai County 蓬萊縣, Beigou 北溝鎮, 4/30/84.

Gao Xuyuan 高緒元, Penglai County 蓬萊縣, Beigou 北溝鎮, 4/30/84.

Gong Wenxue 恭溫學, Laiyang County 萊陽縣, Chengxiang 城鄉鎮, 4/28/84.

Guo Baomeng 郭寶孟, Zouping County 鄒平縣, Weiqiao Commune 魏橋公社, 4/20/84.

Guo Honghuang 郭宏凰, Boxing County 博興縣, Chenhu 陳戶鎮, 4/18/84.

Hou Shangjian 侯尚檢, Ling County 陵縣, Fenghuang Township 鳳凰鄉, 4/13/84.

Hou Shangrui 侯尚瑞, Ling County 陵縣, Fenghuang Township 鳳凰鄉, 4/13/84.

Hou Shangyu 侯尚玉, Ling County 陵縣, Fenghuang Township 鳳凰鄉, 4/13/84.

Hou Xiaolun 侯孝倫, Ling County 陵縣, Fenghuang Township 鳳凰鄉, 4/13/84.

Hu Huiliang 胡惠亮, Zouping County 鄒平縣, Sunzhen Township 孫鎮鄉, 4/19/84.

Jiang Lanqi 姜蘭起, Laiyang County 萊陽縣, Chengxiang 城鄉鎮, 4/29/84.

Jiang Xiuxiang 姜秀香, Gaomi County 高密縣, Kangzhuang 康莊鎮, 4/25/84.

Jing Wenguang 井文光, Linqu County 臨朐縣, Chengguan 城關鎮, 4/23/84.

Kang Guangwen 康光文, Gaomi County 高密縣, Kangzhuang 康莊鎮, 4/25/84.

Lan Junde 藍俊德, Penglai County 蓬萊縣, Beigou 北溝鎮, 4/30/84.

Li Chuanzhen 李傳眞, Ling County 陵縣, Zhangxiqiao Township 張西橋鄉, 4/11/84.

Li Dingjie 李定傑, Binzhou City 濱州市, Pucheng Township 普城鄉, 4/16/84.

Li Gongshui 李公水, Zouping County 鄒平縣, Sunzhen Township 孫鎮鄉, 4/19/84.

Li Yunpeng 李雲鵬, Zouping County 鄒平縣, Sunzhen Township 孫鎮鄉, 4/19/84.

Liu Changxin 劉長新, Dalian Institute of Demography 大連市人口學會, 5/4/84.

Liu Guangpu 劉光譜, Gaomi County 高密縣, Kangzhuang 康莊鎮, 4/25/84.

Liu Huanwu 劉煥武, Binzhou City 濱州市, Pucheng Township 普城鄉, 4/16/84.

Liu Zhangtai 劉長太, Penglai County 蓬萊縣, Liujiagou 劉家溝, 5/1/84.

Liu Zhengzhong 劉正忠, Binzhou City 濱州市, Pucheng Township 普城鄉, 4/16/84.

Ma Xiuqing 馬修慶, Shandong Provincial Government, Foreign Affairs Office 山東省省政府外事辦公室, 4/18/84.

Meng Jingen 孟敬恩, Ling County 陵縣, Zhangxiqiao Township 張西橋鄉, 4/11/84.

Qu Rongyu 曲榮玉, Laiyang County 萊陽縣, Chengxiang 城鄉鎮, 4/29/84.

Sun Hongshan 孫洪山, Laiyang County 萊陽縣, Chengxiang 城鄉鎮, 4/28/84.

Sun Zhiguo 孫志國, Zouping County 鄒平縣, Weiqiao Commune 魏橋公社, 4/20/84.

Wang Bingguang 王炳廣, Boxing County 博興縣, Chenhu 陳戶鎮, 4/18/84.

Wang Duxian 王篤先, Gaomi County 高密縣, Chengguan 城關鎮, 4/26/84.

Wang Guiqian 王貴前, Zouping County 鄒平縣, Weiqiao Commune 魏橋公社, 4/20/84.

Wang Xibin 王希彬, Boxing County 博興縣, Chenhu 陳戶鎮, 4/18/84.

Wang Yuxiang 土土香, Laiyang County 萊陽縣, Chengxiang 城鄉鎮, 4/29/84.

Wei Xianxing 尉先星, Laiyang County 萊陽縣, Chengxiang 城鄉鎮, 4/28/84.

Wu Benzhi 吳本芝, Laiyang County 萊陽縣, Chengxiang 城鄉鎮, 4/29/84.

Wu Shutian 吳書田, Laiyang County 萊陽縣, Chengxiang 城鄉鎮, 4/28/84.

Wu Yuzhen 吳玉珍, Boxing County 博興縣, Pangjia Township 龐家鄉, 4/17/84.

Xiao Lianhe 肖連河, Boxing County 博興縣, Chenhu 陳戶鎮, 4/18/84.

Yu Shulian 于書連, Boxing County 博興縣, Yangji Village 楊集村, 4/17/84.

Yu Shulin 于書林, Boxing County 博興縣, Pangjia Township 龐家鄉, 4/12/84.

Zhang Guangwen 張光文, Gaomi County 高密縣, Kangzhuang 康莊鎮, 4/25/84.

Zhang Hongbao 張宏保, Zouping County 鄒平縣, Sunzhen Township 孫鎮鄉, 4/19/84.

Zhang Shuyun 張書雲, Ling County 陵縣, Zhangxiqiao Township 張西橋鄉, 4/14/84.

Zhang Wenjie 張文傑, Huimin County 惠民縣, Zaohuli Commune 皂戶李公社, 4/15/84.

Zhang Xincheng 張新成, Ling County 陵縣, Fenghuang Township 鳳凰鄉, 4/13/84.

Zhang Xuelun 張學論, Zouping County 鄒平縣, Weiqiao Commune 魏橋公社, 4/20/84.

Zhang Zhenbao 張振寶, Laiyang County 萊陽縣, Chengxiang 城鄉鎮, 4/28/84.

Zhao Guiqian 趙桂謙, Laiyang County 萊陽縣, Chengxiang 城鄉鎮, 4/28/84.

Zhao Qingfu 趙慶福, Gaomi County 高密縣, Kangzhuang 康莊鎮, 4/15/84.

Zhao Yonghu 趙永戶, Linqu County 臨朐縣, Daxingzhong Production Brigade 大幸中大隊 4/23/84.

Zhao Yongting 趙永庭, Linqu County 臨朐縣, Daxingzhong Production Brigade 大幸中大隊, 4/22/84.

Zheng Fulin 鄭府林, Ling County 陵縣, Zhangxiqiao Township 張西橋鄉, 4/14/84.

Zu Chengheng 組成衡, Huimin County 惠民縣, Zaohuli Commune 皂戶李公社 4/15/84.

Local Government Briefings

Binzhou City 濱州市. Introduction, 4/16/84.

Boxing County 博興縣. Introduction, 4/17/84.

Boxing County 博興縣. Pangjia Township 龐家鄉. Introduction, 4/17/84.

Dalian Institute of Demography 大連市人口學會. Introduction, 5/4/84.

Gaomi County 高密縣. Introduction, 4/24/84.

Huimin County 惠民縣. Introduction, 4/15/84.

Laiyang County 萊陽縣. Introduction, 4/27/84.

Laiyang County 萊陽縣. Chengxiang 城鄉鎮. Introduction, 4/27/84.

Ling County 陵縣. Introduction, 4/11/84.

Ling County 陵縣. Bianjian 邊監鎮. Introduction, 4/12/84.

Ling County 陵縣. Fenghuang Township 鳳凰鄉. Introduction, 4/13/84.

Ling County 陵縣. Zhangxiqiao Township 張西橋鄉. Introduction, 4/14/84.

Linqu County 臨朐縣. Introduction, 4/21/84.

Linqu County 臨朐縣. Chengguan 城關鎮. Introduction, 4/23/84.

Linqu County 臨朐縣. Daxingzhong Production Brigade 大幸中大隊. Introduction, 4/22/84.

Linqu County 臨朐縣. Daxingzhong Village 大幸中村. Introduction, 4/21/84.

Penglai County 蓬萊縣. Introduction, 4/30/84.

Penglai County 蓬萊縣. Beigou 北溝鎮. Introduction, 4/30/84.

Penglai County 蓬萊縣. Liujiagou 劉家溝. Introduction, 5/1/84.

Zouping County 鄒平縣. Sunzhen Township 孫鎮鄉. Introduction, 4/19/84.

Zouping County 鄒平縣. Weiqiao Commune 魏橋公社. Introduction, 4/20/84.

Secondary Sources

Note: Minami manshu tetsudo kabushiki kaisha 南滿洲鐵道株式會社 (South Manchuria Railway Company) is abbreviated throughout as MMTKK. All Japanese language publications of the MMTKK are listed under this abbreviation, alphabetically by title; the office of the MMTKK that produced the publication appears after the publication location. English language publications of the SMR are listed under South Manchuria Railway Company.

1993 Zhongguo jingji nianjian 中國經濟年鑒 (1993 almanac of China's economy). Beijing: Jingji guanli chubanshe, 1993.

Adachi Kinnosuke. *Manchuria: A Survey.* New York: R.M. McBride, 1925.

Aird, John S. "Population Growth." In *Economic Trends in Communist China*, 183–327. Ed. Alexander Eckstein, Walter Galenson, and Ta-chung Liu. Chicago: Aldine, 1968.

———. "Recent Demographic Data from China: Problems and Prospects," U.S. Congress, Joint Economic Committee, *China Under the Four Modernizations*, Part 1. Washington, D.C.: U.S. Government Printing Office, 1982.

———. *The Size, Composition, and Growth of the Population of Mainland China*. Washington, D.C.: U.S. Bureau of the Census, International Population Statistics Reports, Series P-90, No. 15, 1961.

Alitto, Guy. *The Last Confucian: Liang Shu-ming and the Chinese Dilemma of Modernity*. Berkeley: University of California Press, 1979.

Almanac of China's Economy, 1981. Compiled by the Economic Research Centre, the State Council of the People's Republic of China and the State Statistical Bureau. New York and Hong Kong: Modern Cultural Company Limited, 1981.

Anderson, Barbara. *Internal Migration During Modernization in Late Nineteenth-Century Russia*. Princeton: Princeton University Press, 1980.

Armstrong, Alex. *Shantung*. Shanghai: Mercury, 1891.

Atwell, Pamela. *British Mandarins and Chinese Reformers*. Oxford: Oxford University Press, 1985.

Banister, Judith. *China's Changing Population*. Stanford: Stanford University Press, 1987.

Berensmann, Wilhelm. *Wirtschaftsgeographie Shantungs unter besondere Beruchsichtigung des Kiautchougebiet*. Berlin: Susserott, 1904.

Bix, Herbert. "Japanese Imperialism and the Manchurian Economy, 1900–31." *China Quarterly* (July–September 1972): 425–43.

Brown, Alan, and E. Neuberger. *Internal Migration, A Comparative Perspective*. New York: Academic Press, 1977.

Buck, David D. *Urban Change in China: Politics and Development in Tsinan, Shantung, 1890–1949*. Madison: University of Wisconsin Press, 1978.

Buck, John Lossing. *The Chinese Farm Economy*. Chicago: University of Chicago Press, 1930.

———. *Land Utilization in China*. Chicago: University of Chicago Press, 1937.

———. *Land Utilization in China: Statistics*. Chicago: University of Chicago Press, 1937.

Burt, E. W. *Fifty Years in China: The Story of the Baptist Mission in Shantung, Shansi, and Shensi*. London: Carey Press, 1925.

Campbell, Persia Crawford. *Chinese Coolie Emigration to Countries within the British Empire.* London: P. S. King, 1923.

Cao Richang 曹日昌. "Nongcun yundong yu xinlixue" 農村運動與心理學 (The rural movement and psychology). *Minjian banyuekan* 民間半月刊 1.9 (September 1934), Beiping.

Cao Zhongmin 曹仲敏. "Yijiuerba nian qianhou Jiaodong de shehui zhuangkuang" 一九二八年前後膠東的社會狀況 (The social situation in Jiaodong before and after 1928). In *Shandong shizhi congkan* 山東史志叢刊, vol. 4. Jinan: Difang shizhi bianzuan weiyuanhui, 1989.

Carlson, Elsworth. *The Kaiping Mines, 1877-1912.* Cambridge, Mass.: Harvard University Press, 1971.

Ceng Lu 曾魯. *Shandong sheng gexian gaikuang yilan* 山東省各縣概況一覽. (A brief survey of the counties in Shandong). Beiping: Xinminhui zhongyang conghui, 1942.

Chang, Kwang-chih. *The Archaeology of Ancient China.* Rev. ed. New Haven: Yale University Press, 1968.

Chao, Chung-fu 趙中孚. "1920-30 niandai di dongsansheng yimin" 1920-30 年代的東三省移民 (Migrants to the Three Eastern Provinces, 1920-1930). In *Zhongyang yanjiuyuan, jindaishi yanjiusuo jikan* 中央研究院近代史研究所 季刊 2 (June 1971): 325-43.

———. "Jindai dongsansheng yimin wenti zhi yanjiu" 近代東三省移民問題 之研究 (Research on the problem of migration to the Three Eastern Provinces in the modern period). In *Zhongyang yanjiuyuan jindaishi yanjiusuo jikan* 中央研究院近代史研究所季刊 4 (December 1974): 613-64.

Chao, Kang. *The Economic Development of Manchuria.* Ann Arbor: Center for Chinese Studies, University of Michigan, 1982.

Chen Bozhuang 陳伯莊. *Ping Han yanxian nongcun jingji diaocha* 平漢延線 農村經濟調查 (Study of the economy along the extension of the Ping-Han line). Shanghai: Jiaotong daxue yanjiusuo, 1936.

Chen Hansheng 陳韓笙 (Chen, Han-seng). "Nanmin de Dongbei liuwang" 難民的東北流亡 (The Manchurian exile of refugees). In *Zhongguo nongcun jingji lun* 中國農村經濟論. Edited by Feng Hefa 馮合法. Shanghai: Liming shuju, 1934.

———. *Heilongjiang liuyu de nongmin yu dizhu* 黑龍江流域的農民與地主. (Farmers and landlords of the Heilongjiang valley). Shanghai: Shehui kexue yanjiu suo, 1929.

Chen, Ta. *Chinese Migrations, with Special Reference to Labor Conditions.* Bulletin of the United States Bureau of Labor Statistics, No. 340;

Washington: Government Printing Office, 1923. Reprinted, Taipei: Ch'eng-wen Publishing Company, 1967.

Chen Zhenlu 陳振鷺. *Zhongguo nongcun jingji wenti* 中國農村經濟問題 (Chinese rural economic issues). Shanghai: Daxue shudian, 1938.

Cheng, Lin [H. Lin Cheng]. *The Chinese Railways, A Historical Survey.* Shanghai: China United Press, 1935.

China Imperial Maritime Customs. *Decennial Reports, 1892-1901.* 2 vols. Shanghai: The Statistical Department of the Inspectorate General of Customs, 1902.

China Maritime Customs (CMC). *Decennial Reports, 1902-1911.* 2 vols. Shanghai: The Statistical Department of the Inspectorate General of Customs, 1913.

———. *Decennial Reports, 1922-1931.* 2 vols. Shanghai: The Statistical Department of the Inspectorate General of Customs, 1933.

———. (before 1911, Imperial Maritime Customs). *Returns of Trade and Trade Reports.* 1869-1928. Annual, published in year following the year covered. Shanghai: Statistical Department of the Inspectorate General of Customs.

China Ministry of Railways, Bureau of Railway Statistics. *Statistics of Chinese National Railways 1915-1929.* Nanjing, 1931.

The China Yearbook. H. T. Montegue Bell, and H.G.W. Woodhead, eds. London: George Routledge and Sons, Ltd.; New York: E. P. Dutton and Co, 1912. 1913. 1914. 1916.

The China Yearbook. H.G.W. Woodhead, ed. Tianjin: The Tientsin Press, Ltd., 1921-1922. 1923. 1924-1925.

The China Yearbook. H.G.W. Woodhead, ed. Shanghai: The North-China Daily News and Herald, Ltd., 1931. 1932. 1933.

Chou, Shun-hsin. "Railway Development and Economic Growth in Manchuria," *China Quarterly* 45 (January–March 1971): 57–84.

Chu Chia-hua. *China's Postal and Other Communications Services.* Shanghai: China United Press, 1937.

Chu, Hsiao. "Manchuria: A Statistical Survey of Its Resources, Industries, Trade, Railways, and Immigration." In *Problems of the Pacific, 1929.* Proceedings of the Third Conference of the Institute of Pacific Relations. Kyoto, 1929. Edited by J. B. Condliffe, 350–422. Chicago: University of Chicago Press, 1930.

Coble, Parks. *Facing Japan.* Cambridge, Mass.: Harvard University Press, 1991.

Cochran, Sherman. *Big Business in China.* Cambridge, Mass.: Harvard University Press, 1980.

Croll, Elizabeth, and Huang Ping, "Migration For and Against Agriculture in Eight Chinese Villages," *China Quarterly* 149 (March 1997): 128–146.

"The Currency Situation." *Chinese Economic Journal* 1.5 (1927).

Day, Lincoln, and Ma Xia, eds. *Migration and Urbanization in China.* Armonk: M. E. Sharpe, 1994.

"De xian zhi jingji gaikuang" 德縣之經濟概況 (Overview of the De County economy). *Zhongguo jingji zhoukan* 中國經濟周刊 July 23, 1927.

Dezhou diqu chuban gongsi 德州地區出版公司. *Lubei fenghuo* 魯北烽火 (North Shandong disasters). Jinan: Shandong wenyi chubanshe, 1985.

Dong Ruzhou 董汝舟. "Zhongguo nongmin licun wenti zhi jiantao" 中國農民離村問題之檢討 (Examination of the problem of Chinese farmers leaving the countryside). *Xin Zhonghua* 新中華 1.9 (May 1933): 14–21.

Dong Shijin 董時進. "Nongmin de chulu" 農民的出路 (The way out for farmers). *Minjian banyuekan* 民間半月刊 1.11 (October 1934).

Dongbei nianjian 東北年鑒. Shenyang: Dongbei wenhua she, 1931.

Duara, Prasanjit. *Culture, Power and the State: Rural North China, 1900–1942.* Stanford: Stanford University Press, 1988.

Eastman, Lloyd E. *Family, Fields, and Ancestors.* New York: Oxford University Press, 1988.

Eckstein, Alexander, Kang Chao, and John Chang. "The Economic Development of Manchuria: The Rise of a Frontier Economy." *The Journal of Economic History* 34.1 (March 1974): 239–64.

Esherick, Joseph W. *The Origins of the Boxer Uprising.* Berkeley: University of California Press, 1987.

Fang Qiuwei 方秋葦. "Ji-Lu pinnong quguan wenti" 濟魯貧農出關問題 (The problem of poor Shandong farmers going beyond the pass). *Xin Zhonghua* 新中華 2.9 (May 1934):15–20.

Fang Xianting 方顯廷. *Zhongguo jingji yanjiu* 中國經濟研究 (China economic research). Shanghai: Shangwu, 1938.

Fei, John and Gustav Ranis. "A Theory of Economic Development." *The American Labor Review* (September 1961): 533–65.

Fei Xiaotong 費孝通. "Chengxiang lianxi de yimian" 城鄉聯係的一面 (One aspect of rural-urban relations). *Zhongguo jianshe* 中國建設 7.1 (1948): 32–35.

———. *Neidi nongmin* 內地農民 (Inland farmers). Shanghai: Shenghuo shudian, 1946.

Feng Hefa 馮和法, ed. *Zhongguo nongcun jingji lun* 中國農村經濟論 (Discussions on the Chinese rural economy). Shanghai: Liming shuju, 1934.

———. *Zhongguo nongcun jingji ziliao* 中國農村經濟資料 (Materials on the Chinese rural economy). Shanghai: Liming shuju, 1935

Feuerwerker, Albert. *Economic Trends in the Republic of China, 1912-1949.* Ann Arbor: The University of Michigan, Center for Chinese Studies, 1977.

———. *The Foreign Establishment in China in the Early Twentieth Century.* Ann Arbor: The University of Michigan, Center for Chinese Studies, 1976.

Forsyth, Robert Coventry. *Shantung: The Sacred Province of China.* Shanghai: Christian Literature Society, 1912.

Fukai Koichi 深井幸一. *Manshu ni okeru hokushi rodosha oyobi rodo tosei ni tsuite* 滿洲に於ける北支勞動者及勞動統制に就て (On North Chinese laborers and labor regulations in Manchuria). Tokyo: Yokohama Specie Bank, Research Department, 1942.

Gao Jiong 高炯. "Women shenyang gaicao tufei?" 我們什樣改操土匪 (How can we reform the behavior of the bandits?). In *Kangzhan zhong di Zhongguo nongcun dong tai* 抗戰中的中國農村動態 (Developments in the Chinese countryside during the War of Resistance). Edited by Qian Jiaju 千家駒. Guilin: Xinzhi shju, 1939. Reprinted, Center for Chinese Research Materials, Washington, D. C., 1972.

"Gesheng nongcun jingji yu nongmin yundong" 各省農村經濟與農民運動 (The rural economy and the rural movement in each province). *Cunzhi* 村治 2.6 (31 October 1931).

Gibert, Lucien. *Dictionnaire historique et géographique de la Mandchourie.* Hong Kong: Société des Missions étrangères, 1934.

Gongye bu 工業部, Quanguo nongye yanjiuyuan 全國農業研究院. "Gesheng nongmin licun diaocha" 各省農民離村調查 (A survey of the rural exodus in China). *Nongqing baogao* 農情報告 4.7 (July 1936).

Gottschang, Thomas R. "Economic Change, Disasters, and Migration: The Historical Case of Manchuria." *Economic Development and Cultural Change* 35.3 (April 1987): 461-90.

———. "Migration from North China to Manchuria: An Economic History, 1891-1942." Ph.D. dissertation, University of Michigan, 1982.

Guo Yizhi 郭異之. "Pochan sheng zhong de yige Jinan nongcun" 破產聲中的 一個冀南農村 (A south Hebei village in the midst of impoverishment). In *Zhongguo nongcun jingji lunwenji* 中國農村經濟論文集 (The Chinese rural economy: A collection of articles). Edited by Qian Jiaju 千家駒. Shanghai: Zhonghua shuju, 1935.

Guomin zhengfu zhuji chu tongji ju 國民政府主計處統計局, *Zhonghua minguo tongji tiyao* 中華民國統計提要 (Statistical abstract of the Republic of China). Nanking, 1936.

Hareven, Tamara. *Family Time and Industrial Time.* Cambridge, Mass.: Harvard University Press, 1982.

He Lian 何廉 [Franklin L. Ho]. *Dongsansheng zhi neidi yimin yanjiu* 東三省之內地移民研究 (Research on domestic migration to the Three Eastern Provinces). Tianjin: Nankai daxue jingji yanjiu suo, 1932.

Hitano Kenichiro. "The Japanese in Manchuria 1906–1931: A study of the historical background of Manchukuo." Ph.D. dissertation, Harvard University, 1993.

Ho, Franklin L. [He Lian]. *Population Movement to the North Eastern Frontier in China.* Shanghai: China Institute of Pacific Relations, 1931.

———. "Reminiscences of Franklin Lien Ho." As told to Crystal Lorch. 2 vols. Manuscript in the possession of Dr. Samuel P. S. Ho, Department of Economics, University of British Columbia.

Ho, Ping-ti 何炳棣. *Studies on the Population of China, 1368–1953.* Cambridge, Mass.: Harvard University Press, 1959.

———. *Zhongguo huiguan shilun* 中國會館史論 (On the History of Landsmannschaften in China). Taipei: Taiwan xuesheng shuju, 1966.

Hosie, Alexander. *Manchuria, Its People, Resources and Recent History.* London: Methuen, 1901; Boston: J. B. Millet Company, 1910.

Hou, Chi-ming. *Foreign Investment and Economic Development in China 1840–1937.* Cambridge, Mass.: Harvard University Press, 1965.

Hsiao, Liang-lin. *China's Foreign Trade Statistics, 1864–1949.* Cambridge, Mass.: Harvard University Press, 1974.

Hsu, Immanuel C. Y. *The Rise of Modern China.* New York and London: Oxford University Press, 1970.

Hsueh Tien-tung, Li Qiang, Liu Shucheng, eds. *China's Provincial Statistics, 1949–1989.* Boulder: Westview Press, 1993.

Huai Xi 槐西. "Zhongguo laodong yimin shigao" 中國勞動移民史稿 (Draft history of Chinese labor migration). *Zhongguo laodong* 中國勞動 1.10 (1935): 217–264.

Huang Jinyan 黃金炎. "Jiuyiba hou Shandong Hebei liangsheng laiwang Dongbei sansheng zhi nonggong shuzi tongji" 九一八後山東河北兩省來往東北三省之農工數字統計 (Statistics on the movement of farmers and laborers between Shandong and Hebei and the three Northeast Provinces after September 18). *Zhongguo shiye zazhi* 中國實業雜誌 1.9 (1935): 1659–1664.

Huang, Philip C. C. *The Peasant Economy and Social Change in North China.* Stanford: Stanford University Press, 1983.

Huang Puze 黃浦澤. "Woguo nongmin licun wenti" 我國農民離村問題 (On China's rural exodus). *Fuxing yuekan* 復興月刊 4.1 (September 1935): 29–52.

Huang Zecang 黃澤蒼. *Shandong* 山東. Shanghai: Zhonghua shuju, 1936.

Hucker, Charles O. *China's Imperial Past: An Introduction to Chinese History and Culture.* Stanford: Stanford University Press, 1975.

Huenemann, Ralph W. *The Dragon and the Iron Horse: The Economics of Railroads in China, 1876–1937.* Cambridge: Harvard University Press, 1984.

Institute of Pacific Relations. *Problems of the Pacific, 1929.* Proceedings of the Third Conference, Kyoto, 1929. Edited by J. B. Condliffe. Chicago: University of Chicago Press, 1930.

Ito Takeo. *Life Along the South Manchurian Railway: The Memoirs of Ito Takeo.* Translated by Joshua A. Fogel. Armonk, N.Y.: M. E. Sharpe, Inc., 1988.

Jiang Wenhan 蔣文漢. "Manzhou yimin" 滿洲移民 (Manchurian migration). In *Zhongguo renkou wenti* 中國人口問題 (China's population problems). Edited by Sun Benwen 孫本文. Shanghai: Zhongguo shehui kexue she, 1932.

Jing Su, and Luo Lun. *Landlord and Labour in Late Imperial China.* Translated by Endymion Wilkinson. Cambridge, Mass.: Harvard University Press, 1978.

Johnston, Reginald. *Lion and Dragon in Northern China.* Oxford: Oxford University Press, 1987.

Jones, Francis Clifford. *Manchuria Since 1931.* London: Royal Institute of International Affairs, 1949.

Kinney, Henry. *Modern Manchuria and the South Manchurian Railway Company.* Dalian: Japanese Advertiser Press, 1928.

"Ko-sai tetsudo" 膠濟鐵道 (The Jiao-Ji Railway). *Mantetsu chosa geppo* 滿鐵調查月報 16.3 (March 1936): 135–46.

Lary, Diana. *Warlord Soldiers.* Cambridge: Cambridge University Press, 1985.

———. "Hidden Migrations: Movement of Shandong People, 1949 to 1978." *Chinese Environment and Development* 7.1–7.2 (Spring/Summer 1996): 56–72.

Lattimore, Owen. *Manchuria: Cradle of Conflict.* New York: MacMillan, 1932.

————. *Inner Asian Frontiers of China.* New York: American Geographical Society, 1940. Reprinted, Boston: Beacon Press, 1962.

Lee, James. "Migration and Expansion in Chinese History." In *Human Migration, Patterns and Policies.* Edited by William H. McNeill and Ruth S. Adams, 20–47. Bloomington: Indiana University Press, 1978.

Lee, Robert H. G. *The Manchurian Frontier in Ch'ing History.* Cambridge, Mass.: Harvard University Press, 1970.

Li Jinghan 李景漢. "Ding Xian renmin chuwai mousheng de diaocha" 定縣人民出外謀生的 調查 (A study of Ding County people going elsewhere to seek a livelihood). *Minjian banyuekan* 民間半月刊 1.7 (August 1934): 18–24.

————. "Nongcun jiating renkou tongji fenxi" 農村家庭人口統計分析 (Statistical analysis of rural household population). *Shehui kexue* 社會科學 2.1 (October 1936): 7–9.

Li, Lillian. "Life and Death in a Chinese Famine: Infanticide as a Demographic Consequence of the 1935 Yellow River Flood." *Comparative Studies in Society and History* 33.3 (July 1991): 466–510.

Lin Qingshan. *Kang [Sheng] waizhuan* 康外傳. (Unauthorized biography of Kang Sheng). Beijing: Zhongguo qingnian chubanshe, 1988.

Lin Xiuzhu 林修竹. *Shandong gexian xiangtu diaocha lu* 山東各縣鄉土調查錄 (Collection of local studies of Shandong counties). Jinan, 1920. Reprinted, Washington: Center for Chinese Research Materials, 1977.

Liu Nanming. "Contribution à l'étude de la population chinoise." Ph.D. dissertation, Faculté des lettres de l'Université de Paris, Geneva, 1935.

Liu Sufen 劉素芬. *Yantai maoyi yanjiu* 煙台貿易研究, *1867–1919* (Research on the foreign trade of Yantai, 1867–1919). Taibei: Zhongguo lishi xiehui, 1990.

Liu Yanmian 劉延冕. "Jin shibanian Zhongguo youzheng zhi lianhuan zhishu" 近十八年中國郵政之連環指數 (Index of Chinese postal service links in the last eighteen years). *Tongji yuebao* 1.5 統計月報 (July 1929).

Lochow, H. J. von. *China's National Railways: Historical Survey and Postwar Planning.* Peiping: By the Author, 1948.

Lowe Chuan-hua. *Facing Labour Issues in China.* Shanghai: China Institute of Pacific Relations, 1933.

Lu Yu 路遇. *Qingdai he minguo Shandong yimin dongbei shilue* 清代合民國山東移民東北史略 (Outline history of Shandong migration to Manchuria in the Qing and Republican periods). Shanghai: Shanghai shehui kexueyuan chubanshe, 1987.

———. *Renkou wenti lun* 人口問題論 (Discussions on demography). Jinan: Zhongguo guangbo dianshi chubanshe, 1989.

———. *Shandong renkou qianyi he chengzhenhua yanjiu* 山東人口遷移合城鎮化研究 (Research on Shandong population movement and urbanization). Jinan: Shandong daxue chubanshe, 1988.

MacNair, Harley Farnsworth. *The Chinese Abroad.* Shanghai: Commercial Press, 1925.

Mallory, Walter H. *China: Land of Famine.* New York: American Geographical Society, 1926.

Manchoukuo Yearbook, 1934. Tokyo: Toa-keizai chosakyoku (East-Asiatic Economic Investigation Bureau), 1934.

Manchuria Yearbook, 1931. Tokyo: Toa-keizai chosakyoku [East-Asiatic Economic Investigation Bureau], 1932–33.

McCormack, Gavin. *Chang Tso-lin in Northeast China, 1911–1928: China, Japan and the Manchurian Idea.* Stanford: Stanford University Press, 1977.

McNeill, William H., and Ruth S. Adams, eds. *Human Migration, Patterns and Policies.* Bloomington: Indiana University Press, 1978.

Ministry of Industry, National Agricultural Research Bureau, "Survey of the rural exodus." *Nonqing baogao* 4.7 (July 1936): 171–75.

MMTKK. *Chugokujin rodosha no chingin* 中國人勞動者の賃銀 (Wages of Chinese laborers). Series: Manshu rodo jijo 滿洲勞動事情, no. 1. Dalian: Sosaishitsu Hitogotoka 總裁室人事課, 1933.

———. *Dairen ni okeru chugokujin rodosha no seikatsu jotai* 大連に於けろ中國人勞動者の生活狀態 (Standard of living of Chinese workers in Dalian). Dalian: Shachoshitsu Jinjika 社長室人事課, 1928.

———. *Dairen shichu ni okeru kaso chugokujin no inshokubutsu shirabe* 大連市中に於けろ下層中國人の飲食物調べ (Study of the diet of lower class Chinese in the city of Dalian). By Yamamato Kiko 山本紀綱. Dalian: Shachoshitsu Jinjika 社長室人事課, 1927.

———. *Gaikoku rodosha nyuman torishimari kyoka go ni okeru hokushi jijo chosasho* 外國勞動者入滿 取締強化後に於けろ北支事情調查書 (A study of matters in North China following the strengthening of controls over foreign workers entering Manchuria). Xinjing: Keizai Chosakai 濟調查會, 1935.

———. *Hokushi keizai tokei kiho* 北支經濟統計季報 (Quarterly bulletin of the statistics of North China). Nos. 1–3, Tianjin: Tenshin Jimusho, Chosaka 天津事務所調查課, January–July 1937; Nos. 4–14, Dalian: Chosabu, Hokushi Jimukyoku, Beijing 調查部北支事務局北京 and Hokushi Keizai Chosa-kyoku 北支經濟調查所, April 1939–March 1942.

———. *Jihen to nyuman rodosha mondai* 事變と入滿勞動者問題 (The problem of the Incident and laborers entering Manchuria). By Oyaki Saigo 尾崎西鄉. Series: Hokkei keizai shiryo 北經經濟資料, no. 100. Harbin: Hokuman Keizai Chosajo 北滿經濟調查所, 1938.

———. *Kako jugonenkan no manshu ni okeru nihonjin oyobi chugokujin shukogyo rodosha chingin no susei* 過去十五年間の滿洲に於けろ日本人及中國人手工業勞動者賃銀の趨勢 (Trends in the wages of Japanese and Chinese manual laborers in Manchuria during the last 15 years). By Yamamoto Kiko 山本紀綱. Dalian: Shachoshitsu Jinjika 社長室人事課, 1927.

———. *Kita shina keizai tokei teiyo* 北支那經濟統計提要 (Summary of North China economic statistics). Dalian: Chosabu Hokushi Jimukyoku, Beijing 調查部北支事務局北京, 1943.

———. *Man-mo nosei shian* 滿蒙農政私案 (Private plan for administering agriculture in Manchuria and Mongolia). Dalian: Chihobu Chihoka 地方部地方課, 1918.

———. *Manshu dekasegi iju kammin no suteki kosatsu* 滿洲出稼移住漢民の數的考察 (A statistical examination of the seasonal migration of Han Chinese in Manchuria). By Kurimoto Yutaka 栗本豐. (Series: Mantetsu chosa shiryo 滿鐵調查資, no. 154.) Dalian: Shomubu Chosaka 庶務部調查課, 1931.

———. *Manshu keizai tokei nempo showa 12-13 nen* 滿洲經濟統計年報昭和12-13年 (Annual report on Manchurian economic statistics, 1937-1938). Dalian: Chosabu 調查部, 1939.

———. *Manshu ni okeru shina ijumin ni kansuru suteki kenkyu* 滿洲に於けろ支那移住民に關すろ數的研究 (A numerical study of Chinese immigrants in Manchuria). By Kurimoto Yutaka. Dalian: Taiheiyo Mondai Chosa Jumbikai 太平洋問題調查準備會, 1931.

———. *Manshu ni taisuru shina no shokumin* 滿洲に對すろ支那の植民 (Chinese settlers in Manchuria). Dalian: Shomubu Chosaka 庶務部調查課, 1929.

———. *Manshu noka no seisan to shohi* 滿洲農家の生產と消費 (Production and consumption of Manchurian farmers). Dalian: Shachoshitsu Chosaka 社長室調查課, 1922.

———. *Manshu no kuri* 滿洲の苦力 (Coolies in Manchuria). By Takei Goichi 武居鄉一. Dalian: Keizai Chosakai 經濟調查會, 1934.

———. *Manshu rodo jijo soran* 滿洲勞動事情綜覽 (Handbook on labor conditions in Manchuria). Dalian: Keizai Chosakai 經濟調查會, 1936.

214 *SWALLOWS AND SETTLERS*

────. *Manshu rodo mondai no suteki ichikosatsu* 滿洲勞動問題の數的一考察 (A numerical study of Manchuria's labor problem). Tokyo: Toa Keizai Chosakyoku 東亞經濟調查所, 1927.

────. *Mantetsu chugokujin seikeihi chosa* 滿鐵中國人生計費調查 (Study of cost of living of South Manchuria Railway Company Chinese). Dalian: Shachoshitsu Jinjika 社長室人事課, 1926.

────. *Minkoku juhachinen manshu dekasegi imin ido jokyo* 民國十八年滿洲出稼移民移動狀況 (Movement of migrant workers in Manchuria in 1929). By Kurimoto Yutaka 栗本豐. Dalian: Shomubu Chosaka 庶務部調查課, 1930.

────. *Minkoku jukyunen manshu dekasegi imin ido jokyo* 民國十九年滿洲出稼移民移動狀況 (Movement of migrant workers in Manchuria in 1930). By Kurimoto Yutaka 栗本豐. Series: Mantetsu chosa shiryo 滿鐵調查資料, no. 161. Dalian: Shomubu Chosaka 庶務部調查課, 1931.

────. *Minkoku jurokunen no manshu dekasegi sha* 民國十六年の滿洲出稼者 (Migrant workers in Manchuria in 1927). By Nakashima Soichi 中島宗一. Series: Mantetsu chosa shiryo 滿鐵調查資料, no. 70. Dalian: Shomubu Chosaka 庶務部調查課, 1927.

────. *Minkoku jushichinen no manshu dekasegi sha* 民國十七年の滿洲出稼者 (Migrant workers in Manchuria in 1928). By Kurimoto Yutaka 栗本豐. Series: Mantetsu chosa shiryo 滿鐵調查資料, no. 100. Dalian: Shomubu Chosaka 庶務部調查課, 1929.

────.*Nyu-ri man kuri tokei* 入離滿苦力統計 (Statistics on coolies entering and leaving Manchuria). Dalian: Sangyobu 產業部, 1937.

────. *Shina keizai nempo* 支那經濟年報 (China economic yearbook). Dalian: Chosabu 調查部, 1940.

Myers, Ramon H. *The Chinese Peasant Economy, Agricultural Development in Hopei and Shantung, 1890–1949.* Cambridge, Mass.: Harvard University Press, 1970.

────. "Economic Development in Manchuria Under Japanese Imperialism: A Dissenting View." *China Quarterly* 55 (July–September 1973): 547–56.

────. "Socioeconomic Change in Villages of Manchuria During the Ch'ing and Republican Periods: Some Preliminary Findings." *Modern Asian Studies* 10.4 (1976): 491–620.

Nankai Institute of Economics. *Nankai Index Numbers, 1936.* Tientsin: Nankai University 1937.

"Nyu man rodosha no jotai" 入滿勞動者の狀態 (The situation of laborers entering Manchuria). *Mantetsu chosa geppo* 滿鐵調查月報 15.9 (September 1935): 111–36.

"Nyu-ri man hokushi rodosha no keitai kin oyobi so kingaku" 入離滿北支
勞動者の攜帶金及び送金額 (Money carried along and remitted by North
Chinese laborers entering and leaving Manchuria). *Mantetsu chosa geppo*
滿鐵調查月報 21.2 (January 1941): 205–14.

Pan Junguo 潘鈞國. *Huimin diqu fengwu zonglan* 惠民地區風務綜覽 (A comprehensive survey of local customs and products of Huimin prefecture).
Jinan: Shandong youyi shushe, 1988.

Peking United International Famine Relief Committee. *The Report of the Peking
United International Famine Relief Committee: The North China Famine of
1920–1921, With Special Reference to the West Chihli Area.* Peking, 1922.

Peloquin, R. P. Bonaventure. *Debuts d'un Missionaire.* Montreal: n.p., 1922.

Perry, Elizabeth J. *Rebels and Revolutionaries in North China, 1845–1945.*
Stanford: Stanford University Press, 1980.

———. *Shanghai on Strike: The Politics of Chinese Labor.* Stanford: Stanford
University Press, 1993.

Pomeranz, Kenneth. *The Making of a Hinterland: State, society and economy in
inland North China, 1853–1937.* Berkeley: University of California Press,
1993.

Pruitt, Ida. *A Daughter of Han: The Autobiography of a Chinese Working
Woman.* Stanford: Stanford University Press, 1967.

Qian Jiaju 千家駒. *Kangzhan zhong de Zhongguo nongcun dong tai.* 抗戰中
的中國農村動態 (Developments in the Chinese countryside during the War
of Resistance). Guilin: Xinzhi shuju, 1939. Reprinted, Center for Chinese
Research Materials, Washington, D. C., 1972.)

———. *Zhongguo nongcun jingji lunwen ji* 中國農村經濟論文集 (The Chinese
rural economy: A collection of articles). Shanghai: Zhonghua shuju, 1936.

Rawski, Thomas G. *China's Republican Economy: An Introduction.* Toronto:
University of Toronto-York University Joint Centre on Modern East Asia,
Discussion Paper, 1978.

———. "Economic Growth and Integration in Prewar China." Toronto: Joint
Centre on Modern East Asia, Discussion Paper no. 5, 1982.

———. *Economic Growth in Prewar China.* Berkeley: University of California
Press, 1989.

Ren Meixi 任美錫. "Hanren yizhi Dongbei zhi yanjiu" 漢人移植東北之研究
(Research on Chinese settlement in Manchuria). *Xin Yaxiya* 新亞西亞 4.5
(September 1932).

Richard, L. *Comprehensive Geography of the Chinese Empire and Dependencies.* Shanghai: T'usewei Press, 1908.

Richardson, Peter. "Chinese indentured labour in the Transvaal gold mining industry." In *Indentured Labour in the British Empire, 1834–1920.* Edited by Kay Saunders. London: Croom Helm, 1984.

Richthofen, Ferdinand von. *Schantung und seine Eingangspforte Kiautchou.* Berlin: D. Reimer, 1898.

Rietveld, Harriet. "Women and Children in Industry in Chefoo." *Chinese Economic Monthly* (December 1936).

Roll, Charles Robert, Jr. *The Distribution of Rural Incomes in China: A Comparison of the 1930s and the 1950s.* New York: Garland Publishing, Inc., 1980.

Sakatani, Y. *Manchuria: A Survey of Its Economic Development.* New York: Garland Publishing, Inc., 1980. (Originally prepared for the Division of Economics and History of the Carnegie Endowment for International Peace. 1932.)

Saunders, Kay, ed. *Indentured Labour in the British Empire, 1834–1920.* London: Croom Helm, 1984.

Schmidt, Vera. *Die deutsche Eisenbahnpolitik in Shantung, 1898–1914.* Wiesbaden: Harassowitz, 1976.

Schrecker, John E. *Imperialism and Chinese Nationalism: Germany in Shantung.* Cambridge, Mass.: Harvard University Press, 1971.

Shaffer, Lynda. *Mao and the Workers: The Hunan Labor Movement, 1920–1923.* Armonk: M. E. Sharpe, 1982.

Shan Man et al. *Shandong minsu* 山東民俗 (Shandong folkways). Jinan: Shandongsheng xinhua shudian, 1988.

"Shandong de nongcun jingji yu nongmin yundong" 山東的農村經濟與農民運動 (Shandong's rural economy and the rural movement). *Cunzhi* 村治 2.5 (September 1931): 6–20.

Shandong nongye diaochahui 山東農業調查會. *Shandong zhi nongye gaikuang* 山東之農業概況 (Agricultural conditions in Shandong). Jinan, 1922.

Shandongsheng difang shizhi bianji weiyuanhui 山東省地方史志編輯委員會. *Shandong shizhi ziliao* 山東史志資料 (Shandong historical materials). Vol. 2. Jinan, 1982.

Shao Fujun 邵覆均. "Shandong Ju xian Shaoquan xiang shehui zhuangkuang diaocha" 山東莒縣邵泉鄉社會狀況調查 (Study of social conditions in Shaoquan Township, Ju County, Shandong). *Cunzhi* 村治 2.1 (December 1930).

Sheridan, James E. *Chinese Warlord: The Career of Feng Yu-hsiang.* Stanford: Stanford University Press, 1966.

"Shi ichigatsu ita gogatsu dairen keiyiu santo jikirei kuri ido soku tokei" 自一月至五月大連經由山東直隸苦力移動數統計 (Statistics on migration of laborers from Shantung and Chihli through Dairen, from January to May 1928). *Mantetsu chosa geppo* 滿鐵調查月報 (here, *Chosa jiho*) 8.7 (July 1928): 174–99.

"Showa san nendo kami hanki minami manshu ni okeru santo jikirei kuri ido soku tokei" 昭和三年度上半期南滿洲に於けろ山東直隸苦力移動數統計 (Statistics on migration of laborers from Shantung and Chihli in South Manchuria in the first half of 1928). *Mantetsu chosa geppo* 滿鐵調查月報 (here, *Chosa jiho*). In two parts: 8.9 (September 1928): 117–51, and 8.10 (October 1928): 78–104.

Shryock, Henry S., Jr. *Population Mobility Within the United States*. Chicago: Community and Family Study Center, University of Chicago, 1964.

Skinner, G. William, ed. *The City in Late Imperial China*. Stanford: Stanford University Press, 1977.

———. "Marketing and Social Structure in Rural China." Parts I, II, III. *The Journal of Asian Studies* 24.1 (November 1964): 3–43; 24.2 (January 1965): 195–228; 24, 3 (May 1965): 363–99.

———. "Regional Urbanization in Nineteenth-Century China." In *The City in Late Imperial China*. Edited by G. William Skinner. Stanford: Stanford University Press, 1977.

South Manchuria Railway Company (SMR). *Second Report on Progress in Manchuria to 1930*. Dairen, 1931.

———. *Fifth Report on Progress in Manchuria to 1936*. Dairen, 1936.

———. *Sixth Report on Progress in Manchuria to 1939*. Dairen, 1939.

Spengler, Joseph J., and George C. Meyers. "Migration and Socioeconomic Development: Today and Yesterday." In *Migration, A Comparative Perspective*, 11–35. Edited by Alan A. Brown and Egon Neuberger. New York: Academic Press, 1977.

Stark, Oded. *The Migration of Labor*. Cambridge, Mass.: Blackwell Publishers, 1991.

Statistical Yearbook of China 1983. Compiled by the State Statistical Bureau, People's Republic of China. Hong Kong: Economic Information and Agency, 1983.

Stewart, John R. *Manchuria Since 1931*. New York: Secretariat, Institute of Pacific Relations, 1936.

218 *SWALLOWS AND SETTLERS*

Suleski, Ronald Stanley. "Regional Development in Manchuria: Immigrant Laborers and Provincial Officials in the 1920s." *Modern China* 4.4 (October 1978): 419–34.

———. "Manchuria Under Chang Tso-lin." Ph.D. dissertation, The University of Michigan, 1974.

Sun Qingji 孫慶基. *Shandongsheng dili* 山東省地理 (The geography of Shandong). Jinan: Shandongsheng xinhua shudian, 1987.

Taeuber, Irene B. "Manchuria as a Demographic Frontier." *Population Index* 11 (1945): 260–74.

———. "Migrants and Cities in Japan, Taiwan, and Northeast China." In *The Chinese City Between Two Worlds*, 359–84. Edited by Mark Elvin and G. William Skinner. Stanford: Stanford University Press, 1974

Taeuber, Irene B. and Nai-chi Wang. "Population Reports in the Ch'ing Dynasty." *The Journal of Asian Studies* 19 (August 1960): 403–17.

———. "Questions on Population Growth in China." In *Population Trends in Eastern Europe, the U.S.S.R., and Mainland China*, 263–310. New York: Milbank Memorial Fund, 1960.

Tan Qixiang 潭其驤, ed. *Huang He shi lunzong* 黃河史論綜 (Survey history of the Yellow River). Shanghai: Fudan daxue chubanshe, 1986.

Tanaka Tadao 田中忠夫. "Zhongguo nongmin de licun wenti" 中國農民的離村問題 (Problems of Chinese farmers leaving the countryside). In *Zhongguo nongmin wenti yu nongmin yundong* 中國農民問題與農民運動. (Problems of Chinese farmers and the rural movement). Edited by Wang Zhongwu 王仲鳴. Shanghai: Pingfan shuju, 1929.

Thomas, Brinley. *Migration and Economic Growth: A Study of Great Britain and the Atlantic Economy*. Cambridge: Cambridge University Press, 1954.

Tian Fang 田方 and Zhang Dongliang 張東亮. *Zhongguo renkou qianyi xintan* 中國人口遷移新探 (A new exploration of Chinese population movement). Beijing: Zhishi chubanshe, 1989.

Tian Keshen 田克深 and Wang Zhaoliang 王兆良. *Guanghui de bainian licheng* 光輝的百年歷程 (The course of a glorious century). Jinan: Shandong renmin chubanshe, 1984.

Tilly, Charles. "Migration in Modern European History." In *Human Migration, Patterns and Policies*. Edited by William H. McNeill and Ruth S. Adams, 48–72. Bloomington: Indiana University Press, 1978.

Toiku, Shiro 桶口士郎. "Hokushi ni okeru tai man rodo ryoku kyokyu no kinkyo" 北支における對滿勞動力供給の近況 (The recent condition of the labor supply for Manchuria in North China). *Mantetsu chosa geppo* 滿鐵調查月報 21.1 (January 1941): 178–87.

Tong Zhang 童璋. "Zhongguo nongmin licun de yanzhongxing" 中國農民離村 的嚴重性 (The gravity of China's rural exodus). *Jianshe pinglun* 建設評論 2 (May–July 1936):2–4.

Torgasheff, Boris. "Mining labour in China." *Chinese Economic Journal* 6.4 (1930): 324–417; 6.5 (1930): 510–541; 6.6 (1930): 652–676.

Treadgold, Donald W. *The Great Siberian Migration*. Princeton: Princeton University Press, 1957.

Tsao Lien-en. *Chinese Migration and the Three Eastern Provinces*. Shanghai: Bureau of Industrial and Commercial Information, 1931.

United States Central Intelligence Agency. *People's Republic of China: Atlas*. Washington, D.C.: U.S. Government Printing Office, 1971.

Wagner, Wilhelm. *Die chinesische Landwirtschaft*. Berlin: P. Parey, 1926.

Wang Haibo 王海波. *Dongbei yimin wenti* 東北移民問題 (Manchuria migration issues). Shanghai: Zhonghua shuju, 1932.

Wang, I-shou. "Chinese Migration and Population Change in Manchuria, 1900–1940." Ph.D. dissertation, University of Minnesota, 1971.

Wang Kuixi 王魁喜 et al. *Jindai Dongbeishi* 近代東北史 (Modern Manchurian history). Ha'erbin: Heilongjiang renmin chubanshe, 1984.

Wang Pilian 王丕廉. "Zhang Zongchang zhi sinanguai" 張宗昌之死難怪 (Zhang Zongchang's strange accidental death). *Jinan wenshi ziliao* 濟南文史資料, vol. 2. Jinan, 1984.

Wang Yaoyu 王藥雨. "Jin ershinian Shandong Yidu wushige nongcun de nongmin he gengdong suoyou quan zhi bianqian" 近二十年山東益都五十 個農村的農民合更動所有權之變遷 (Changes in joint ownership rights of farmers in fifty villages of Yidu, Shandong, over the last twenty years). *Jingji yanjiu* 經濟研究 115 (1935): 178–187.

———. "Shandong nongmin licun di yige jiantao" 山東農民離村的一個檢討 (An examination of rural exodus in Shandong). In *Zhongguo jingji yanjiu* 中國經濟研究. Edited by Fang Xianting 方顯廷. Changsha: Shangwu, 1938.

Williamson, Jeffrey G. "Migration to the New World: Long Term Influences and Impact." *Explorations in Economic History* 11.4 (Summer 1974): 357–89.

Wright, Tim. *Coal Mining in China's Economy and Society, 1895–1937*. Cambridge: Cambridge University Press, 1984.

Wu Gumin 吳顧敏. "Zouping renkou wenti de fenxi" 鄒平人口問題的分析 (Analysis of Zouping population questions). *Xiangcun jianshe* 鄉村建設 5 (October–November 1935): 6–7.

———. *Zouping shiyan xian hukou diaocha baogao* 鄒平實驗縣戶口調查報告 (Research report on the population of Zouping Experimental County). Shanghai: Zhonghua shuju, 1935.

Wu Yulin 吳玉林, ed. *Zhongguo renkou Shandong fence* 中國人口山東分冊 (China's population, Shandong volume). Beijing: Zhongguo caizheng jingji chubanshe, 1986.

Wu Zhixin 吳至信. "Zhongguo nongmin licun wenti" 中國農民離村問題 (The problem of China's rural exodus). *Minzu* 民族 5.7 (July 1937); reprinted in *Dongfang zazhi* 東方雜誌 34.15 (August 1937) and 34.22 (December 1937).

Wynne, Waller. *The Population of Manchuria*. Washington, D.C.: Bureau of the Census, International Population Reports P-90, No. 7, 1958.

Xiangcun jianshe yanjiuyuan 鄉村建設研究院. *Shandong xiangcun jianshe yanjiuyuan ji Zouping shiyan qu* 山東鄉村建設研究院及鄒平實驗區 (Shandong Rural Construction Research Institute and the Zouping Experimental District). Zouping: Shandong nongcun jianshe yanjiuyuan chubanshe, 1936.

Xiao Wan 曉蔓. "Shandong Zhaoyuan xian nongcun gaikuang" 山東招遠縣農村概況 (Survey of rural Zhaoyuan County, Shandong). In *Zhongguo nongcun jingji lunwenji* 中國農村經濟論文集. Edited by Qian Jiaju 千家駒. Shanghai: Zhonghua shuju, 1935.

Xu Hengyao 徐恒耀. "Man Meng de laodong zhuangkuang yu yimin" 滿蒙的勞動狀況與移民 (Labor and migration in Manchuria and Mongolia). *Dongfang zazhi* 東方雜誌 22 (November 1925): 21–22.

Xu Shilian 許仕廉 (Leonard Hsu). *Zhongguo renkou wenti* 中國人口問題 (China's population problem). Shanghai: Shangwu, 1930.

Yan Yunxiang. *The Flow of Gifts: Reciprocity and Social Networks in a Chinese Village*. Stanford: Stanford University Press, 1996.

Yan Zhongping 嚴中平. *Zhongguo jindai jingjishi tongji ziliao xuanji* 中國近代經濟史統計資料選輯 (Selected statistics on China's modern economic history). Beijing: Kexue, 1955.

Yang, Ch'ing-k'un (C. K. Yang). *Chinese Society: The Family and the Village*. Cambridge, Mass.: Harvard University Press, 1966.

———. *A North China Local Market Economy*. New York: Institute of Pacific Relations, 1944.

Yang, Martin C. *A Chinese Village: Taitou, Shantung Province*. New York: Columbia University Press, 1945.

Yeh Ch'ing-kuang. *Coolies and Mandarins: China's Protection of Overseas Chinese During the Late Ch'ing Period (1851–1911)*. Singapore: Singapore University Press, 1985.

Young, C. Walter. "Chinese Colonization and the Development of Manchuria." In *Problems of the Pacific, 1929,* Proceedings of the Institute for Pacific Relations, Third Conference, Kyoto, 1929. Edited by J.B. Condliffe, 423–66. Chicago: University of Chicago Press, 1930.

————. "Chinese Colonization in Manchuria." *The Far Eastern Review* 24 (1928): 241–50, 296–303.

————. "Chinese Immigration and Colonization in Manchuria." In *Pioneer Settlement: Cooperative Studies by Twenty-Six Authors.* American Geographical Society, Special Publication No. 14. Edited by W.L.G. Joerg, 330–59. New York: American Geographical Society, 1932.

————. "Chinese labour emigration to Manchuria." *Chinese Economic Journal* 1.7 (July 1927). 613–33

————. *The International Relations of Manchuria.* Chicago: The University of Chicago Press, 1929.

————. "Manchuria, a New Homeland for the Chinese." *Current History* (1928): 529–36.

Young, John. *The Research Activities of the South Manchurian Railway Company, 1907–1945: A History and Bibliography.* New York: East Asian Institute, Columbia University, 1966.

Zhang Ruide 張瑞德. *Ping-Han tielu yu Huabei de jingji fazhan* 平漢鐵路與華北的經濟發展 (The Ping-Han Railway and economic development in North China). Taipei: Zhongyang yanjiuyuan, Jindaishi yanjiusuo, 1979.

Zhang Yufa 張玉法. *Zhongguo xiandaihua de yanjiu: Shandongsheng 1860–1919* 中國現代化的研究: 山東省 1860–1919 (Research on modernization in China: Shandong, 1860–1919). Taipei: Zhongyang yanjiuyuan Jindaishi yanjiusuo, 1982.

Zhang Zhenyi 張振一. "Renhuo tianzai xia zhi Shandong renmin yu Dongbei yimin" 人禍天災下之山東人民與東北移民 (The people of Shandong and migrants to Manchuria [in times of] manmade and natural disasters). *Xin Yaxiya* 2 (June 1921): 3.

Zou Yilin 鄒逸麟. "Huang He xiayou hedao bianyan ji qi yinxiang gaishu" 黃河下游河道邊沿及其印象概述 (General impressions of the fringes of the Yellow River's lower reaches.). In *Huang He shi lunzong* 黃河史論綜 (Historical survey of the Yellow River). Edited by Tan Qixiang 潭其驤. Shanghai: Fudan daxue chubanshe, 1986.

INDEX

influenza, 58
inheritance systems, 71–72
interviews, of former migrants,
    18–22

Japan, activities in Shandong, 21, 132;
    aggression against China, 128–
    133; annexation of Korea, 67;
    defeat in 1945, 76, 124;
    and Korean settlers in Manchuria,
    68; and Manchuria, 48, 128, 129;
    migration to Manchuria from, 67;
    occupation of Shandong, 132;
    suppression of opposition in
    Manchuria, 131
Japanese Army, 50; and atrocities,
    132; German holdings in
    Shandong attacked by, 119;
    Manchuria seized by, 76, 118, 120,
    129; North China invaded by, 21,
    28, 121. *See also* Jinan Incident
Japanese industrialists, strike against
    by workers in Qingdao, 80
Jiao-Ji Railway. *See* Shandong
    Railway
Jiaodong, 23, 89. *See also* Shandong
    Peninsula
Jiaozhou, 61
Jilin Province, xi, 49, 68, 82, 117–118;
    and migration, post-1949, 140
Jin-Pu Railway. *See* Tianjin-Pukou
    Railway
Jinan, 24, 27, 81, 89, 138; travel costs
    from, 122–124
Jinan Incident, 120
Jinan-Qingdao Railway. *See*
    Shandong Railway
Johnston, Reginald, 72, 80, 84, 85
Juye County, 126
junks, 36, 51

Kaiping Mines, 51, 60
Kaitong, Jilin, 76, 77
Kangxi Emperor, 47
kinship terminology, 97

Kirin. *See* Jilin Province
Korea, 67

labor, contract system, 60–62;
    contractors, (*batou*), 60–62, 81, 94,
    116, 117; contracts, 61, 65–66;
    markets, 11; scarcity in
    Manchuria, 44, 48, 127, 128
Laipigou, Jilin, 118
Laiyang County, 8, 30–31, 75, 77, 87–
    88, 90, 117; return migration in,
    121; and return rights, in 1980s,
    126
land leases, distribution in 1980s, 125
land ownership, concentration, 25, 26,
    29, 30; as goal of migration, 11, 74
land reform, 124
land route, to Manchuria, 35, 121
laoxiang (fellow locals), 62, 89, 96–97,
    131, 143
Lattimore, Owen, 13, 77
League of Nations, 128
letters, from migrants, 87
Li Yunsheng, 84
Liang Shuming, 27
Liangshanbo, 17, 23
Liao River, 46, 51
Liaodong Peninsula, 22, 23, 45, 48
Liaoning Province, xi, 68; economic
    structure, 141; and migration,
    post-1949, 140
Liaoyang, 140
Ling County, 24–25, 70, 76, 89;
    return migration in, 116, 122, 124,
    125, 127; and return rights in
    1980s, 124
Linqing, 44
Linqu County, 8, 27–29, 76, 77, 122,
    125; drought in, 117; family
    migration from, 82–83; return
    migration in, 121, 124
Lobei settlement, 63
local government, transition in 1980s,
    123